More or Less

By the same author

HAPPY GO LUCKY
KINDLY LEAVE THE STAGE

KENNETH MORE

More or Less

HODDER AND STOUGHTON
LONDON SYDNEY AUCKLAND TORONTO

British Library Cataloguing in Publication Data

More, Kenneth
    More or less.
    1. More, Kenneth   2. Actors – England – Biography
    I. Title
    792'028'0924   PN2598.M65

    ISBN 0 340 22603 X

Hodder and Stoughton Editorial Office: 47 Bedford Square, London WC1B 3DP

For 'Shrimp', whose laughter and tears
make it all possible, and for
Pat and Cyril Porter, whose friendship
never wavered.

Illustrations

ACKNOWLEDGMENTS

 1 Author's collection
 2 The Rank Organisation
 3 BBC copyright
 4 Twentieth Century-Fox
 5 Maurice Aubry
 6 Daily Mirror Newspapers Ltd.
 7 ATV
 8 *Woman* Magazine
 9 Anglia Television
10 EMI

From the writer to the reader

SOME YEARS AGO, when I was working in Spain on a film of Verne's *Journey to the Centre of the Earth*, I was stopped by an old peasant woman with a most unusual request. She wanted me to hear her confession. I explained through an interpreter that I was neither a Catholic nor a priest, but this did not put her off. She had seen me as 'Padre Brown' in the *Father Brown* TV series, then showing in Spain with phenomenal success; and as she had bad legs and the place was remote and mountainous, and she hated her parish priest who lived way down the hill, she decided that I was her man. In fact, it was me or no one. Unable to oblige, I left the poor old soul muttering to herself about the inconsistencies of actors. If a man plays the part of a priest, why can't he really be one?

It's a fair question, I suppose. If all the world's a stage I have, in real life, played many parts: engineering apprentice, shop assistant, emigrant to Canada, stage-hand, naval officer, club-man. And in the make-believe world of stage and films and TV I have played many more: medical student, legless pilot, business-man, barrister, man of property, innkeeper and priest, to name only a few.

But – as every actor asks himself in front of his mirror – who am I? What connection was there between Freddie in *The Deep Blue Sea* and the player who slipped anonymously from the stage door at the end of the evening? More complicated, what was the link-up between the two of them and Ambrose Claverhouse, the breezy young bloke with the passion for veteran cars, whom Freddie became each day while making the film of *Genevieve*? All three of them were me, but in what sense exactly? And what was – and is – the 'I' behind the mask of my real-life roles?

Many years ago, in a book called *Happy Go Lucky*, I made a first shot at answering these questions. But that was back in 1959 and a lot has happened since then. Young Jolyon and Father Brown are only two of the characters who have added to my actor's problems of 'multiple personality'. Friends have died, my domestic life has changed, and the ups-and-downs of nearly twenty years have brought me many new experiences, some good, some bad, to alter the viewpoint of the man I once was. I feel this is the moment to put it all down, in as true a perspective as I shall ever hope to achieve . . . more or less.

More or Less

1

MY FIRST PUBLIC appearance was a matinée – and on a Sunday of all days, traditionally the actor's day of rest. I played to an intimate audience of three: my mother, our local doctor and a nurse. My mother was delighted, the doctor possibly less so, for he had to miss an afternoon's golf in order to deliver me.

I was born on Sunday, September 20, 1914. The first world war was about six weeks old and everyone was sure it would all be over by Christmas. I spent my childhood in the shadow of that war and its aftermath, yet, looking back, I remember little of the dark side of life, and so much of the fun and warmth and laughter which surrounded our family.

I had a sister, Kate, eighteen months older than me, and for the first four years of my life I rarely saw my father because he was a pilot in the Royal Naval Air Service.

My mother, sister and I lived in a house in Vicarage Road, Gerrards Cross, then a very small town surrounded by fields and woods. I had a nurse, Nanny Gething, whom I regarded as being very old; she was probably all of thirty, but my parents were both much younger.

My mother was the daughter of a Cardiff solicitor, but had nothing of the law's solemnity about her. She bubbled with vivacity like a glass of champagne. Perhaps because of this she was never called Edith, which was her name, but 'Tops', 'Topsy' or 'Toppy'. She loved dressing up and had the most wonderful and infectious laugh. Life to her was what I have always tried to make it for myself (sometimes without notable success) – a time to enjoy and to share with others of like mind. I am forever in her debt for this.

So far as I know, the Mores have nothing theatrical in their past, although the life of my most distinguished ancestor, Sir Thomas More, Henry VIII's Lord Chancellor, was so dramatic, it inspired Robert Bolt to write his classic play, *A Man For All Seasons*. There was certainly nothing theatrical about my father, except perhaps the Christian name Gilbert, which he also gave to me. My father had a civil engineering degree from King's College,

13

London, and his only connection with the theatre was as a theatre-goer. From him I inherit an easy-going attitude to life though not the casual attitude which was to bring him twice to the edge of ruin. I am also indebted to him for a certain inventiveness of mind which has helped me in my career, and for memories of his prodigal and sometimes misplaced generosity. There was nothing small-minded or mean about him.

So my immediate background on both sides of the family was conventional and cheerful. In qualifying as an engineer my father followed his father, who had designed the Richmond lock and weir and supervised the construction of two Thames bridges. Later, he became Chief Engineer to the Port of London Authority.

My grandfather lived in style in a large house in Sutherland Avenue, Maida Vale, waited on by a full staff of servants. I never met him, because he died before I was born, but I heard a great deal about him. He influenced our family enormously, for on his death he left my father an inheritance of £40,000, a fortune in those days. This was without doubt the worst thing that ever happened to his son. It changed his life completely, and so changed ours, in a way Grandpa More could never have foreseen.

In terms of today's values, this legacy would be worth about £500,000, and so it meant that my father, though still a young man, had no need to work. He felt he could do as he pleased all day and every day, for with the income from this money, and virtually no income tax to worry about, to work was a waste of time.

Without this windfall, I believe my father would have been as successful an engineer as his father. With it, he frittered away his life and energies along with all the money.

He had an extremely quick, alert mind, and early on realised the potential of flying, which was then in its very early days. Thus, shortly after I was born, he joined the Royal Naval Air Service to train as a pilot, and was posted to a camp at an airfield in Chingford, Essex. Here the regular naval officer in charge of his batch of trainee pilots was a Lieutenant-Commander Travers. As Ben Travers, he later achieved fame and a considerable fortune through writing the brilliant Aldwych farces.

I later came to know Ben well, but it was some time before I realised he was also the Travers my father had so frequently mentioned to us. Ben is now ninety-one, and remembers those first days of war with amazing clarity – including a night when he shot down a German Zeppelin.

Once, over a drink at the Garrick Club, he was recalling such wartime experiences, and mentioned he had taught a man named More to fly. All he could remember was his name, Bertie. That was my father, I told him. Next time we met, Ben presented me with a photograph. This shows my father's squad of about twenty serious-faced young men, all wearing brand-new wings on the left sleeves of their naval uniforms. My father was one of the few in that group who survived the war.

While my father was still at Chingford, the rest of us moved to Richmond to a small Regency house, Bute Lodge, the lease of which we purchased in Park Road. Nowadays, Bute Lodge is ringed by multi-storey flats. I believe it survives only because a preservation order protects it. But I never pass by without seeing it as it was then in my childhood, with a long garden, thick green hedges, and smooth lawns. The sight of it, the sound of the name, recalls, with a quickening of the heart, happiness and fulfilment of long ago.

One night there was an air-raid warning. A German Zeppelin was overhead. I saw its long silver cigar-shape with the spinning propeller blades, caught like haloes in the crossbeams of search-lights. It seemed to hang just above our local church steeple as though unable to move, a moment of supreme excitement.

This was in 1917, so I would have been three. I have always had a long and vivid memory – a gift which has helped me in my career. I also remember the celebrations on Armistice Day very clearly. The parties and red, white and blue streamers. I remember a lot of music and bands played in Richmond streets. Three or four ex-servicemen, one of them sometimes blind or on crutches, would play trumpets and flutes and concertinas in the gutter, an empty cap at their feet to catch the coins of passers-by.

During the latter part of the war, my father transferred to the Royal Flying Corps and was demobilised with the rank of major. Like many others at that time, he kept his rank, and was often addressed as Major More by people who wished to be respectful, and as Bertie by his friends.

One of the strongest memories of my early years is of him leaving the house every morning to walk down the garden to a splendid workshop he had built. Here, he had installed a lathe and other expensive and sophisticated engineering equipment. A born optimist, he was convinced he would eventually produce some gadget that would be marketed at phenomenal profit. Others had done this – look at the safety pin, the gramophone needle, the simple box camera – so why couldn't he? Certainly he worked hard. All day there came a sound of drilling and

15

grinding and whirring of metal from his workshop. Sometimes he hired mechanics and draughtsmen to help him; sometimes he worked alone. Over the years, he produced a number of household gadgets and made improvements to valves and taps around the house. But nothing showed the expected and longed for potential of which he dreamed.

He was keen on motoring and motor-cycling, and gradually his interests and enthusiasm turned towards producing a carburettor which could improve a car's petrol consumption by ten or fifteen miles a gallon. He had gauged the market astutely, for motoring was becoming popular with thousands of people who had learned to drive during their war service. The Austin Seven had also just been announced and was the first full-size car which ordinary people could afford. Although petrol was then about a shilling a gallon, wages were correspondingly low, and these new owners were always eager to cut their running costs. For months my father applied himself resolutely to this problem.

One day, I was playing in the garden on my tricycle – which I remember well because it had bone handles – when a man drove up to our front gate in a touring car with a funny round radiator. Years later I owned one myself, so I can say now that it was a bull-nose Morris Cowley. The man walked up the garden path to our front door. He was of medium height and had a fresh face, and was neatly dressed. He was smoking a cigarette. He saw me on my tricycle and nodded.

'Are you Bertie More's son?' he asked.

I said, 'Yes.'

That was the extent of our conversation because at that moment, Elsie, our parlourmaid, who had also seen him arrive, opened the front door and he went into the house. I carried on tricycling, and watched him come out with my father. He lit another cigarette and they went down to the workshop together.

When they left they were deep in conversation, but the visitor saw I was still there, and as they walked past, he put his hand in his pocket and gave me a shilling.

'Buy some sweets with that,' he told me, and went on to his car. I was only five or six, and I don't think I even knew what a shilling was, until my sister Kate tried to take it off me and I punched her in the face.

Years later, after we had left Bute House, the subject of this carburettor came up in conversation, and I asked my mother: 'Who was that man?'

'Mr. Morris,' she replied. 'And to think – he offered your father a partnership.'

16

My father had refused because he felt he could market his invention himself. Mr. Morris, for his part, went on to become Lord Nuffield, and the most successful British motor manufacturer of the 1930s.

My father's mind flitted like a butterfly from one enthusiasm to another. Indeed, he tried his hand at so many inventions, so many strange projects, that he was known to his friends as Ubiquitous More. One Sunday, Kate was dressed in her best clothes to go to church – a white coat with fur trimming, a white hat and gloves and shoes – when he decided he must dismantle a motor cycle in order to redesign some part of it, and he needed someone to help him. He enlisted Kate's aid and they took the machine to pieces on the lawn. Afterwards, Kate looked like a refugee from the Black and White Minstrels. But as quickly as my father's interests were aroused, they could also easily be diverted. The motor cycle was never put together. Its component pieces joined dismantled clocks and bits of the economical carburettor lying about the house, and gradually it just melted away.

An invention on which he spent a lot of time, and even more money, was a waterproofing fluid he called 'Roomac'. This, he was sure, could make raincoats, mackintoshes and gum-boots quite unnecessary, because if jackets and trousers and shoes could be rendered rainproof who would need to buy such things?

Everyone in the family rallied to test this strange liquid. We immersed our shirts and trousers and shoes and socks in a barrel of the stuff, and afterwards I poured water over them to test its properties. The water ran off quickly enough, but everything else looked as though it had been covered in thick green pond slime. The clothes smelled so strongly of chemicals that none of us could bring ourselves to wear them. And there was worse to come. 'Roomac' was so strong that not only did it repel water *and* us; within a few weeks it also repelled everything to which it was applied. Shirt and shoes and suits just rotted away to a mass of sticky goo.

Another invention was a liqueur my father called Vespatrio. This looked like liquid gold and tasted like a mixture of Benedictine and apricot brandy. I know, because I sipped some illicitly to try it. Again, my father was enthusiastic about its prospects. Bottles were ordered by the gross, and attractive labels specially designed and printed, but distribution to the wine trade proved impossible, and so this joined an increasingly long list of expensive failures.

In an attempt to recoup such losses, my father turned to the stock exchange. But whereas a safe and steady share would have brought in a regular if small income, he was attracted to high risk areas as the moth is drawn to the candle flame. Something about the promises in the prospectuses of South African diamond mines stirred his imagination. But, alas, their promises regularly outran their performance. My father lost again and again.

People with ideas, who needed money to promote them, businessmen, entrepreneurs and others, would find their way to our house. Of them all, there was one whose name even then stuck in my mind, because it had a certain flamboyance. I cannot now remember on what venture he sought my father's assistance but I remember him coming to the house several times. He was Vivian Van Damm. Little did I realise how much, and in what unpredictable circumstances, he would one day influence my life.

It was one thing being approached by people with a genuine proposition to promote, but my father's generosity extended to any friend, any neighbour, even a casual acquaintance or the friend of a friend. The person had only to ask for a loan of five pounds and my father would immediately reply, 'Five pounds, did you say? Goodness me, you couldn't possibly manage on that. Here's ten.' Of course, the money and the acquaintance were often never seen again.

My father and Topsy would have made a perfect childless couple; her interests were his. I don't think he was ever particularly fond of children. For this reason, my sister spent a great deal of time with Topsy while I gravitated to the companionship of Nanny Gething. Once she took me to Blackpool where her brother ran a stall amid all the glitter and excitement of the Golden Mile. I grew very close to her and I was secretly concerned in case she died and I was left alone.

Apart from this worry, life in those days seems to have been one long summer, with no shadows to darken the enjoyment. Yet behind the façade of affluence, of a cook and housemaid, a gardener and a nurse, there must have lurked worries which our parents carefully concealed from Kate and me. Either that, or else we were too innocent to observe them, for I cannot remember one single angry word between my father and my mother. But all the while the money was steadily diminishing, a thousand here, five hundred elsewhere, a tenner to a needy neighbour.

My father bought an interest in a car-sales business in Gerrard Street off Shaftesbury Avenue, and after a trip to London to this showroom, he would visit us in our night-nursery. My sister slept in one small bed and I in another. Father would blow smoke rings around the door and shout 'Boo' at us to frighten us.

This was part of his strange approach to his children. He would alarm us one minute, and then praise us the next, and say: 'Well done,' and give us each a shilling. Sometimes, though, his generosity to us was really a gift to himself. When I was five, for example, he went to Gamages and bought a most expensive steam engine with a funnel and a brass boiler. In theory, this was a present to me, but I was never allowed to touch the thing. He spent hours playing with it himself. I would walk past his study and hear the engine hissing and blowing off steam behind the door, and smell its unforgettable and exciting aroma of methylated spirits and warm oil, and long to play with it but never be allowed to join in.

When I was six, father decided that Kate and I had been at home long enough and so we should be sent to a boarding school, out of the way. We were very young for this separation, and it caused the first upset in our lives, for neither of us really knew or even imagined what boarding school would be like.

Mother and Nanny Gething burst into tears at the news, and Kate and I howled to see them cry. We were entered for a preparatory school, Steyne School in Worthing, Sussex, which had one section for little girls, and the other for boys up to the age of fourteen. Nanny must have been very worried at the prospect that her own livelihood might disappear, but she bravely concealed her feelings, and explained to us that going to a boarding school was really like entering an outpost of fairyland. Gnomes would join our games. There would be fun of all kinds. Life would be an endless playtime, infinitely better than anything we had so far experienced, with chocolate cake and honey buns for tea.

My sister received Nanny's assurance with all the reservation of a girl aged seven and a half, but I believed it entirely. My excitement and anticipation grew when we went to Whiteleys department store in Bayswater to buy our new school clothes and tuck-boxes. It was the fashion then for little boys to wear sailor suits with reefer jackets with brass buttons and little sailor hats. Kate had a reefer jacket and a skirt. I felt very proud of this rigout, and also of my new tuck-box. This was like a small trunk of unpainted wood with black metal corners and hinges, and a tray inside for cakes and tins of sweets.

On the first day of term my father drove us both to Victoria to catch what was grandly known as the school train. Here we saw parents with other children, some of our age, some older, who all wore sailor suits and were going down to Worthing under the supervision of a master. As a parting present, my father gave Kate and me a miniature fountain pen each, known as a Dinky pen, made of a pearly mottled celluloid material. This was new in those days, and had a neat metal lever on the side of the barrel of the pen to fill it.

On the journey, Kate and I kept telling ourselves how exciting going to school was, and gradually she shed her initial reservations. But what an awakening when we arrived at Worthing! Not even my Dinky pen could comfort me. We were immediately split up into our sections, and instead of fairyland, we found we had come to stay in a cold house which seemed to have a chill wind scouring it perpetually, as though no doors were ever closed. The walls of rooms and corridors were dirty and the light came from gas lamps so old they had fishtail burners instead of mantles.

I sat down with other boys to tea at a long table, without any cloth, and not a chocolate cake or honey bun in sight. Slices of bread were piled on a plate and the margarine was so yellow that it looked like squashed buttercups. It tasted sour and rancid, and I could hardly swallow the stuff. We had a pot of fish paste to spread on this bread and margarine, but this was quite inedible.

I felt more miserable and lonely in this bleak unfriendly place than I have ever felt since. The pervading smells seemed symbolic of Steyne School's pretensions contrasted with its reality – crude carbolic soap and cabbage water. Ahead stretched terms, years, an infinity. The prospect was so unbearable that for the first time in my life I wet my bed that night. And from then on, every night in term time, I either wet or dirtied the bed. We had a young matron to look after the dormitories, and she moved me into a small room reserved for cry-babies. There were three of us, and we all found it incredible to comprehend why or how we had left our homes and mothers and fathers and exchanged homely nurseries for this exile.

The matron, with increasing irritation, changed my sheets every day. I could never meet my sister except to speak to her briefly through a chicken-run wire fence that separated boys from the girls. Kate was more resilient than me and bore her isolation stoically.

I used to tell her miserably, 'I am so unhappy, Kate.' She would reply, 'I can't do anything for you, Kenny. I just can't. But I am sure you will be all right.'

Every day we would meet like this, like prisoners, with the wire between us, and in response to my misery she would try to give me reassurance, but I was not to be reassured.

20

There was a group of boys who set out to make life even more unpleasant than it was already for newer and smaller boys like me. They certainly succeeded. They behaved like a sort of mini-Mafia, and deliberately removed the only source of comfort I had during all the terms I survived at Steyne. This comfort consisted of a brand of sweets called snowballs, which were (and still are) toffees dusted with sugar powder.

Every Sunday morning all of us boys were given a penny each to put in the plate of the local church on the front, to which we were marched in a crocodile for morning service. This was the only money we were allowed each week, so I followed the example of others in trying to spend it on secular rather than ecclesiastical purposes. We would ignore the offertory plate in church, and after the service would turn down the tops of our stockings, so that the telltale red school colours would not show, and then dash across the street to a corner shop to spend our pennies on sweets.

The 'Mafia' lacked the courage to risk running to the shop themselves to buy their own sweets. Instead, they would approach us smaller boys after we had returned to school and ask menacingly, 'Got any suckers?' When they asked us this, we would all hand over one or two sweets reluctantly rather than face a punching from someone who seemed twice our size. On this particular occasion, I handed over one snowball as tribute, but the gang insisted I gave them all I had bought. I was so scared that I did so, and so miserable at my own weakness, that I wept.

For this display of feeling, one of the bullies gave me what the school called a 'toe-er' – a vicious kick up my backside with the toe of his shoe as opposed to the flat of the instep.

I fell to the ground almost paralysed with pain and he left me sobbing. Sometimes I wonder whether that incident made any impression on him, as it did on me, mentally more than physically. For this traumatic experience at such a young age taught me a wariness about dealing with some fellow human beings which has stood me in good stead during my career. It also gave me a personal insight into the depths of suffering a child can endure, and like every other experience in my life, for good or ill, this has been also of value to me as an actor. You have to know pain and pleasure yourself before you can begin to demonstrate them to an audience.

Finally chance – or providence – allowed me to escape from the Dickensian atmosphere of Steyne School. My sister developed diphtheria and I caught mumps. To be ill in such surroundings was impossible, and to our relief we were allowed home. But here we became involved in another crises of a totally different kind in which we were not so much actors, as audience, powerless to help. My father had spent all his legacy. He was on the verge of bankruptcy.

Nanny Gething, who was still living at Bute House, would write to us every week at Worthing, so we had some idea what was happening at home, but she had never mentioned how low were family funds, if indeed she had any inkling of this. Kate and I therefore knew nothing about it, for we had never been bothered because our father did not go out to work like other fathers. We knew he worked at home, and we did not realise that his work was unpaid, and virtually a hobby. Now, he had run through his fortune. Bills were coming in with that speed which financial depression induces, and creditors were calling at the house. This was the appalling situation to which we returned, weak and pale from school.

In the years since then, I have on several occasions been without money – once without even a shilling for the gas meter or food throughout an entire winter weekend – but each time I have been saved by what I can only describe as an act of providence. And so it was here. I will never forget the deep sense of doom and foreboding that hung over our house.

My father would receive registered letters from lawyers demanding sums they claimed he owed to their clients. They threatened all kinds of dire retribution if what they quaintly called 'these monies' were not paid immediately. My mother went silently from room to room, trying to be cheerful. Nanny Gething bravely pretended that all was as it had been and always would be, but Kate and I could now see the worry behind all their optimistic pretences.

Then suddenly – salvation, in the form of a letter from a lawyer. My father opened the envelope, imagining that it must only contain another bill, another threat, but as he read the letter, a remarkable transformation came over his face – as well it might.

This lawyer informed us of the death of my father's great-aunt, whom we called Auntie More. Like many unmarried women of her time, Auntie More was not trained for any career, and so became the paid companion of a rich old widow. When this lady died, she left Auntie More her money, and now Auntie More had died at the age of eighty-three, and left everything to my father, her only relation. One moment he was almost destitute; the next, he was heir to £30,000.

This time, my father decided to be more careful with his

money. He still spent a considerable amount on his search for a lucrative invention, but not on the same scale as before, and the greatest change in his outlook was that he decided to take a job.

He was unexpectedly offered the post of general manager of Jersey Eastern Railways in the Channel Islands. The salary was £500 a year, quite a lot of money in those days, and added to the interest from his investments, we could all live comfortably once more.

I see from my schoolboy's diary that on July 29, 1924, I made this entry: 'Crossed to Jersey on the S.S.*Reindeer.*' This was the ship in which we sailed to a totally new phase in our lives. We sold our furniture and the lease of Bute Lodge, and arrived in Jersey as virtual immigrants, our possessions limited to what we could carry.

My father plunged into his new job with the enthusiasm of a schoolboy with a new mechanical toy. As manager of the railway, he controlled several steam locomotives, with rolling stock and twelve stations spread out over a total distance of nine miles, running from St. Helier to Gorey Castle. Now he had real steam engines with which to occupy his time, not toys like the one he had bought for me, and his pleasure knew no bounds. This spread to us, and our only sadness was saying goodbye to Nanny Gething, who was leaving to join another family as nurse to their children.

Until we could find a house, we lived in a small private hotel. My father bought a Chevrolet car, and then a house, Ellengowan, at Le Fauvic, half-way up a hill.

My mother engaged a French couple to help in this house, the man to do odd jobs, his wife to cook. They came from Normandy or Brittany and lived in our house. The first meal the wife cooked for us was a Sunday lunch of roast lamb. I was starving hungry, but when I took a mouthful, it tasted so strange that I instinctively spat it out on my plate.

'What's the matter, darling?' my mother asked, annoyed and puzzled.

'I can't eat this. It tastes awful.'

My father was furious.

'What do you mean, it tastes awful? How dare the boy behave like this at the lunch table?' he appealed to Topsy rhetorically in the way that fathers did then.

'It tastes funny,' I told him.

'How can roast lamb taste funny?' he demanded. Then he took a mouthful himself and his face showed that he agreed it did indeed taste funny, and not funny ha-ha either, but funny peculiar. Apparently, our new French cook had been far too liberal with the garlic, and my father apologised to me – one of the few times he ever did so.

'You were quite right, my boy,' he said. 'It *was* awful.' And he went straight down to the kitchen to dismiss the couple on the spot, after a violent argument about the value of garlic.

We lived in Ellengowan for about a year and then moved to another house in Green Street, St. Helier. My grandmother, my mother's mother, whom we called 'Dear One', had a flat near us. This overlooked the local swimming pool, where Kate and I swam on most warm days during the holidays. We had a ritual every morning at eleven o'clock when we would go up to Dear One's flat, and she would give us each a biscuit and a glass of port to help keep our circulation going after the cold bathe – no heating in pools in those days.

I attended school, Victoria College Preparatory, where I fell in love for the first time. This was with the headmistress, Miss Bunny, a lady with big teeth, a big bosom and a big heart. For some reason, I became her special favourite. I was in the first eleven football team and even worked hard in class in my efforts to please her. Everybody loved Miss Bunny. I was not the only one to feel warmly towards her, for she took a genuine interest in all her pupils, and her school was the complete antithesis of Steyne. She lived to a great old age, and died only a few years ago, remembered with affection by everyone she had ever taught.

For all of us in our family our years in Jersey had a specially warm glow about them. Every Christmas Eve, I would accompany my father on the train from one end of the line to the other. We would travel in the cab of the engine with the driver and fireman. At each station, the train would stop, and I would step down with my father to greet the local station master, and wish him a Merry Christmas.

My father would bring a bottle of whisky, a turkey, and a box of cigars as his Christmas present for each of the twelve station masters. He paid for these presents himself, and when anyone asked why, he would reply: 'If I don't do it, who else will?'

The station masters, naturally enough, held him in the highest regard; he was a gentleman, which was the supreme compliment they could pay anyone. I remember Mr. Drury, the station master at Le Fauvic, our local station, coming out of his house with tears in his eyes to receive his Christmas box.

'Oh, Major,' he said. 'There has never been anybody like you.' I felt so proud of my father then, for I loved him dearly.

But his second legacy was now melting away with chilling speed. The value of his shares went down suddenly in the late 1920s owing to the general recession. Some companies in which he had invested went out of business altogether; others could not afford to pay any dividend. This slump was also felt on the railway. Takings dropped sharply, and once more we began to be haunted by the spectre of harder times. But now my father, though still barely in his forties, was beginning to feel his age. He complained of pain in the right side of his back. He had in fact suffered from such pains for years, as we all knew, and the local doctor in Richmond had said he thought they might be caused by a stone in a kidney. An X-Ray was suggested, but nothing was ever done. Then one day my father collapsed at work and was taken to the general hospital in Jersey.

He was told he must have an operation to remove a stone, but what would have been a relatively simple operation if tackled in its earlier stages, was now infinitely more complicated, for the stone had calcified and grown very large.

For a long time after the operation he lay in great pain, seriously ill. Gradually, he began to recover, but never again did he regain the resilience and ebullience which had been one of his greatest characteristics.

When he was able to return to work, my father found that the finances of the railway had steadily worsened. In an attempt to increase its profitably he introduced new steam rail cars instead of the traditional locomotives, because they would be cheaper to operate. These rail cars were built by Sentinel-Cammell in Shrewsbury. After seeing various tests at the factory, my father ordered four rail cars, and for the next few months travelled regularly between Shrewsbury and Jersey while they were being built to his exact specification. During these visits, he came to know the directors well. They were grateful to him for such an important order, and his easy-going manner and air of bonhomie impressed them so much that they offered him a job at £750 a year, to sell their products in the East.

The railway was still in decline and there was some doubt as to whether it could even stay solvent. My father, therefore, decided to give up his job as manager before the whole company folded and accepted the Sentinel offer. A few weeks later he sailed East on a two-year contract, involving travel to Singapore, Ceylon and Australia.

My mother went out to join him after six months, and Kate and I stayed on in Jersey. Obviously, we could not live alone in the house in Green Street, so this was sold and we boarded with a family friend, Captain Oldham, in his house, Brookhill Farm. Like my father, Captain Oldham had kept his service rank after the war and he was, I think, rather attracted to my mother and eager to do anything to help her.

In due course, I moved up to the big school, Victoria College, where I had my first part in a school play, *The Sport of Kings*. In the play I took the part of a red-haired girl, and when I put on my wig and my dress, all the senior boys came sidling up to me, saying in a meaningful way, 'I say, More, you *are* a bit of all right!' Somehow their unexpected adulation made me feel sexy.

The first school play in which I played a male was J. M. Barrie's *The Admirable Crichton* which years later I filmed and also took the lead when it was made into a musical. The critic of the school magazine wrote pompously: 'Watch Mr. More. He should go places.' Just what places, and when and why, I had no idea, but I was glad someone believed I was on the move.

Our headmaster was A. H. Worrall, who had taught my father at Bradfield, and he took a special interest in me. This school had a profound effect on my whole life and attitude, for it taught me the importance of fair play, and the hard basic fact that doing a dirty trick is not only unnecessary; it invariably rebounds on the doer, to his disadvantage. I have nothing but warm memories of Victoria College, and particularly of its teaching staff, led by Worrall, who lived to be ninety-two. But when the time came to leave, I did not have a great deal more than memories. When I sat for School Certificate examinations – we did not have 'O' Levels and 'A' Levels then – I received two and a half per cent for mathematics. I think the examiners only gave me this mark because they were sorry that I had produced such an appalling paper. I can still remember the disappointment of all the masters at this deplorable result. I also remember my own feelings, and those of my parents, for how could I earn my living without this absolutely vital subject?

Many of my friends were the sons and daughters of retired Army officers who had served in India and now lived on small pensions, which went farther in Jersey than in England. Jersey was a tax free island, and whisky was 7s. 6d. a bottle and cigarettes, twenty for 4d. Several of my contemporaries went on to Sandhurst, but it was clear I would never pass the entrance exam. And even if I had been capable of doing so, money was once more a serious problem in the family.

My father had come back to England before his contract expired because he was clearly very unwell. His other kidney was now affected, the infection had spread, and he could not continue working. The firm generously kept him on the payroll for a further year, but at the end of this time his health had deteriorated beyond any prospect of working again. He was extremely worried about the future, for by now his second legacy had almost gone the way of the first. His surgeons' and doctors' fees and the hospital bills were so high that if it had not been for the generosity of Dear One neither Kate nor I would have been able to continue at school. She paid the fees for both of us.

My father must have realised he had no hope of a permanent cure, and he worried that I would not be trained for any career. But I was seventeen and I had to do something, for I was due to leave school at a time when about two million other people in Britain were also looking for jobs.

My father decided that the best chance was for me to join Sentinel-Cammell. This was, in fact, the only company where he knew anyone who might help. He took me up to London to meet Commander Gaud, the London sales director, to ask him whether he could find a place for me. I remember that interview very clearly. My father came straight to the point.

'Can you do anything about my son, because frankly I am not in a position to do much for him myself?'

This was a heart-cry from one ex-officer to another. The good Commander Gaud must have heard it often enough before, and he was immediately helpful.

'I can put him into the works as an apprentice, to see how he shapes,' he replied at once. 'Then, if he is any good, he could come into the Sales Department, Bertie, and follow in your footsteps.'

So in two minutes my future appeared decided.

The prospect did not fill me with much enthusiasm. I had hoped for some more exciting job than working for two years in a factory in Shrewsbury making steam engines, to prepare me for a lifetime selling them. But I had no alternative proposal to offer and I realised I was lucky to be offered any kind of job, and so did my best to appear pleased at a prospect that secretly depressed me.

Father and I went home with the news, and Tops helped me to pack my belongings in a suitcase. I said goodbye to everyone, and with a parting present of a few pounds in my pocket, travelled to Shrewsbury.

Commander Gaud had very kindly arranged digs for me, literally opposite the factory whistle, with a Mrs. Anslow, whose husband also worked at Sentinel. My room was small but very clean, with gleaming lino and a pervading smell of polish. Mrs.

Anslow greeted me on the morning of my arrival very correctly as Mr. More, but by the evening, I was Ken, which made me feel at home.

On the Monday morning at eight o'clock, when the whistle blew, I presented myself at the factory gates. Wearing a set of brand new blue denim overalls, I certainly looked the part of the industrious apprentice.

I was being paid a pound a week, and since I was what was called quaintly 'a privileged apprentice' and being trained for an executive position, I was told that I could wear white overalls. I bought a pair of these, one of the great mistakes of my life, because in a week they showed every single mark, whereas the other apprentices could wear their blue overalls for at least six weeks without having them washed.

I was relieved to find no hostility from them or anyone else. Although I spoke rather differently from them, and some would mimic my accent, which until then I had always assumed was a very ordinary one, they all accepted me. I came in for some leg-pulling from the older men, of course. I was sent to fetch 'rubber nails', 'left-handed tea cups' and 'glass hammers', but this was all part of the initiation of the newcomer. I had put up with much worse at school, and accepted it.

In order to learn the rudiments of engineering, I was put to work for weeks at a time with different men in different sections of the huge factory.

My first job was with a Welshman, Wat Thomas. He was a big man and I could see at once that he also had a big thirst. Not to put too fine a point on it, Thomas was nearly always suffering from the effects of having drunk too much beer on the previous evening. I worked with him in what we called the wheel-bay. Our job was to convert the wheels of old-fashioned steam wagons, that had originally been fitted with solid rubber tyres, to the more modern pneumatic tyres. This job was known as a DC4 conversion, DC being the type of steam wagon, and the number 4, referring to its wheels. There was a constant stream of these old wagons waiting to be modernised.

The work was very heavy, because the axles and wheels were built on a massive scale. My task, as the unskilled trainee, was to remove the old axles, which seemed to weigh about half a ton each, clean the congealed mud and grease of years from them and then help to modify them. Removing these axles was an extremely difficult task. Locking pins that held them to the springs had generally rusted into their holes over five or ten years' hard use. The only way to extract them was to hammer them out. My part in this operation was to hold a tapering metal spike about a foot long against the end of one of these pins, while Wat Thomas, the skilled engineer, swung a sledge-hammer and knocked them free with three or four tremendous blows.

Wat Thomas would be on the beer every night, and so each morning I dreaded holding this spike while he swayed about with his enormous hammer, peering blearily in the general direction of the pin, as though not quite sure where it was. Half an inch off target, and my hand and wrist would have been smashed. I therefore decided to increase the odds against this happening as best I could.

In addition to my pound a week wages, my mother managed to scrape together another thirty shillings a week to send me. Since my digs cost twenty-five shillings a week, I had twenty-five shillings left for myself each week. This was not a lot, even then, but I felt it would be enough to buy myself out of this predicament which was a living nightmare to me. I told Wat about it.

'I am worried that one day you'll miss and break my wrist.'

'I've never missed so far in my life, so why should I start now?' he asked me rhetorically. But he looked so green with beer as he spoke that this sounded a very empty boast to me. And, in addition, he was talking about the past; I was looking to the future. Now Wat Thomas smoked as much as he drank, and so I went on to ask him, in the accent that the others liked to mimic:

'Does smoking mean a lot to you?'

He nodded.

'Course it does. Obvious, isn't it?'

'Then I'll make a bet with you,' I told him. 'You give up the beer for a week, and I'll buy you a hundred Players.'

That meant an outlay of five shillings, but it should keep my wrist intact for another seven days. I regarded the expenditure as being in the nature of an insurance policy. Thomas regarded it as a wonderful gift; five shillings was a lot of money to both of us.

'I can give up drinking any time I like,' he told me confidently.

'You're on.'

This conversation took place on a Friday. On Monday morning, he came in bright-eyed, with healthy colour in his cheeks.

'I'm going to win those fags,' he assured me, as he prepared to hit the spike. His stroke was surer and more certain already, so it seemed to me, and it grew sharper and more precise with each day that passed. I began to feel more confident that I would survive my time in the wheel-bay without mutilation. A subsidiary bonus was the fact that I did not have to suffer from Wat's awful beery breath any more.

When Friday came round, he swore he hadn't drunk for a whole week, and I believed him. He was healthier than I'd ever seen him; even his teeth looked whiter. I was short of ready money that week so I borrowed half a crown from a friend and presented Wat with the hundred Players. They came in a fine blue box with gold lettering. Wat Thomas was delighted. Beaming all over his face, he picked up his giant hammer, swung it at the spike, missed – and took the nail off my right thumb. I put him back on the beer after that, and he never missed again.

There didn't seem a lot of social life in Shrewsbury at that time, or if there was, I wasn't in it.

Of course, people were very much more aware of social and class divisions, sometimes real, sometimes imaginary, and I did not mix much with my workmates outside of factory hours. But I did make some friends, not in the factory, and we used to go to dances on Saturday evenings, either in pairs or in a group. One of these dances was particularly memorable for me for it led to my first real sexual adventure, which must be a milestone in any man's life.

I must point out that I was still a very shy boy. I suppose that we all were shy and backward and remarkably innocent then. Of course, I would boast to my friends of my conquests, but nothing had happened to me at all – and I suppose nothing much had happened to them either, although they stoutly claimed it had.

On this particular night, I went to the dance with a friend, Walter Gee, and picked up a nurse from one of the local hospitals. She was no particular beauty, by any means, but she was great fun and as soon as I put my arm around her in a two-step she pressed hard against me. I realised even in my young innocence that she was not one of the thin anaemic type of girls who sat around the walls waiting for a partner. She knew what she wanted, and what she wanted was sex. I also knew, as though I had seen the future written in letters of fire, that I was to be the means of gratifying her need, and this knowledge, which I felt in my blood and bones and elsewhere in my body, was profoundly exciting.

After previous dances there had been a bit of fumbling with other girls, and the undoing of blouse buttons behind the dance hall, while music from the band pounded through the walls, but, in the crude phrase of the day, I had never actually 'put it in'.

Now I realised, with a feeling of expectation and trepidation, that I would not be able to say this for much longer. I might have started the evening as a boy, but I was determined to end it a man.

We danced well together – so well that we won the spot prize for waltzing, which seemed to me a good augury of success in other more intimate associations. At the end of the evening the nurse mentioned casually that she shared a flat above a local hair-dresser's shop with a friend. The friend was away for the weekend. Would I care to go home with her after the dance? Would I *care* to? I could hardly wait.

I had ridden to the dance on my bicycle, for I could not afford even a motor bike on my pay. She had walked, and we covered the 300 yards back to her flat in the same way, me pedalling while she ran alongside holding on to the saddle with one hand. This was the view Walter Gee had of us as he stood in the dance hall doorway, preparing to go back to his digs alone. He thought she was holding on to the saddle in case I should try to escape.

The nurse and I went upstairs above the shop and into her bedroom. We undressed and climbed into a remarkably cold bed, the chill of which was speedily obliterated by her generous warmth. She instructed me in my part of the proceedings – or at least what she hoped my part would be. But my state of nervousness and excitement was such that it was all over before I really began.

Next morning, still half asleep from my delightful if unpro-tracted exertions, I was awakened by a strange sound outside. I listened for a moment and realised that someone was throwing pebbles at the bedroom window. I glanced at the nurse. She was still asleep. I crept cautiously out of bed, crossed the carpet and looked out of the window. Faithful Walter Gee was outside in the street, one arm raised to throw another pebble at the window.

'I know you're up there because your bike's outside,' he called. 'And it's about time you came home. We are due at church in an hour with my parents!'

Poor Walter! He meant so well. We had not been to church for months, either of us, but I think he feared some dreadful harm would befall me at the hands of such an experienced woman, and this was his way of trying to save me – and incidentally, surprise his family.

I dressed quickly and quietly and tip-toed down the stairs. I felt ashamed of my sexual performance, but my embarrassment was soon outweighed by a growing worry that the eager nurse might be pregnant. I knew nothing of birth control, and so for the next few weeks, which my friends maliciously assured me would be crucial, I lived the life of a hunted man.

31

I dreaded every letter that came through the post in case it was from a lawyer to inform me that his client, the nurse, had 'joined the club'!

When I went out, I walked furtively through the streets of Shrewsbury. I would glance behind me from time to time, in case her father or a brother were following me to touch me on the shoulder and demand to know my intentions towards her. These intentions, I must cravenly now admit, were simply never to set eyes upon her again. Gradually the weeks passed without incident or alarm and my fears diminished.

It was just at this time that I heard from Tops that my father had only a short time to live. The surgeons had discovered that his remaining kidney was infected and there was no cure. This was before the days of kidney transplants and antibiotics, but a man could still live indefinitely with one kidney. It was only if the second became diseased that he received sentence of death. My father died within days. He was only forty-five.

2

MY MOTHER AND I shared the melancholy task of going
through his papers in an attempt to sort out his affairs.
The drawers of his desk were stuffed with share certificates in companies that had either ceased trading or had not paid
dividends for years. There was an overdraft of £3,000 at the bank
about which the manager was becoming tetchy, and a number of
unpaid bills which somehow had to be met. In his wallet we
found three one pound notes.

Amid the mass of worthless certificates, however, we discovered a life insurance policy which he had taken out without
any of us knowing. Goodness only knows how he had ever
managed to pass the medical. This helped us to pay off his debts,
but afterwards only a few pounds were left. My mother went to
live with her mother, Dear One, in Weston-super-Mare where
she had moved from Jersey. Fortunately, Dear One had some
capital of her own and she believed they could live quietly on it
together now both Kate and I were off her hands. But Tops, as a
relatively young woman, could not bear to exist on what she felt
was virtually charity. She was therefore extremely thankful when
a friend of hers from Jersey, one Miriam Fallah, wrote to her to
sympathise on father's death, and quite unexpectedly offered her
a job. Miriam explained that she had recently bought a large hotel
in Malvern, Worcestershire, where she had moved. Knowing
how capable my mother was, she wondered whether she would
be interested in running this for her.

Miriam was a rich, middle-aged woman who required someone to run the hotel because all her time and energies were otherwise accounted for. She had fairly recently married a man much
younger than herself, Bobby Pinnegar, and she had discovered
that marriage had not caused Bobby's eye to cease roving. He
was, in fact, quite a charmer. He took great pains to give everyone the impression of being top-drawer, but I think he came from
several drawers down. He would ride to hounds, but he still
liked a bit of 'how's your father' as well, and this was what was
worrying Miriam.

Bobby had no money. His capital was his charm. He had lived

by his wits, or by the prowess of other parts of his anatomy pleasurable to middle-aged ladies, until he met and married Miriam. Now he was living like a lord in her hotel.

Strangers assumed that Bobby must be the local squire. He wore well-cut tweed suits, hand-made brogues and silk shirts. He drove a fast and expensive car, and enjoyed the finest wines and cigars. Miriam feared he also enjoyed the favours of other ladies more attractive than herself and she realised with concern that marriage had not closed the gap in their ages, but increased it. She tended to sit in her front parlour and worry about life in general, and especially how she had got herself into this awful situation.

With this on her mind, the last thing she wanted at her time of life was to have the additional worry of running a hotel.

My mother accepted Miriam's offer gratefully and thoroughly enjoyed the challenge of her job.

One weekend, she wrote to me from Malvern, and asked if I could join them for a dance that Bobby Pinnegar had decided to hold to celebrate something. He had been promoted Master of Hounds, or had received some other signal recognition in the hunting field which he felt deserved celebrating. All he really wanted was an excuse for a big dance, and this seemed as good a reason as any other.

'Kenny, darling,' my mother. wrote. 'Wouldn't it be lovely if you could come for the weekend from Shrewsbury? Kate could come from London, and then we would all be together as in the old days.'

Kate was then married to John Tilly, the comedian, who could not join us because he was in a show. I would have loved to go but I had no car, and by train the distance and changes involved seemed daunting, to say nothing of the expense.

Then I remembered two friends, Tim and Dolly, who owned a small car. They were a sweet couple and had virtually adopted me. I suppose they were in their early thirties, and I used to spend many weekends with them, and loved them. I suggested they should come to the ball as well. They would have a free weekend and I would have a free ride to Malvern and back in their Austin Ten. They were delighted to accept.

We arrived, had dinner, and then the dance began. As the evening wore on, and the wine flowed freely in both senses of the word, I noticed that my sister and Bobby Pinnegar were dancing closer and closer together. I could hardly help noticing this, for Bobby was gripping her as though she would fall if he released his hold. I also saw that old Miriam Fallah was not unaware of this and was giving them dirty looks. Even my mother was growing a little uncomfortable.

Dolly and Tim were dancing and drinking away happily, and I am sure they did not sense our concern. But then, they did not know Kate's reputation for what was called 'fast living', a description which boys did not want to hear applied to their sisters.

An hour before the last waltz, when the floor was absolutely packed, Kate and Bobby Pinnegar suddenly disappeared. Miriam had been watching them as usual, but her attention was distracted for a moment, and in that instant they left the floor. The dance continued. Miriam turned to my mother and asked anxiously: 'Where's Bobby? Where's Kate?'

My mother said nothing, but went very red in the face. Miriam sat on, puzzled by the couple's disappearance, but still unable to believe there could be anything sinister behind it.

After the last waltz, I went up the stairs to my room. My mother followed me, and Miriam was a few paces behind her. We reached the floor on which she and Bobby had their suite. At that moment, Miriam's bedroom door burst open and Kate, drunk out of her mind and naked as Mother Eve, ran squealing down the corridor. Bobby was just behind her. To use a phrase popular when I was in the Navy, he was 'Harry Starkers' and was chasing her with enthusiasm and clearly one purpose in mind.

I was so startled and ashamed to see my sister behave like this – as I have already said, I was very innocent – that I burst into tears. My mother gave a great gasp of horror.

'Oh, my God!'

Miriam said nothing, but pursed her lips and shook her head in a way that left us in no doubt that this marked the beginning of the end of Bobby Pinnegar's time as the squire of Malvern, at least at her expense.

The worst thing for all of us was that Kate and Bobby both clearly thought the whole incident hysterically funny and of no consequence whatever. They were screaming with laughter.

I drew my mother gently into my bedroom, and we sat down on the edge of the bed.

'What's going to happen to us?' I said, as though she could possibly know.

'I don't know,' she replied, holding my hand. 'But your sister has let us down. It's terrible. Terrible. I can't stay here after this.'

She began to cry, for her own future, on which she had set such high hopes, was now in ruins.

Miriam followed us into the room. She was also weeping. Then Tim and Dolly arrived, and wanted to know why we were all crying. We told them. They didn't cry, but they instantly realised that the party was over.

Tim said that they should really go home as he had just remembered he had to make an early start for somewhere. They offered me a lift back to Shrewsbury. I accepted. So, at about three o'clock in the morning, I packed my clothes and climbed into their car for the long drive back.

I was too naïve to consider it odd that Tim should tell me to sit in the back with Dolly. We both climbed into the back seat obediently, and suddenly, while Tim was hunched over the wheel, and we were grinding along at about thirty miles an hour in the light of the Austin's feeble headlamps, Dolly was all over me.

I was terrified. There was Tim, twice my size, barely a foot in front of us, while his wife was all but raping me in the back seat.

This was my second sexual experience, and what an experience! Dolly was puffing and blowing and feeling, and God knows what else. We did things to each other during that journey I had not even heard of before. We must have been making the most awful noises and yet Tim never once looked over his shoulder. Was he also immensely naïve, or was he immensely sophisticated? I still am not sure. But what I am sure about is that this was the most memorable car ride of my life. And the curious thing was, it was never referred to afterwards by any of us.

I was now nearing the end of my privileged apprenticeship at Shrewsbury, and I knew what I had previously strongly suspected, that engineering was not for me. I spent my final six months in the sales office, where they tried to train me as a representative. I was told that after many years I might become a sales manager, a kind of glorified salesman, like my father. This was not the way I wanted to spend my life.

As it happened, another friend of mine, John Hulton-Harrop, was also dissatisfied with his job, and he suggested we should both volunteer for the Royal Air Force. This seemed a good idea, and we wrote off for interviews. Commander Gaud tried to talk me out of this, by assuring me there was a great future for me in the firm if I stayed, but my mind was made up.

'No, sir,' I told him. 'I am going to try for the RAF.'

He then very sportingly promised to do everything he could to help me realise this ambition, and gave me a fine reference.

I told Tops of my intention, and she somehow scraped together fifty pounds, because I would have to stay in London for several days and might need money to buy some new clothes for my various interviews.

John and I set off together for London, and we found digs in a house of bed-sitters in Gloucester Terrace. Then we presented ourselves at the Air Ministry in Adastral House, Kingsway.

John passed as fit on all counts for the RAF but I failed on two. First, I had no school certificate. I should have realised that without this document I would not get very far, for this had been drummed into me often enough at school, but somehow I had not expected to fail on what still seemed to me to be a small point – literally an academic point.

As if this was not sufficient reason for the RAF to decline my services, I also failed their medical. I was placed in a swivel chair and an orderly spun it around and then I was told to walk a chalk line. I started, staggered and fell over, through some lack of ability to balance.

So there I was, out of Sentinel, and out of the RAF before I'd even been in. I was bitterly disappointed.

John duly qualified as a fighter pilot, and a first rate one, at that. Shortly after the outbreak of war, he was returning from one of the very early sweeps over France when British anti-aircraft batteries on the Kent coast confused his flight with a flight of German planes that had also been reported – and shot him down. He was one of the first RAF casualties in the war. I am pretty certain that had I been accepted with him, I would not have survived much longer. As in the first world war, nearly all the early pilots had very short lives.

This was the first of several incidents which have increasingly drawn me to the conclusion that our lives do have a set and definite pattern – if only we do not struggle against it. Sometimes we try so hard to achieve something that seems important at the time, and only years later do we realise that if we had but let events take their course, and been content to be carried on their tide, we would have achieved quite a different aim, for which we were probably much better suited. But, at nineteen, this philosophic approach had no attractions for me. I had no job and no qualifications for one, yet it was absolutely imperative that I found some employment that would at least keep me in food and lodging.

Of course, I wrote to Tops to explain what had happened, and she replied with a proposal. Sainsbury's, the grocers, were advertising for staff. She suggested that I should join them and then, in the phrase of those days, work my way right up to the top. Again, this prospect did not exactly light my star, but at least

I would be paid, so I applied for a job. I passed the interview, was told of the excellent prospects then, clad in a white apron was put to work behind the butter-and-eggs counter in Sainsbury's branch in the Strand. So began my first face-to-face association with the British public.

One thing that surprised me when working in Sainsbury's was the number of customers who were so shy that they could barely bring themselves to ask for half-a-dozen eggs or a pound of butter. They could only do so in a whisper, as though it was a guilty transaction of which they were ashamed. What a blessing supermarkets must be for them, where no words need be spoken at all.

Another surprise was that my maths had not improved since my disastrous showing in the school certificate examination. In fact, they were probably rather worse. Other counter-hands could work out in their heads complicated sums involving half-a-dozen eggs, two ounces of margarine, a quarter of New Zealand butter and a half of lard. This was totally beyond my ability, then or now. Also, I seemed to break a surprising number of eggs I handled. I had no idea how thin their shells were, until I picked them up. Soon, I noticed the manager pursing his lips in a brooding sort of way whenever he looked in my direction. I was not therefore wholly surprised when after a couple of weeks' trial, it was suggested to me that Mr. Sainsbury could manage his shops more profitably without my assistance.

So I was back again in my digs, unemployed and seemingly unemployable.

One morning, on the stairs, I met the man in the room next door, Bill Manfield, who was about my own age with a similar background. After a fruitless visit to the local employment exchange, I met him again for a beer in a pub that lunchtime. I explained my situation to him. I had still about ten pounds left from the fifty my mother had given me, but this would not last for very long, and when it was gone – what then?

'Tell you what,' he said brightly. 'Let's go to Canada.'

'Canada?' I repeated. 'What can we do in Canada?'

'Make a fortune there, that's what. Trapping. Shooting bears. Selling furs. It's quite easy when you know people, and in Canada I've got the best contact in the world. An uncle in the Hudson Bay Trading Company. He knows all kinds of people who'll help us. Think about that, Kenny.'

I thought about it, and we had another beer, then I thought about it a bit more. Already, I could see myself tracking through frozen wastes in snow-shoes, spearing polar bears, leaping from ice floe to ice floe, shooting rapids and grizzlies. Trapper More Goes North. It was an agreeable picture.

'Sounds a great idea,' I admitted. 'But how do we go about it?'

'We just sail to Canada, and ring him up,' said Bill. 'That's how.'

'Won't we need a lot of kit?'

'Oh, a few old tents, rifles, boots, breeches. That sort of thing.'

'It's as easy as that?' I asked in surprise. 'But these things will cost a lot of money.'

'Haven't you got *any* money?'

'Not much,' I admitted. 'But I suppose I could ask my mother.'

'You do that,' Bill advised me gravely.

I had decided not to ask Tops for any more money, but now I told myself that this should not be regarded as a gift or even as a loan, but as an investment. Within months, I should be able to pay her back, and with interest. But in order to explain this fact fully, I felt I should go to see her instead of writing.

Tops was a very soft, sweet, generous-hearted person. She listened to me patiently, while I told her of this wonderful opportunity, how I could start a completely new career in Canada, and on only a hundred pounds.

'Kenny,' she said when she had heard me out. 'Just how long have you actually known this Mr. Manfield?'

'I've really only met him a day or so ago,' I admitted. 'But what's that got to do with it?'

Tops sat with her hands folded, considering my proposition.

'Darling,' she said at last. 'A hundred pounds is an awful lot of money, and I just cannot spare that much. But I'll ask Dear One, and if she has it, then I know she'll give it to you.'

And Dear One did just that. I went back to my digs, and within a few days a registered letter arrived. The envelope felt thick and crinkly. I opened it and counted out twenty huge white old-fashioned five pound notes, twice the size and possibly ten times the value of our present little blue fivers. There was also a letter from my mother.

'With this money, you will have to find a career for yourself, Kenny,' she wrote. 'I can offer you no more. I am sorry, but there it is. This is your life now.'

Bill Manfield was understandably delighted when he heard that I could now finance our trip. Our two most expensive items were two trans-Atlantic steamer tickets aboard the Cunard liner, SS *Montcalm*. We bought the cheapest singles obtainable for there seemed no point in buying return fares. By the time we wanted to come back, we would both be rich enough to travel in staterooms.

Then we went to the Army and Navy Stores in Victoria Street, and bought a two-man tent, which Bill said would be absolutely necessary when we were tracking. Next, we visited a gunsmith and bought two second-hand Schneider rifles, which the salesman assured us were surplus stock from the Boer War, and two single-barrel shotguns guaranteed to stop a bear in its tracks at twenty paces. Then we bought hunting knives, ex-Army boots, puttees, breeches, shirts, a Primus stove and two sleeping bags. All this made a big hole in my hundred pounds, but at least we were booked outward bound from Liverpool to Quebec, and possessed sufficient kit to start our new careers in Canada.

A few days before we were due to sail, we were drinking beer in a pub near Gloucester Terrace, when into the bar walked one of the most beautiful girls I have ever seen in my life.

I know I am susceptible to feminine beauty, but this girl still stays in my mind as a face apart. Her figure was pretty good too.

Bill glanced across at her, and suddenly he went pale. He put his tankard on the bar with a trembling hand.

'What's the matter?' I asked. 'Do you know her?'

It seemed inconceivable that homely Bill could actually be acquainted with such a ravishing creature.

'Yes,' he admitted hoarsely. 'I do know her. She's Joan Spencer. We've been sort of, well, together.'

'How did she find you were here?' I asked.

'I don't know,' he replied gloomily. 'But she has.'

'Aren't you lucky?' I told him. 'I wish she'd find me.'

'She's trouble, Kenny.'

'She doesn't look like trouble to me.'

I can see her now, with short shingled hair, and beautiful eyes, and I fell for her instantly. Of course, she hardly noticed me. Her big blue eyes were on Bill, and she was furious with him. She started a long recriminatory argument as to where he had been, and why he had not been in touch with her for weeks. I tried to help Bill with his halting and unconvincing excuses, by explaining we were both about to leave for Canada, to make our fortunes.

'You are not leaving this country without me,' she told Bill bluntly.

'I'm sorry,' said Bill, without much conviction. 'We just have to. We've already booked our tickets.'

'You go without me, and I'll make such a fuss, you'll never forget it.'

40

Bill did not answer her. He paused for a moment, and then turned to me.

'Kenny, how much money have we got left?'

'Thirty quid,' I said, noticing the use of the editorial or royal plural. Hang it all, this was my money – or, rather, Dear One's. 'And that's all we *have* got.' On this we had to reach Montreal and then travel up to the Arctic Circle.

'Well,' he said, 'the tickets are only fifteen pounds each. We can at least buy another ticket, and still have some over.' The tickets were third class, of course!

So Dear One's money bought another ticket, and we all took the train up to Liverpool, and went aboard. I was in one cabin with Bill and several other men. Joan was elsewhere, with three or four women.

Both cabins were down in the bowels of the ship, virtually in the steerage. As the *Montcalm* moved down the Mersey, we could hear the propeller thundering near us and the creak of the rudder chains and the hammering of waves against her hull. Indeed, these noises were so loud, we could hear little else. Over everything in our cabin hung a strong and most disagreeable smell of sickness and vomit, for ventilation so far down was minimal.

This was a horrible beginning, but I endured it, for I was on my way to riches and travelling with this unbelievable girl. I was already madly in love with her – but she hardly ever spoke to me. I don't know whether she even remembered my name. She was Bill's girl. He was very good-looking, which I'd never noticed until I saw them together. I didn't stand a chance, and was heartbroken. I felt so out of things that I walked five paces behind them as we strolled round the decks.

For the first two days at sea, some of our companions in the cabin never left their bunks, they were so ill, groaning away, and finally I thought, to hell with this. I didn't belong down here in this foetid, airless cell, with these wretched emigrant mechanics and their carpet-bags of tools. I felt I belonged up in the first-class section of the ship, where there was air and light and music and hot baths and good meals. *Montcalm* was divided into classes, first, second, third, with gates between one deck and another to keep everyone in their sections. These gates were kept locked, but we three discovered a way around them. By going down one companionway, then along a corridor, up a staircase and through a couple of doors marked 'No Admittance: Crew Only', we found we could reach the sanctuary of the first-class section.

We therefore began to lead double lives. By day we would

suffer in our part of the ship, but at dusk we would join the richer voyagers in the first-class areas, drinking at the bar and dancing. Then, like three Cinderellas, we would creep back to our filthy stinking cabins below sea-level before we could be discovered.

The classes were so rigidly segregated because the first-class fare cost a great deal more than the second or third, and there was a strongly-built member of the crew, the ship's Master-at-Arms, whose job was to keep passengers in their social stations.

'Hey, you, sirs, and you, miss!' he would call sharply, when he spotted us, and if we ignored his shout, he would give chase.

As soon as we heard his feet drum on the deck, we used to scatter, running down gangways, and in and out of doors, like characters in a French farce.

At long last the good ship *Montcalm* steamed up the St. Lawrence River and approached Quebec. A launch drew alongside and immigration officials climbed aboard. They set up tables in one of the lounges, and the passengers formed up in line in front of them to have their passports checked. It was a formality to stamp and return their passports with a smile, but when Bill and Joan and I appeared, the officials held ours back.

'The three of you are coming ashore,' one of them informed us briefly.

'Why?' I asked.

'For questioning.'

'What about?'

'We need some more information about you.'

'What sort of information? Can't we give it to you here? Where are we going?'

They refused to answer any of our questions. We had to wait in the lounge until the ship docked, and then, with our luggage, we were marched unceremoniously down the gangway and into a car that took us to the immigration building. From this we were moved to a detention centre for illegal immigrants.

No one would tell us why we were there. Bill and I were put into separate cells, and Joan was taken off to the women's section. In the cell next to me was a Chinese drug addict who screamed all night and rattled the bars like a gorilla in his attempts to go free. When this produced no results, he beat his head on the floor almost as forcefully as Wat Thomas had wielded his sledge-hammer. No one took any notice of him or of us. We were given food in our cells, and for each of the three days we spent in the detention centre, officials took us out every morning for exercise on the flat roof.

I told them that I was a British subject. They showed no

42

surprise. I read out the splendid exhortation in the front of my passport: 'His Britannic Majesty's Principal Secretary for Foreign Affairs requests and requires in the name of His Majesty all those whom it may concern to allow the bearer to pass freely without let or hindrance, and to afford the bearer such assistance and protection as may be necessary.'

'What about that, then?' I asked them, as though this should settle all doubts.

The guards just shrugged.

Finally, I was taken in front of the governor of the detention centre and declaimed this front page, which I knew by heart. He was also unimpressed.

'Listen, young fellow,' he said. 'Do you know why you are here?'

'Of course I don't. I have been asking that for days, but no one will tell me.'

'Well, before *I* tell you, what exactly do you intend to do here in Canada?'

'Do in Canada? I'm going to shoot polar bears, trap foxes, sell furs. My friend's uncle is a director of the Hudson Bay Company. What do you think we've brought all this kit for?'

'I've really no idea,' he admitted. 'How much Canadian money have you got?'

'About forty-seven dollars. Say ten pounds.'

'And that is going to take you a long way in a big country, isn't it?' he asked sarcastically.

'I don't need money,' I assured him. 'My friend's uncle will look after us. Just as soon as we get to Montreal and contact him, we'll be in clover.'

'You think so? Well, you've got forty-seven bucks. I suggest you use a few of them to put a phone call in to your friend's uncle.'

'I don't know his name or his number,' I admitted. 'But you ask my friend. He'll do it.'

'No,' he said. 'He won't. And you know why? Because we've already asked him. He hasn't got any uncle in the Hudson Bay Company, so he hasn't got any phone number he can ring.'

'He has,' I insisted stubbornly, for the alternative was too terrible to contemplate.

'What about the woman?' the governor went on.

'She's with us,' I said.

'Maybe. But do you know she's already married?'

'Rubbish! She's Bill Manfield's girl friend.'

'I don't deny that. But she is also married to an Italian in

London. One of the charges you are being held on here is the very serious one of smuggling a married woman over a state border without the permission of her husband.'

I stood aghast at this, and as though to confound me further, the governor opened a folder on his desk and began to read out the story of my life so far. What my father had been. My mother's maiden name. Where I went to school. How I had been a privileged apprentice at Sentinel. Even the melancholy fact that I had been rejected for the RAF. Somehow, they had gathered all this information from London in the three days we had been in the cells.

He closed the folder and we looked at each other in silence.

'Well,' he said at last. 'I have nothing against you personally. Nothing at all. If you can find someone who will stand guarantee for you, you can come right into Canada. But your friend and the girl – no. They are going to be deported.'

'What on?'

'The same ship that brought you here.'

I thought, my God, that will drive the Master-at-Arms mad.

'She's gone up-river to Montreal,' the governor continued. 'On the way back, she'll call here and take them back to Liverpool. But, as I say, you can stay.'

'But what can I do on my own? I don't know anybody here.'

'Right,' he replied smartly. 'Then pack your kit. You're going back with them.'

We were all served with deportation orders, and when *Montcalm* docked, there at the top of the gangway stood the Master-at-Arms. Suddenly, he saw us and his face was terrible to behold. As we were being deported, the shipping company had to carry us for nothing. This time, though, the Master-at-Arms did not have to pursue us through the first-class section. We felt so depressed, we stayed in our cabins.

'What the hell do you mean by doing this to me?' I asked Bill bitterly, as we headed back into the Atlantic.

'Kenny,' he replied. 'It was a fair risk. I thought we'd just get off the boat and go.'

When we arrived back in England, Joan went off to her mother, or maybe her husband, and Bill and I went to the only place we could afford – our digs in Gloucester Terrace. Then he found a job somewhere and moved out of my life.

Back in London with no money, I found that the market for second-hand snow shoes, breeches, puttees, and Boer War rifles stood at a very low ebb.

I wrote to my mother and explained what had happened. This,

44

I felt, was the least I could do. Then I thought that it was all too little. So I tore up the letter and went down to Weston-super-Mare to tell her and Dear One personally just why I was back again and broke.

They heard me out and then gave me a good stripping down for being such a fool. I deserved it, but I didn't improve matters by saying that most of all I wanted to find Joan, wherever she was.

'Don't be so stupid,' my mother told me, angry for once. 'Let her go, and good riddance.'

We had a long conference about my future without reaching any conclusion, and then Dear One made her contribution. As was so often the case with her, this was in kind and not in conversation.

'Whatever you do, Kenny,' she said. 'You'll have to have some money to stay alive while you do it. Here is my contribution. All I can spare. And after this has gone, well, there *is* no more.'

She handed me an envelope. I opened it. Inside was a further hundred pounds in fivers.

I felt immensely grateful, but where could I find a job? It was obvious I would not find one in Weston-super-Mare, so back I went to London to my digs. I wrote for jobs that were advertised in newspapers; I applied for interviews; I queued up at the Labour Exchange, and in between all these unsuccessful attempts to find work, I walked the streets.

I hoped vaguely, and seemingly without any reason, for some sign or portent that would point my life in a worthwhile direction.

Hands in pockets, face creased with worry, I walked through the West End of London. Chauffeurs were opening the doors of Rolls-Royces outside the Ritz. The commissionaire at Fortnum's bowed dowagers into Daimlers. All around was evidence of wealth and success, but I was on the outside, looking in.

I walked on down Piccadilly, paused at the Circus with the old flower-sellers, watched the bootblacks, wondering in which direction I should go. I considered going down the Haymarket, and then thought about Leicester Square – or what about Regent Street, curving away to the north? For some reason, I know not what or why, I took none of these directions. Instead, I took the middle road – up Shaftesbury Avenue. Perhaps I was drawn by a childhood association with my father's car showroom in Gerrard Street, which I had visited with him, or perhaps it was something else. I do not know. All I know is that I walked up that street of theatres.

Fifty yards on, a road led to the left – Windmill Street – a narrow thoroughfare of snack bars and shops. On the right of this street stood a small theatre, named after a landmark that stood there a century earlier: The Windmill.

Having no other goal, I strolled up to this theatre and looked at the photographs outside. Then above the main entrance door, I saw four words that made my heart stop for a second: 'General Manager – Vivian Van Damm.'

I remembered the name now, and the visitor to Bute Lodge. Until then, I had forgotten all about him – or had I? Had my subconscious memory stored away this strange name for just such a purpose? Had this guided my feet like a lodestone through London to this one particular theatre? I decided to ask him for a job.

I crossed the road to a telephone box, looked up the number of the theatre in the directory and telephoned.

I got through, spoke to his secretary, and finally to the man himself.

'Mr. Van Damm, I would like to see you,' I said.

'What about?'

'I want a job.'

'Who are you?'

'My name is Kenneth More.'

There was a pause.

'Are you Bertie More's son?'

I said, 'Yes.'

'Well . . .'

Van Damm paused again, and then he went on, in words I will always remember.

'Bertie More was the whitest man I ever met. If I can do anything for you, I will. Come and see me at my office here tomorrow. Half past ten.'

This description of my father had a Kiplingesque ring to it, nothing whatever to do with colour. It simply meant that he was straight and honourable, a man with no dark side to his nature, who would willingly help anyone, without thought of personal gain or personal cost.

The following morning, I went up the stairs to Van Damm's office. It was rather like a film set of a study with a huge desk and shelves of books. Van Damm was smoking a cigar. We shook hands.

'Now what can I do for you, exactly?' he asked.

'I want a job, sir,' I replied. I called most men older than me, 'sir'.

'What have you been doing so far?'

46

'Engineering, sir. But I'm not interested in going on with that.'

'You're Bertie More's son, and that's good enough for me. Start next Monday.'

'Start doing what, sir?'

'Start at the bottom like the rest, as a stagehand. Then, when you've been here a few months, I'll teach you front-of-the-house management. Put you through all the parts of the theatre. One day, I intend to branch out into other things, and then maybe you can take over this theatre.'

He laughed. I didn't know whether what he said was meant as a joke or seriously. I laughed too. I had something to be cheerful about. I had a job.

'Thank you very much, sir,' I told him. 'That's very good of you.'

So my father's kindness and generosity on innumerable occasions to so many people over so many years had paid an unexpected dividend after his death.

'There is one thing you must remember, Kenny,' Vivian Van Damm went on, waving aside my thanks. 'There are girls here. Girls without any clothes on.'

'I can't believe it,' I said. I was that innocent.

'Yes, yes, there are.'

He must have seen how green I was, for whatever he had been going to say, he decided against it.

'Start on Monday, then.'

'Er, how much, sir?'

'Two pounds ten shillings a week to begin with. What do your digs cost you?'

'Thirty shillings, sir.'

'That leaves you one pound for your food. You will have to manage on that for a while.'

In those days, a skilled mechanic with a family was only earning five shillings more, so this salary, with the prospect of naked ladies thrown in, was manna from heaven for a young lad.

'There is just one thing I would like to warn you about,' said Van Damm seriously. 'Not drink. And not girls. Acting. You must never, *ever* become a bloody actor. Acting is the end. It is death and destruction to become an actor, and I know what I'm talking about. You stick to me, Kenny, and I'll teach you how to run a theatre. But whatever you do, forget acting. Put that right out of your mind.'

'I've never had it in my mind at all, sir,' I assured him. 'I give you my word, sir. The last thing I intend to do, sir, is to become an actor.'

47

3

A T NINE O'CLOCK on the following Monday morning, I was waiting outside the stage door of the Windmill. I knew nothing about the theatre and did not know what clothes I should wear for my new job. Actors for me were people who wore cloaks and wide-brimmed hats – but did such dress also extend to stagehands?

I still had my dungarees from Sentinel but felt that these were unsuitable. I possessed one good suit, but did not want to wear this in case I had to move scenery, which might dirty it. I therefore compromised by wearing what was the 1930s equivalent of jeans, a tweed sports jacket and grey flannel trousers.

The Windmill Theatre was owned by a widow, Mrs. Laura Henderson, who had inherited a fortune through a family shipping line. This theatre was her abiding interest and somehow she had persuaded the Lord Chamberlain, who was a personal friend, that *tableaux vivants* with bare-breasted girls were harmless entertainment and not conducive to public immorality, as her critics sometimes claimed. Indeed, the Windmill Theatre was one of the most moral places in which I have ever worked. Mrs. Henderson took a personal interest in all the staff. She would come to see the show regularly every month from a box, and frequently brought along the Lord Chamberlain as her guest, so that he could see for himself that everything was being conducted in a decorous manner. One of the conditions under which the theatre was allowed to feature semi-nude show girls was that they must remain perfectly still and static on stage. One move, and the theatre's licence would be in danger; two, and it could be revoked.

When I arrived, other stagehands were moving around the stage, which soon filled up with lovely girls. Vivian Van Damm had two companies, 'A' and 'B', one presenting the current show, which ran for six weeks, and the other which would be rehearsing the show to follow this.

Everyone was extremely friendly to me as a new arrival. I was told to report to Rudolph, the stage manager, an oldish man, known as 'Old Rudy'. He had started his career as a stage carpenter, and so knew exactly how scenery should be made and how 'flats' – the large sections of background scenery, such as painted trees or castle walls – should be held when being moved so they would not be damaged.

'What am I to do?' I asked him. 'Move scenery?'

'No,' he said. 'That takes skill to learn. Your job now is to get the girls off stage quickly. When they come to the end of a tableau, the lights all go out – what we call a black-out. As soon as this happens, you dash on stage with their dressing gowns, because they are not allowed to be seen moving without their clothes. You must get them off-stage fast, so we can get the next scene set.'

'But they're almost naked,' I pointed out.

'You'll soon get used to that,' he assured me. I felt less certain.

The first time I had to do this, three girls were standing in a giant papier mâché oyster. They were supposed to be pearls, and to emphasise this they each wore a pearl necklace, and not much else. They each held one hand in front of their fannies, and bits of seaweed dangled in odd places.

A tenor, dressed as a deep-sea fisherman, strolled down in front of the footlights and sang: 'When I'm beneath the ocean, all my cares are gone', an awful shanty someone had specially composed for him.

Of course, the audience didn't care a damn about the tenor or what he sang, or whether he could even sing (which was a pity, because Geoffrey Denton sang very well). Their eyes were on the girls. As the singer reached his final top note, Rudy gave me a nod. The lights snapped out and down came the curtain.

One tiny pilot light lit the stage sufficiently for me to see my way across it. I ran on, holding three dressing gowns, and pushed them over the girls' shoulders, blushing scarlet as I did so. When they followed me into the wings, they were all laughing at my embarrassment.

'Don't worry, love,' one told me. 'You'll get used to it. And we promise we won't get you into any trouble.'

And I thought, I hope they don't – or do I hope they do?

That was how I began my career in the theatre.

Many other actors also started at the Windmill, so it is sad to reflect that nowadays a youngster could not be given the chance Van Damm gave me and all the others, because of trade union rules. There were no unions then back-stage, and Equity, the actors' union, was bohemian and easy-going and not at all militant. Nowadays, someone who wishes to go on the stage professionally can find it impossible to get a part without holding an Equity card – but an actor or actress has to appear in a given number of professional performances before being able to qualify for membership. Looking back, I realise how lucky I was to have started when I did. So were others like me; together, we enjoyed the last of the wine.

As days and weeks passed, I progressed from carrying dressing gowns for naked girls to moving scenery, and to working the complicated switchboard that controlled the lights and opened and closed the curtains. I also learned, from watching comics at rehearsals, how they built up a sketch, perhaps originally from a remark or from something someone saw in the street, into a sequence of funny happenings, lasting for three or four minutes.

Gradually, I came to realise the dangerous attraction of acting, and the thrill of applause, a rare, heady pleasure that no money can buy, only talent, and timing, and much hard work. Various comics would join the company for a few weeks at a time. I remember Barry Lupino, Dick Tubb and Ken Blain. They each had loyal and enthusiastic followers and all possessed an aura which I found difficult to explain or describe.

Their warm, outgoing personalities made them appear somehow larger than life. Their clothes had just a little more colour than the clothes of others of their age in more sedate and orthodox jobs. Their characters had the chemistry of excitement. They were fun to be with, even to watch at work, for they gave where others were content to take.

I began to realise how right Van Damm had been to warn me against being an actor, because I found myself strongly drawn to a world about which I had never previously given a moment's thought.

Vivian Van Damm used to come to rehearsals on most days, and then he would see one of the performances in the afternoon or evening. On these occasions he always had a cheerful word for me. Was I doing all right? How did I like the business? And so on.

After one of these visits, I watched Dick Tubb, a tall thin lugubrious comic, rehearsing his act. Dick used several stage-hands as his helpers and throughout this particular sketch he smoked a long cigar. At the very end, he threw it away. The climax was, that all the stagehands rushed on, and pounced on the stub. One would seize it. He would then puff away at it like a tycoon, while the others fell in behind him, with Dick at the end of the line. Then they would all march away, one behind the other. This may seem pretty feeble now, but then it had a great deal of relevance, because, few people could afford to smoke cigars and no one would throw away a smokable stub. After the rehearsal, I asked Dick if I could be one of the pouncers.

'Certainly,' he said at once. 'Go on with the others, Ken.'

This was kind of him, because he paid two shillings and six-pence to each of us at the end of the week for our efforts, and half-a-crown could buy quite a lot of beer in those days.

That night, when Dick threw away his cigar stub, I pounced with the rest of the lads and managed to seize it. Such was my excitement that I forgot the rest of the sketch, and instead of putting the stub in my mouth and smoking it triumphantly, I handed it back to Dick, completely ruining his exit. For some reason, the audience loved this, and cheered and clapped their hands enthusiastically. When the curtain came down, Dick Tubb approached me. I thought he was going to be angry, but instead he was delighted with the change.

'Keep it in,' he told me. 'That's good.'

And so, from then on, Dick's act finished with me handing back the cigar stub to him, while he walked off, puffing it. And he did this to much greater applause than he had received before.

I could not understand why this worked, but it did, and I thought, it can't be bad, being an actor, if all you have to do is pick up a cigar stub, hand it back to the comic – and get a big laugh. This seemed to me like money for jam – in spite of Mr. Van Damm's warning.

I felt rather proud of my contribution and the applause it received, so when that company ended its run and 'B' company were due to take their place, I approached Ken Douglas, their comedian.

'If you have any bit parts for the boys, I would like to volunteer,' I told him.

Ken was immediately helpful.

'I am doing a sketch in which a policeman has to open a door and come in,' he explained. 'I'll be in a sitting room with my wife. The policeman has to ask: "Is that your car outside, sir?" Have that part, if you like.'

'Is that all I have to say?'

'Absolutely all. Just dress yourself up as a policeman, and say that one line.'

'Right, I will – and thank you.'

There was one small complication. I was able to obtain a policeman's helmet and uniform jacket from the wardrobe mistress, but I could not find any suitable trousers, and did not want to appear on stage wearing old flannel bags. Then I saw that the set had a window near the door, and thought, there's no need for me to wear black trousers. All I have to do is to speak through this window. Usually, glass is not fixed in a stage window in case of accidents, and because of reflections from the lights. So when my cue came, I simply pushed my helmeted head through the empty window frame and asked: 'Is that your car outside, sir?'

Again, this brought down the house. The audience seemed to imagine I was putting my head through a sheet of plate glass. As soon as the performance was over, Ken came up to me. 'Keep that in, Kenny,' he told me. 'That's funny.'

Again I thought, I must be a bit of a comic, and I decided to gain all the experience I could. Already, life on stage seemed more attractive than life back-stage.

My next chance came with our most popular resident comedian, a Cockney, Gus Chevalier. Audiences loved him and he appeared at the Windmill more than any other comic. I suppose his salary would be all of fifteen pounds a week – three white ones, as we used to say – which was a lot of money.

I asked Gus if I could help him in his sketches, playing straight man or feed to him as the comic. He agreed immediately. I had a little more confidence now, and Gus gave me a great deal more by explaining how important the straight man is to the comedian. Unless the straight man times his ripostes absolutely correctly, the comic loses a laugh. The art in a double act is timing – just look at Morecambe and Wise. Timing words and inflection is, in fact, the secret of all comedy acting, and I began to learn a great deal at the hands of Gus Chevalier. He taught me in front of an audience, so by a process of public humiliation and embarrassment when I did something wrong, I learned how to avoid that mistake in future.

For example, if I made a mess of my timing, instead of being angry, Gus would turn to the audience and appeal to them, while I stood on the stage, scarlet with confusion.

'He made a mess of that now, didn't he?' Gus would ask the audience.

'Yes!' one or two of them would shout in reply.

'Well, he's only a young lad. Let's give him another chance. Shall we ask him to do that again?'

Meanwhile, I would be standing there shivering with fright as the audience shouted: 'Yes! Give him another go!'

So Gus would turn to me and say:

'Let's have that line again, Ken. What *you* have to say is: "Who was that lady I saw you with last night?" And what *I* reply is, "That was no lady, that was my wife." So let's try it again, and don't mess it up this time, or you're fired.'

The audience loved all this and I grew to value it too because I knew that although he was making me feel an utter fool in front of them, he really liked me, and was teaching me how to play comedy.

What the audience appreciated was his frankness in letting them into the secret that I was learning. I have never forgotten the patience and kindness of my teacher – or the strange way in which he taught me.

Each time we perfected something Gus would say to me afterwards: 'Let's do it like that for a few days, Kenny. Perhaps we can work it up into something better.' And so I learned how, from the basic platform of a single joke or action, we could construct a complete sketch.

As well as these minute bits of business on stage, I was learning all I could about my real work back-stage. Old Rudy took a shine to me.

'Young Ken's doing all right,' he told Van Damm. 'And I'd like you to make him assistant stage manager.'

Van Damm agreed, and when Rudy told me, I asked him what was involved.

'Pretty well everything,' he explained. 'Running the show from the corner, controlling the tabs and black-outs, all the switches, the cue lights, and so on.'

The tabs are the front curtains, and as assistant stage manager I had to lower them, control light changes, give the cue to the orchestra to begin, and generally make sure that everything was running smoothly. This was a very worrying job, and Rudy stayed with me in the corner for a few dummy runs until I could run the show myself. Being assistant stage manager also involved me in seeing to the girls' welfare.

On one occasion, I had just brought the lights up for a long sketch that lasted for about four or five minutes. This meant that I could sit on a bench in the corner for a rest and a cigarette, for there was nothing for me to do until the black-out. At that moment, a call boy ran up to me and said in a hoarse whisper:

'Bobbie's sat on a bit of glass and cut her bum. Come and do something.'

I looked at him in horror.

'I can't do anything to Bobbie's bum,' I said. 'What can I possibly do? I've only a few minutes, anyhow.'

Bobbie Bradshaw was one of our chief posing girls, a most beautiful creature, engaged to a man working in a high government position in Malaya.

'You must help her,' the boy persisted. 'There's no one else.'

I collected the first aid box and raced down to the girls' dressing-room. Bobbie was standing without a stitch on, holding a handkerchief to her backside.

'What can I do to help?' I asked her.

'Put something on it, darling,' she told me. She leaned forward over a chair with her bum in the air so that I could see where the cut was. At first I found this sort of thing rather embarrassing, but then I began to enjoy myself. I thought, I'm in a position of power here. Not only am I running the show, but I'm also sticking plaster on girls' backsides. That can't be bad. My day was made when I heard from Van Damm that he was increasing my salary from two pounds ten shillings to four pounds a week.

Because the Windmill was the only theatre in London allowed to present semi-nude girls, it was extremely popular with young bloods, and also with older men of a different style whose blood still ran too warm in their ageing veins.

Boat Race nights, the evening of the University rugger match at Twickenham, and the aftermath of other such contests were chaotic for us. Because it was well known that the Lord Chamberlain had strictly decreed that our girls were not to move when their breasts were bare, young men from Oxford and Cambridge, and other supporters, came to the theatre in crowds, determined to *make* them move. Many would arrive with pea-shooters, and sit in the front rows and blow dried peas at the girls. Others put little bags of joke sneezing powder into their pea-shooters and blew these out, hoping to make the girls sneeze. Others fired pellets of chewing gum – anything to make them move or sneeze, because any slight movement in a girl's face would be reflected in her body. When she sneezed, her breasts bobbed up and down and the whole audience would shriek with laughter.

One of my tasks as assistant stage manager was to spot exactly what was going on in every audience. On nights like these I could then warn the girls where trouble-makers were sitting. We had a little peephole covered by a small piece of dark velvet. I would lift this velvet and look out into the auditorium without anyone in the audience knowing I was doing so. The disturbing thing to us back-stage was that if any girl was forced to move under these assaults, we became immediately aware of a violent mass sexual reaction from the audience.

54

The Windmill had a strict rule that no member of the audience could bring in what our notices in the auditorium described as 'artificial aids to vision', such as telescopes, binoculars or opera glasses. Despite this, one regular visitor, an ex-sea-captain, would come in regularly and sit in the front row of the circle, pull a telescope out of an attaché case, steady it with his left hand, and play with himself with his right. Other middle-aged men, usually wearing raincoats, would place The *Evening News* and *The Times* on their laps and do the same thing under the newspaper when the tableaux were in progress. More dignified customers of this kind would sit, similarly engaged, with their bowler hats on their laps. This sort of behaviour could be embarrassing to other members of the audience, and also might result in our licence being revoked if anyone complained to the police about it.

I was told to keep a lookout for these undesirable activities and I had a simple code with the front office when I spotted anything. I would pick up the house telephone and say: 'A4, Wanker, *Times*. C 17, *Daily Mail.*'

The commissionaire would then stride down the aisle to Seat A4, and then to Seat C 17, tap the man on the shoulder, and say, 'The manager wishes to see you in his office.'

The commissionaire, an old soldier, was under strict instructions not to say 'Stop wanking', or some other more forthright comment, in case there had been a misunderstanding, or the client denied the charge. His defence could be, 'I was just scratching myself,' or something like that. But always the men concerned realised they had been rumbled, buttoned up their flies and left quietly. Some of these customers would even arrive wearing overcoats with both pockets removed so they could reach themselves more easily.

During the summer months it was very hot back-stage and we would be glad to snatch a few moments of fresh air at the stage-door, which opened on to Archer Street. The girls would come out scantily dressed and have a cigarette before they had to dash back for their next appearance. One afternoon, when I was enjoying the sunshine for a few minutes, I noticed that the street contained a Rolls-Royce and other expensive cars parked end to end near the stage-door. I had not seen any there during the winter and wondered with a mild curiosity why they had suddenly appeared. At the wheel of the Rolls sat a uniformed chauffeur, and in the back was a very old gnome-like man, obviously extremely rich. This man, and others, used to wait for the girls to come out in their tiny costumes and would watch

55

them closely. They did not speak to the girls, and indeed never left their cars. They simply sat and watched, in silence.

One day, when I had a free moment, I went up to the nearest car, a silver Phantom Rolls-Royce. The man in the back of it looked as old as God. He wore a stiff white collar, and his neck inside it was wrinkled like a tortoise.

'Is there anything I can do for you, sir?' I asked him very respectfully. He had seen me come out of the stage-door, so he knew I must work there.

'Do you know these girls?' he asked me, indicating a few of the dancers lounging around the doorway.

'Yes, indeed I do. I'm the assistant stage manager.'

'How interesting. Then I wonder if you could do something for me?'

He turned very slowly, because it would have been much too dangerous for him to turn fast; his head might have detached itself from his neck. Then he pointed to Lya, a very pretty show girl, who was smoking a cigarette.

'You see that girl over there? Well, could you get me one of her stockings?'

'A stocking?' I repeated in surprise. I don't know what I had been expecting him to ask me, but not this.

'It would be worth something to you, young man,' he went on.

'It could be difficult,' I said. 'But I'll do my best, sir.'

'You get me one of her stockings, young man,' he said, 'and there will be a few pounds in it for you.'

This opened up a whole new area of enterprise in my mind and I went back into the theatre to discuss this proposition with a stagehand.

'It doesn't have to be one of Lya's stockings,' he pointed out. 'Give him any stocking. He won't know the difference.' The wardrobe mistress wanted to be rid of a number of old laddered stockings and so I took one of these. I folded it neatly in an envelope and handed this to him. The old man in the Rolls was delighted, and gave me four pounds. I decided to expand this unexpected trade, and soon was selling stockings or ribbons that I would say had been worn by Connie or Suzy, or whoever else they fancied. Others back-stage heard of this lucrative exchange, and they also began to sell, at even greater prices, more intimate garments which they claimed had been worn by this or that girl. But I never extended my range beyond ribbons and stockings.

Some men would spend a whole afternoon and evening in the theatre. If they could not get a seat in one of the front rows for the early show, they sat where they could until the interval and as soon as the lights went up, they would make a mad rush for the front rows.

We called these men our stage-door commandos. They would climb over rows and rows of seats to reach one in the front. The result was that the front five rows took a tremendous amount of punishment for which they had not been designed. They had to be reinforced with extra bolts and strips of metal, otherwise they would be torn apart at every show. Sometimes men fought each other because one claimed someone else had taken his seat. Nowadays, I suppose, the counterparts of these people squabble over who has prior claim to a parking meter.

No one in the audience paid much attention to the comedians on the stage; they had come to see the girls. But even less attention, as I have already remarked, was paid to the tenor who had to sing a sea-shanty or some other ballad against a background of a nude tableau.

One sketched starred the 'A' company tenor, a very large and most charming man, Eric Woodburn, who later made a name for himself as Dr. Snoddy in the TV series, *Dr. Finlay's Casebook*. This sketch was about the Tower of London and Eric appeared as a Beefeater. He was tall and broad-shouldered and could, as they say, 'carry the costume', so he looked the part. With the lights very dim, he went into a long pontifical monologue about the glories of the Tower. Slowly the lights would come up to allow the audience to see various characters in the Tower's history, in somewhat scanty costume, pass across the battlements.

Of course, the audience didn't give a damn about the glories of the Tower of London or Eric's song. Their eyes were on Ann Boleyn going past very nearly in the 'altogether', to put her head on the block, or Lady Jane Grey in an equally abbreviated costume, while Eric was gallantly doing his stuff out in front.

As assistant stage manager I had to understudy all the actors in case one of them fell ill, and then I could go through with his performance either until the actor recovered or a permanent substitute could be found.

This particular night was fairly slack for me, and I was doing a crossword puzzle in my room when Rudy ran up to me in a state of agitation.

'You're on!' he announced breathlessly.

'On? Doing what?'

'Eric's part.'

'No,' I cried. 'That's impossible. I can't sing a bloody note. And anyway, Eric's twice my size. His clothes won't fit.'

57

'You're on! You're on! In three minutes!' Rudy kept repeating, as though he had not heard me.

'What's happened to Eric, then?' I asked him. Even as I spoke, I saw Eric being carried past in full costume by two stagehands. He had twisted his ankle.

'Hurry! You've only got two minutes,' said Rudy.

Others were already tearing Eric's costume off him as he was carried away, and feeling that I was taking part in an incredible nightmare, I began to put on his ludicrous gear. The legs of the vast red trousers crinkled around my calves like another skin. My feet had inches to spare in his huge shoes, and his Beefeater's cap came down over my eyes. I could only hold it up sufficiently to see by packing a rolled-up page of a newspaper inside. The ruffle at the throat of the jacket covered my chin. I looked like a Womble or the Incredible Shrunken Man.

Someone stuck a halberd in my hand. Rudy said soothingly, as he propelled me on stage: 'Don't you worry, now, Kenny. I'll read the lines to you from the side.'

Then I was on my own. The stage was pitch dark. I could dimly see girls giggling at my appearance in the wings waiting to cross the battlements. The orchestra played the introduction to the sketch, and then the music faded as the curtain rose for me to begin Eric's monologue. I said nothing, for I did not know what to say. Eric's was the one part I had not learned because by no means of imagination could I double for him physically or as a singer.

The conductor took the musicians through the music for a second time, and now from the wings I heard a faint hissing, and then Rudy's voice reading from the script. He was not a man who found reading easy.

'Great Tower of London,' he said hoarsely.

I repeated in a very small, thin voice: 'Great Tower of London . . .' and stopped. Then I heard him read the next line very slowly, as though he had difficulty in making out the words.

'. . . How little knew the mind.'

'How little knew the mind,' I repeated.

'. . . Who thee created . .'

Line after laborious line had to be whispered and repeated in this way. The audience were, of course, seeing the sketch for the first time and had no idea whether it was meant to be serious or comic. They were forced to assume the latter, and began to laugh.

As the lights went up, I knew that the girls were walking behind me and it was my cue to sing. I could see Alan D'Albert, the musical director, looking up at me from the orchestra pit with an appalled expression I shall not easily forget. I plunged into my song, as usual a line behind Rudy's prompting. I knew nothing of musical keys. The orchestra realised this and changed theirs to help me. I changed mine to help them.

Somehow the humiliation ended and I staggered thankfully off the stage, a grotesque parody of a Beefeater. Stagehands were holding their sides with laughter, and, luckily, so were the audience. Van Damm, who had heard of Eric's accident, was waiting for me. I expected the chop for my miserable performance, but instead he congratulated me.

'The funniest thing I have seen for months,' he said – and meant it.

This unexpected result made me feel I really should do more comic acting on stage, and less work back-stage. Of course, I still remembered Van Damm's warning, but finally I decided I must tell him of my decision. I went to his office with its rich smell of cigar smoke.

'Well, Ken, what can I do for you?' he asked me.

'Sir,' I began awkwardly, 'I don't think you are going to like what I am going to tell you. But I have thought everything over very carefully, and despite your warning to me I would like to be an actor – seriously, and not just a helper-out.'

Van Damm removed the cigar from his mouth, and studied its glowing end as though it was an oracle, before he replied.

'Well,' he said. 'I warned you. And I think you're a bloody fool. Still, if that's what you really want, I'll do all I can to help you.'

At the end of that week, he took me off stage management and I reported to Eve Bradfield who was in charge of production. I now began to take longer parts in sketches, and after a couple of months Van Damm gave me a second rise in pay – to six pounds a week. This was quite a reasonable salary then for my digs only cost me thirty bob, and a four-course meal in a London restaurant was only three shillings.

I had now been working in the Windmill for roughly a year, and began to grow rather fond of Betty Van Damm, Vivian's elder daughter. I don't think that this was frowned on by her father, although he was Jewish, and I am not. Indeed, he rather encouraged it in a quiet way. He was always extremely kind to me and treated me more as a son than an employee. Betty was one of the model girls who posed in the shows, and although many outsiders criticised Van Damm for letting his daughter pose like this, he always replied: 'If it's good enough for other girls, it's good enough for Betty, and Betty can do it.'

Betty certainly could, for she was a well-made girl. She lived with her father and mother and her younger sister, Sheila Van Damm (who later became famous as a British rally driver), in a beautiful flat in a block in Baker Street. Often after the last show of the evening, I would go home with her and have supper with the family. On Saturdays in the summer, Betty and I would sometimes go out punting on the river, and although there was nothing serious between us, and we never went to bed together or anything like that, we always liked each other, and still do.

Also in the company was another beautiful girl, called Ann. I was rehearsing a sketch one morning when the door of the rehearsal room opened and in she walked. I had just celebrated my twenty-first birthday. She was probably four years older and had joined the show as a bubble dancer, which in those days was a very daring thing. Her job was to dance around on the stage holding a huge, semi-transparent balloon.

She was nude except for bits of sticking plaster in strategic places. Of course, nobody saw anything in any case, because the bubble was always discreetly placed and virtually covered up her whole body. The attraction was that the audience felt sure that one day the bubble *must* burst and there Ann would be, naked in all her glory. This had never happened, but people were always optimistic.

To increase Ann's appeal, Van Damm fixed her up with two enormous ostrich feather fans, and she abandoned the bubble and branched out as a fan dancer. Here, she wore the same bits of sticking plaster, but since the audience could not see the plaster, they believed she really was naked. Ann was so clever with these fans that for all any audience ever did see, she might as well have been fully clothed.

I assumed that because of her job Ann would be very fast, a heavy drinker and smoker, willing to jump into bed with anybody, but she was just the reverse, a very quiet, reticent girl. For a long time after our first introduction, I was too shy to speak to her. Not only was she beautiful, she was making a lot more money than me. However, I did finally conquer my shyness and we got on amazingly well.

It was at this moment, after I had been nearly two years at the Windmill, that a coolness developed between Vivian Van Damm and me.

Van Damm was, of course, a very handsome and successful man and consequently extremely attractive to women, a sophisticated, charming employer whose word was law. There was also no doubt that he had his favourites in the company, and up till now, through my father's generosity, I was fortunate to be one of them. At that time, we had two soubrettes in the 'B' Company, as opposed to the 'A' Company. One was Doris Barry, the sister of Alicia Markova, the ballerina, and the other was an equally pretty girl, Meggie Eaton. It was obvious that Van Damm was very fond of Meggie. I am not saying there was a serious affair going on, but so far as all the young men in the company were concerned, the message was, lay off Meggie.

One night, Meggie gave a party in her flat in Lansdowne Gardens. Doris was there with a lot of other young people, some from the show. I must admit right away that I fancied Meggie quite considerably, and had done for some time, but, of course, I had to be very careful, because so far as the Windmill was concerned this was holy ground. However, at her party I drank far too much, and so was in no state to go home. Meggie thoughtfully suggested that I should stay the night. This was by no means a disagreeable proposal to me, but even in my inebriated state I could hear warning bells ring.

'You haven't any room,' I told her. 'I know you have only one bed, and Doris is staying the night, too.'

'We'll *make* room, Kenny,' Meggie said grandly. 'You can sleep in the bed between us.'

This proposition held certain attractions, and although I was secretly absolutely terrified, I had a bath and we all went to bed together, giggling away. I lay between the two girls, Doris on one side, and Meggie on the other.

Doris said to me before she turned out the light: 'Now look, love, please behave yourself. I've kept what I've got a long time – and I don't want to lose it tonight.'

I'll always remember those few words, because virginity then was of considerable importance!

'Don't worry, darling,' I reassured her. 'It's perfectly all right. You can rely on me. There'll be no trouble at all.'

Meggie, I noticed, didn't say anything to me as we all three lay there, thigh to delicious thigh. I remember that night – how can I ever forget it? I felt like a character from some mediaeval morality play, tortured by desire and longing, yet fearful of divine retribution if he succumbed to the thirsts of the flesh. I desperately wanted to make a move towards Meggie, yet I did not dare to do so. I felt that she also wanted to make a move towards me, but the whole thing was spoiled by the vision of Van Damm looking down on us and saying, 'You two are committing sacrilege.' In fact – unfortunately – we were committing nothing, and next morning I caught an early bus back to my digs.

Somehow, word got back to Van Damm that I had spent the night with Meggie. I don't know how this did reach him – but after this night our relationship was never quite the same.

A few days later, Van Damm sent for me, and this time we had a rather frigid interview in his office.

'I understand there was a party at Meggie's flat, and you stayed the night there?' he began.

I said, 'Yes, sir.'

'Well, this is not the sort of thing I expected from you, Kenny. I don't expect you to behave in this manner.'

'I am sorry, sir, but I assure you it was perfectly innocent. Nothing untoward happened at all.'

He gave me a most peculiar look.

'No,' he said coldly. 'I'm sure it didn't.'

Van Damm looked at me so hard that I could feel my colour rising, but he said nothing more, and indeed never again referred to the episode. For my part, I concentrated all my off-duty attentions on Ann. Even so, I knew that I had hurt Van Damm, and where we had previously been on the warmest terms our relationship from then on was cold and formal. This made me even more determined to become a success as a straight actor.

Eve Bradfield suggested I should learn to sing and dance, for this would be useful to me in the Windmill, and would also help me if I left and wanted a part in musical comedy. I attended the singing class which was held regularly in the rehearsal room, but I soon discovered I was no potential Crosby. Dancing, I thought, should be a different matter, so I enrolled with the Buddy Bradley School of Dancing. Buddy Bradley had been a stage dancer, but decided there was more money in teaching others to dance than in dancing himself. He was extremely good at coaching actors and actresses in dance routines, but with me he had to admit failure. So after a few sessions I came back and told Eve that so far as the Windmill was concerned, singing and dancing were out, and I would have to continue as a straight man. I had done as well as I could there, but I felt I had reached my peak. I could probably continue feeding lines and jokes to itinerant comics indefinitely, but this was a treadmill, leading nowhere. If I intended to become what I call a proper actor, then I should leave and find a job in repertory, and learn the craft properly. Yet I was reluctant to give up a regular salary. What should I do?

I asked Van Damm for his opinion, and he repeated he would do all he could to help me, but I could tell from his reaction that he thought I was becoming a bit too cocky, a bit too sure of myself in wishing to strike out on my own. So he did what he felt he had to do in the circumstances. He gave me the sack.

I know now he did this for my own sake. I had ignored his advice about becoming an actor. I had moved away from his proposal that I should make myself proficient in all aspects of theatre management, and I was no longer a potential husband for his daughter. I had learned all the Windmill could teach me, so he put me out.

After nearly two years' steady employment this came as a great shock, especially since Ann and I had decided to live together and had signed the lease of an unfurnished flat in Wellesley Court, Maida Vale. It consisted of a sitting room, a bedroom, a kitchen, a tiny dressing room and a bathroom, at a rent of nine pounds fifteen shillings a month.

I had no money whatever because I always spent everything I had – a habit I suppose inherited from my father. I had been earning six pounds a week, and spending six pounds ten shillings and so I was broke and could contribute nothing towards our new home.

Ann had saved up some money, because she was earning about twenty pounds a week, which was a fortune in those days, and she bailed me out of my digs. I could not have left otherwise, because I owed my landlady seven weeks' rent. Then we moved into the flat in Maida Vale. To be absolutely accurate, Ann moved in alone, and so we started off on the wrong foot. She had lived in a tiny flat in Shoot Up Hill, Hampstead, and on the day she moved her furniture I was supposed to be there to help. I owned no furniture at all, only a few shirts and a suit and a spare pair of trousers, but I promised to bring all my worldly possessions in a suitcase, and help her unload. Moving is a task I absolutely loathe – a fact that has caused me much trouble with wives, for when there has been any moving to be done, I have always taken care to be absent.

Ostensibly, on this occasion, I was scouring the agents' offices in the West End for work, but actually I was simply keeping out of the way. When I returned in the evening, Ann had done all the work and was furious. We had a terrible row. However, she finally forgave me, for we thought we were in love, and with all the misplaced confidence of the young, were certain that everything from then on was going to be wonderful.

I had not paid a National Insurance stamp long enough to be able to draw the dole, so I had to live off Ann's bounty, a situation I disliked intensely.

Van Damm had given me an introduction to a theatrical manager, Bill O'Bryen, a partner in the firm of O'Bryen, Linnit &

Dunfee, in the hope that he could help me find work. Bill was married to Elizabeth Allan, a stage and screen actress of great beauty, and now remembered by TV viewers for her appearances in 'What's My Line?'

At the time I met Bill he was at the height of his influence and he gave me a sympathetic hearing.

'If you were setting yourself up as a professional comic with a turn of some kind, I might be able to help you,' he told me frankly, 'but I don't think I can be very optimistic over what you have done so far.'

For the next few months, I was going to hear this message from every agent and theatrical manager I saw.

I heard that an audition for a touring play was being held at the Globe, so I went along to try for a part. The theatre was cold and dark and grim. I was given a copy of the script and told to walk out on the bare stage and read the part.

I did so, wondering whether anyone was actually out there in the auditorium among the dust sheets. When I finished, a voice from the darkness asked me: 'What experience have you had, young man?' The tone of the question seemed encouraging.

'The Windmill,' I replied.

There was a hush. Then someone laughed. And then the same voice, said, 'Keep in touch, laddie.' The tone was now one of dismissal. And the next candidate was called on to stage.

Whenever I heard that an audition was being held in any theatre I would go and read for a part. And always, just when it seemed that I had a chance, I would have to admit that my only previous experience was at the Windmill, and the result was the same.

I called regularly at a film casting office and once was paid two guineas for appearing in a film with Bebe Daniels and Ben Lyon. Then Ann and I worked out a cabaret act together, and persuaded a little club in Shaftesbury Avenue to engage us. I was to play the piano, while she would sing. The trouble was that I could only play by ear and Ann was a terrible singer.

We went on trial for the first time at ten o'clock one evening when the club was full. No one paid any attention whatever to the manager's announcement that we would entertain them, but Ann sang as best she could and I vamped away at the piano.

We were half way through our act when the manager came up to me.

'You can have your thirty shillings,' he said shortly. 'You'd better wind up and go home now, because no one's listening to you.'

Above left: Kenneth More (aged one year) with
his mother ('Topsy') and sister Kate.
Above right: his father, Bertie, in RAF uniform
in 1918.

Below: the faithful family retainers: nanny, cook and butler in the garden of the house at
Gerrards Cross.

Above: Kenneth More (standing fifth from left), talented left-half for the Windmill Theatre Football team in 1935.

Below: telescope in hand, Lt. Kenneth More, RNVR, serving on HMS *Aurora* – Naples harbour, 1944

So we broke the act off half way, and the people who didn't know we had started didn't know we had finished. Nor did they care.

I felt I could not face living on Ann indefinitely, and yet paradoxically it seemed that I could not afford to live alone. Then one morning I was in a pub in Charing Cross Road, The Salisbury, with some other out-of-work actors, when my luck changed. I had just told them I was down to my last few shillings.

'I know someone who can help you,' one of them said. 'Try Miriam Warner.'

'Who's she?' I asked.

'She has an office above Alkit, the military outfitters in Cambridge Circus. She looks after young actors, especially young actors who want jobs touring. She doesn't touch the West End or anything like that. She's a wonderful old girl and she's got an assistant, 'Smithie', who also loves actors, and everyone loves him. If anyone can help you, they can.'

So I immediately finished my beer and walked down the street to Cambridge Circus. The lift in the building wasn't working that day, so I climbed up four flights of stairs and arrived exhausted at her office. Smithie sat in an outer room and introduced himself. He wore a big black moustache and a big grin to match.

'What do you want?' he asked me.

'A job,' I replied simply.

'Where have you been?' he asked.

'The Windmill.'

'Doing what?'

'A bit of everything. Singing, dancing, feeding comics. But now I want a job in the straight theatre.'

'Have you any other experience? Been to drama school, or anything like that?'

'No, nothing. But I have been an engineer. I have also been turned down for the RAF and deported from Canada. I'm no good at all really. No school certificate, no brain, no hope. But I think I can act a bit.'

'You sound an ideal candidate,' said Smithie drily. 'Come in and see Miss Warner.'

He showed me into Miriam Warner's office.

She was a funny little old girl, sitting in a wooden chair behind a huge desk. In all the years Miriam was to represent me, I never once saw her standing up, and I never met anyone else who did, either. She was so small that her head just came up over the desk. Standing alongside her was the famous tiny comic, Wee Georgie Wood. He only came up to the top of Miriam's head, and she was sitting down. I thought, what an extraordinary sight. Her hair was dyed red with henna, and she had a bald patch on top of her head, and Georgie Wood with his man's face and child's body was cracking jokes. I thought, my God, is this the place to start my dramatic career? Then Georgie Wood smiled and spoke in his squeaky little voice.

'Come in, young man. Don't worry about us. We are just having a chat. Well, I'll see you, Miriam darling.' He gave Miriam a big kiss, and left. I repeated to her what I had already told Smithie.

'I think I could fix you up with repertory,' she said. 'Have you done any acting at all?'

'Apart from the Windmill, nothing.'

'That doesn't matter,' she said. 'All the better, in fact. I'll call you next week.'

And of all the agents I had seen, she did ring me and asked me to come to her office. I was very excited. Ann sent me off to Miriam's as smart as possible.

'How would you like to do rep in Newcastle?' Miriam asked me.

'I'd love to,' I told her. 'Is it the Playhouse?'

The Newcastle Playhouse was a very famous repertory theatre. Miriam shook her head.

'Not actually the Playhouse,' she admitted. 'The Grand Theatre, Byker. A lovely old Edwardian theatre. You'll get on well there.'

I thought, well, it's better than nothing, I suppose.

'Who runs the company?' I asked.

'Charlie Denville.'

I didn't know who Charlie Denville was.

'What does he do there? Dodie Smith? St. John Irvine?'

Miriam shook her head.

'Oh, no, dear. Melodrama. *The Coastguard's Daughter, The Prince and the Beggarmaid, Sweeney Todd, The Sheikh of Araby,* and so forth!'

'Oh, that's different, isn't it?'

'Yes,' she agreed. 'That's quite different.'

'Right. When do I start?'

'Next week.'

'That's fine,' I said. 'How much?'

'Five pounds, dear. All my artists get five pounds a week until they are worth more.'

'That's very good,' I said, and it was, for I knew I'd be able to find digs with full board for thirty shillings a week at the most.

'The others are getting less,' Miriam went on. 'The girls are only getting three pounds ten shillings, and the stage manager, two pounds. They are only paying you five because you've had comedy experience at the Windmill, and Charlie likes comics. He doesn't like anything subtle, mind. He'll give you some non-subtle jokes. You listen to him.'

'Does he have scripts of plays and things?'

'Well, yes. Charlie has his own scripts. He keeps them in a wardrobe or a trunk or somewhere. He's been using them for years. He'll tell you what to say and what to do.'

I thought that this sounded rather funny. I mean, how could he produce plays and comedies without proper scripts? It would be interesting to discover, I thought, and dashed back to see Ann and tell her the good news. We had rather a sad parting, but we would have parted in any case, because she was leaving to do a season with a revue in Edinburgh. She was also pleased about this because she was dancing in clothes, and without her fan or her bubble, and felt that this was a major step forward in her career.

For the time we had been together we had been very happy, but we both realised that now our ways lay in different directions. When she was in Scotland, she met and married a local Scottish comedian, but he drank rather a lot and the marriage went wrong. After the war, when I had been out of touch with her for a long time, I learned she had married Peter Saunders, the London impresario. He has since made theatrical history with Agatha Christie's play *The Mousetrap,* which has enjoyed a longer run than any other play in the history of the stage.

Sometimes I would meet Ann at first nights and we would make light conversation together. But never once did either of us refer to those early days in Wellesley Court. Ann kept her good looks and charm all through her life and died recently after a long and gallant fight against illness.

When she and I locked up our little flat for the last time, we also locked up a section of our lives, which I will always remember with warmth and affection.

Miriam gave me an advance of salary to buy a ticket and when I got out of the train at Newcastle I noticed a very pretty girl with a lovely peaches-and-cream complexion, big blue eyes and blonde hair, stepping down from the next carriage. Somehow, I knew she was an actress. You can always tell, one way or another. I went right up to her.

'Are you joining the theatre?' I asked her.

'Yes,' she said.

'You're not at the Playhouse, are you?'

'No. The Grand.'

'You're with Charlie Denville, too, then?'

'Yes, I am.'

She was of Dutch descent and straight out of drama school. Her name was Julie Boas.

There was nothing like arriving in style, so I suggested we shared a taxi. An old porter was shambling about, so I asked him whether he knew the Grand Theatre, Byker.

'Oh, my God,' he said in his Newcastle accent. 'You're not going *there*, are you?'

'Why not?' I asked him.

'It's tough up there, I tell you. It's over the bridge, and in Newcastle you're either over the bridge, or this side of the bridge. And in Byker you're right over the bridge.'

Later, I knew what he meant. An enormous viaduct bridge separates Byker from Newcastle. It spans sheds and railway lines in a vast cutting, like a huge and sooty canyon. The bridge was known locally as 'the bridge of lost hope' because about twelve people every year used to jump from it to commit suicide.

Julie and I shared the taxi and we began to grow more and more depressed, as the buildings became small and dirtier and the streets slummier.

'I hope we haven't made a terrible mistake, Kenny,' said Julie at last. I already had my own opinion about this, so I did not answer. To change the subject I asked her how much she was being paid. When she said it was only three pounds ten shillings, I felt more cheerful.

The taxi was now going through streets of such wretchedness that it was almost inconceivable that people could live there. Then the driver made another turn, and ahead of us was the Grand, an extraordinary theatre, either Edwardian, as Miriam had said, or late Victorian. We paid off the driver, and carried our luggage through the front door. Everything inside the theatre was beautiful. The auditorium was all gilt, with red plush seats. In the midst of poverty and broken-down houses and mean, shabby streets, the Grand glowed like a temple of enjoyment, and our worst fears began to leave us.

The whole company were already assembled on stage. Charlie Denville and his wife Marjorie introduced themselves. Charlie was dapper and short and spry, full of confidence. He spoke with a slight Cockney accent in what I would call an actor-laddie Cockney voice. You felt that if Charlie paid you five pounds in single notes, he would hang on to the last one if he possibly could.

The producer, E. Hamilton Jordan, was about six feet tall, a very upstanding man, wearing a black Homburg hat, an eye-glass, and a black-and-white polka-dot stock. He also had a rather seedy frock coat, pin-stripe trousers, spats and black, highly-polished shoes. He held a cane and a pair of wash-leather gloves in his left hand, and extended his right hand.

'I am your producer, E. Hamilton Jordan,' he announced in a splendid voice. 'I welcome you here to the Grand Theatre, Byker, and I am sure we are all going to have a most successful season.'

I was then introduced to another girl, Beryl Johnstone, whom later I married; to Arthur Lane, the manager, who also doubled up as leading man; and to Hugh Paddick, who has since made a great name for himself as a TV comic as well as on the London stage.

But the man who impressed me most, I must say, was E. Hamilton Jordan. He did not seem to belong to the seedy district of Byker; he looked too important. But I did notice something out of keeping with the first impression of grandeur. His teeth didn't fit.

As he talked in his wonderful port-wine, dark-brown-fruit-cake-voice his teeth went up and down on their own.

I discovered why, after we both appeared in the play *Love on the Dole* by Walter Greenwood. Our version of it wasn't quite the authorised Walter Greenwood version, but nevertheless it was one of the few recognisable plays we did during my stay at the Grand.

The climax of the play, at least in our version, came when E. Hamilton Jordan as the father of a pretty daughter, learned that, in the phrase of the time, she had been 'selling her body'.

He and I were seated at a table and he had to lean forward towards me and utter the memorable line, 'My God, my daughter's a whore.' With that, his head should fall forward in his hands.

When E. Hamilton Jordan did this at the first performance, his false teeth shot out of his mouth on to the plate, on either side of a pork pie he had been eating.

This brought down the house, and poor E. Hamilton Jordan looked very confused while his teeth rattled around the plate as though they had a will of their own. This also happened at the second performance, and so I offered him some advice.

'Hammy,' I told him. 'You should put a thumb underneath

your top set to stop them falling out, when you jerk your head forward.'

And from then on, as he said 'My God, my daughter's a whore', and his hand went up to his forehead to show the extremity of his grief, he pressed his thumb under his top plate.

I could not understand why he did not have false teeth that fitted.

'Well, laddie,' he explained afterwards. 'There's a story attached to it. Four years ago, I was playing a summer season at Scunthorpe, and we did rather well. To my surprise, we were asked back the following year. I had always had bad teeth, and on the strength of this future engagement, I went to a local dentist. Scunthorpe dentists weren't very good in those days, but he extracted my teeth, which was what I wanted. Of course, I had to wait without any teeth while my gums hardened, and in this interval, our second summer season was cancelled. This meant that I couldn't afford to pay for my new teeth. I went back to the dentist and explained this, for I had to have *some* teeth if I was to make a living, as an actor. He was sympathetic, and gave me an old set he had lying about in his surgery. And, Kenny, I'm sorry to say, I've never had enough money since to buy new ones.'

At our first meeting at the Grand, E. Hamilton Jordan ended his speech of welcome by saying: 'Your agents may not have told you this, but we are going to play twice nightly, twice weekly.'

We all groaned at this news. It meant that while we presented one play during the first half of the week, we would have to spend each morning rehearsing the new play to be presented on Thursday, Friday and Saturday. And on the mornings of those last three days, we would be rehearsing the play for the following Monday, Tuesday and Wednesday, and so on. This meant we would have little or no free time.

'You may also be surprised to hear that the most expensive seat in the house is one and ninepence. But we get good audiences and we have a full orchestra.'

Sure enough, there was an orchestra of twelve, and each of us was given our own little signature tune. Whatever play we appeared in, as we came on stage, our tune greeted us, so the audience could easily recognise who we were.

Now, E. Hamilton Jordan had a warning.

'On Friday nights you needn't bother to speak the lines the author gave you, because Friday night is fish-and-chip night. They come in here with a bottle of beer each and fish-and-chips in newspaper, and they talk among themselves. This is a social gathering, and they don't really care what's happening on stage. They only listen to the music.'

This sounded rather strange to me, but it was too late now to back out.

'Our first production is going to be *The Prince and the Beggar-maid* and Charlie will hand out the parts you are going to play. After that, we will do *Son of the Sheikh*.'

Charlie Denville now handed out to us some very well-thumbed sheets of paper. It was obvious that dozens of actors had played these parts before us, for the edges of the paper were curled and the margins full of pencilled notes. I had two sheets of quarto, very badly typed, with a half red, half black, mixed-up ribbon, and as I began to read it, I heard E. Hamilton Jordan say: 'You're on stage all the time, Kenny.'

'But I've only got two pages here,' I pointed out.

'That's all right. You make it up as you go along. You can improvise, can't you?'

'But I must have a script to improvise from.'

'You have one, Kenny. Pick the bones of it. I'm giving you this part of Prince Rupert. You'll wear a hat with a feather in it, a grand blue uniform. You're in the Imperial Hussars. You're a comic, aren't you?'

'But, Mr. Jordan,' I pointed out. 'I haven't any comic lines. There's nothing here to say.'

'I can't understand you, Kenny. You've been at the Windmill, haven't you? Think of the lines you used to feed comics there.'

'Give me an example, then. I can't think of anything.'

He said, 'It's up me sleeve. What is? Me arm.'

'I don't think that's very funny,' I told him.

'You'll bring the house down up here with it. Here's another. It's over the wall. What is? The other side.'

'I can't say lines like that.'

'Why not? You've got nothing else, so you'll have to try. And I'll give you one more hint, Kenny. If you ever get stuck, just say this magic line quickly: "A bucket of health salts".'

'What?' I asked him in amazement.

'A bucket of health salts,' he repeated.

'What does it mean?' I asked him.

'It's an expression they use up here. But you have to say it quickly. A bucket of health salts. Then it sounds like "Bugger off to hell, ma". You'll bring the house down.'

I stood there in utter bewilderment holding my two sheets of paper. I thought, if this is a straight theatre, it is unbelievable. I should get back to the Windmill as soon as I can.

71

We went into rehearsals virtually right away. Mercifully I remember very little about the opening night, except for some of the terrible lines I had to say. Someone asked me: 'Where is Antoinette?' I didn't even know that Antoinette was in the play, but I remember replying: 'She is here, my pretty one.'

Whenever I dried up or when no one said anything to me – which seemed to be the case for much of the play – I shouted, 'A bucket of health salts!' The audience went wild, just as E. Hamilton Jordan had said they would. In between this, as a very strange officer in the Imperial Hussars, I would say, *à propos* of nothing: 'It's over the wall.' And someone else would call back: 'What is?'

'The other side,' I'd tell him. Loud and prolonged applause.

Somehow the first three days passed with their six performances. Then came *Son of the Sheikh* which we had been busily rehearsing each morning. This involved a big scene around an oasis in the Sahara Desert. We were all tearing around with turbans on, and I was playing a Lancashire businessman who was on holiday there with his wife. Don't ask me why. Anyhow, he was very rich and very common. I had to talk Lancashire, to annoy the leading lady, my wife, who was very posh. To show I was rich, I had a big fat belly – a cushion stuffed under my shirt. Charlie Denville explained the background of the play to all of us.

'This is an eastern play, of course,' he said. 'Tons of atmosphere. It's an oasis, so we've got to have animals and sawdust. Animals for colour and effect.'

'What sort of animals have you in mind, Charlie?' I asked him.

'A camel, for one. The ship of the desert.'

'But where are you going to find a camel in Byker?'

'It's all been taken care of, dear boy. I've been to the local zoo, and they'll let me have one.'

'Do you know what to feed a camel on?'

'No, but it's going to eat anything I give it. We'll also have a few chickens and ducks.'

'But you don't have chickens and ducks in the middle of the Sahara.'

'*I* do,' Charlie replied with finality. 'Anything that moves and flys is good value. The whole stage is going to be covered in sawdust, and the scene will be set for the three nights, so the animals can stay on stage when the theatre's closed.'

Beryl protested, 'But, Charlie, the chickens and all those other animals will make an awful mess in the sawdust. The smell will be terrible.'

I felt especially unhappy about this because in one of my scenes I had to be knocked down by bandits.

'What about the chicken shit?' I asked Charlie. 'That's going to go all over me.'

Charlie Denville laid one hand gently on my shoulder.

'You're an actor,' he declared pontifically. 'That's all part of the fun. If you get a bit of chicken shit hanging out of your hair, they'll laugh.'

This play proved a terrible experience for us all. By the third night, the stage was covered with animal droppings. We had chickens, ducks, two goats and two donkeys, all contributing. The birds fluttered into the orchestra pit and had to be driven out by musicians wielding flutes and cornets like clubs. The whole theatre stank to high heaven. Stagehands, who were playing the bandits, would trip me up and roll my face in the mess, having the time of their lives. And to cap it all, there was no room for the camel to get on the stage properly.

It was essential that he was seen, to prove that a camel was actually in the cast, and ideally the brute should have come loping across the desert with the hero on his back to rescue my wife and me from the villains. But so much other livestock was crowding the stage that there simply wasn't room for him.

So the camel came in, just as far as the base of his neck, with the rest of his body outside in the wings. This semi-entrance at least proved he existed. On this last night, with a fight going on around the stage oasis, the camel suddenly decided he had had enough and started to pee. The sight was as yet unseen, but the sound was unmistakable. Immediately, the audience forgot our fight and shouted: 'Look at that camel! Eeeh! It's pissing, man!'

The man who had hired the camel was supposed to see that his charge performed this function before each performance, but he'd been in the pub and had somehow forgotten to do so.

Water just poured from the beast. It trickled out of the wings and on to the stage. At first, the leading lady tried to ignore this, but finally, realising that the audience knew what was happening, she called at the top of her voice: 'Put a bucket under it!'

One of the stagehands did so and now the water flooded like the Niagara Falls into the bucket, the metal base and sides magnifying the noise. At the same time, someone else had the idea that if he could give the camel a drink, it would stop peeing. So we had the curious sight of one person (an actor!) holding a bucket for the camel to drink from, and another holding a bucket at the other end to catch water coming out – and all the time we on stage were supposed to be playing heavy drama. The audience went wild.

Charlie Denville was a born showman and made the utmost of every chance to publicise his plays. Whenever possible, he would take full (and free) advantage of advertising put out by local cinemas. For example, if a cinema announced that next week it would be showing *Dracula*, he would immediately put on a play of his own devising, which he called *Dracula's Daughter*. All over Newcastle there would be posters for the Metropole: 'Coming next week, "*Dracula*".' And underneath, Charlie would have his poster: 'The Grand: Coming next week, *Dracula's Daughter*.'

He wrote many of these shows himself, or at least an outline of the general plot, and the cast had to fill in the rest as best they could.

Dracula's Daughter, in which I played with Beryl Johnstone, was a good example of his style as a playwright. Bats flew in at the windows, and Beryl, who was the vampire's daughter, came on stage, dressed for a smart dinner party in a London house, wearing a white shroud, two long fangs, and with blood running down her chin. She was called Lady Chumleigh, and I, as Professor Van Helsing, always remember the line the host had to say as she took her place at the dinner table.

'Lady Chumleigh doesn't look too well tonight.' And there was Beryl, sitting down with blood running out of her mouth all down her shroud!

In another play, set in some vague and carefully indefined bygone age, E. Hamilton Jordan was the villain, a hunchback who had to fight the leading man – our stage manager, Arthur Lane. I was the Crown Prince, and our scene was set on top of a castle battlement. Curiously enough, the Grand Theatre had a very good scene-painter and set designer. What he managed to achieve with the minimum of money and materials was quite incredible, so we had a perfectly good top of a castle. The battlements were plywood with metal spikes on top, and on their far side, out of sight of the audience, a mattress had been placed.

The plot demanded that E. Hamilton Jordan and Arthur Lane fight furiously together, and then Lane was to throw 'Hammy' over the battlement. He landed unharmed on this mattress. This had gone very well at rehearsals, but on the first night Arthur did not put enough force into his throw. The result was that E. Hamilton Jordan went up and over the battlements but one of the spikes stuck into the top of one boot. So while his head and body were safely down on the mattress, his left foot and boot were still in the air, and in full view of the audience.

E. Hamilton Jordan panicked. Instead of remaining still as though only the boot had caught there, he wriggled his toes inside it – and was still doing so after Arthur Lane declaimed dramatically: 'He has crashed to his death, the blackhearted villain! He's in the moat!'

I realised I had to do something quickly, so I ad-libbed a line. 'I'll help you!' I cried. 'I'll come to your aid!'

I heaved the boot off the battlement, and at once Hammy's foot, encased in a black and rather holey sock, disappeared. The audience loved this. They went hysterical, throwing chip-bags on to the stage to show their appreciation.

Afterwards, Charlie was furious.

'I couldn't help it,' protested E. Hamilton Jordan, his loose teeth going up and down in his mouth. 'My foot got stuck in the battlements. What else could I do?'

'You should have kept your bloody foot still, that's what.'

Poor E. Hamilton Jordan. I loved him. He was larger than life, an original character of immense ebullience and bravura. He was also one of the last remaining actor-laddies of the old school. His claim to fame was that he had been the original Professor Van Helsing in the touring version of the original production of *Dracula*. He knew the old melodramas backwards, and from the depths of his prodigious memory could dredge up all manner of stage business to enrich any part he played. But even in the late 1930s, and in such a backwater as Byker, E. Hamilton Jordan was already an acting anachronism.

After I had been at the Grand for several months, I think that even the audiences realised this, because the cinema was making them much more sophisticated. Finally, Charlie Denville decided that he should go.

No one gave any explanation as to why he was leaving, and we were too tactful to ask, for, deep down, we all knew the reason. Until that moment, I still thought E. Hamilton Jordan was a man of some standing, despite his teeth, and must have a little money put by. But on his last morning, he came to me in my dressing room and asked, almost pathetically: 'Can you lend me four shillings, Kenny, for the journey home?' He wanted to buy a beer and a sandwich on the London train.

When I went to the station to say goodbye, I never imagined I would see him again, but I did, many months later, in London. There used to be a pub, The Round House, in Wardour Street, much frequented by actors waiting for work. I saw him at the bar, still wearing his outmoded clothes, but now without socks beneath his spats. He explained to me that he was suffering from dropsy and could not bear the constriction of ordinary woollen socks around his ankles. He therefore wore a pair of his wife's silk stockings beneath his spats. At a glance, it seemed that he had bare feet beneath the spats.

Years after this final brief meeting, I casually mentioned this story during a newspaper interview, and thought nothing more about it. At the time, I was making the film, *The Admirable Crichton*, and we were in the studios preparing one of the major scenes. Just as we were about to shoot, with dozens of extras clustered round, I became aware of one of these extras, a middle-aged woman, forcing her way through the crowd towards me.

She came right up to me, as I began to play the scene, and suddenly slapped my face hard on both sides.

'My God!' I cried. 'What have I done? What's the matter?'

Everyone crowded round, wondering what had happened. She stood in the middle, a lonely, wretched figure.

'How dare you talk about my husband like that?' she burst out, almost in tears. 'He could *always* afford a pair of socks.'

Then she turned and ran away, weeping. She was E. Hamilton Jordan's wife. I had never met her before, and I never saw her again, but her proud loyalty to her husband's memory nearly broke my heart.

4

I ENJOYED THE EXCITEMENT and the challenge at Byker but after
seven months, with two performances a night and two different plays a week, I felt I was in a rut, and if I did not move, I
might never move. And if I never moved, I could be there until I
was as old as E. Hamilton Jordan.

So after some deliberation, I told Charlie Denville that I
thought I had learned all I could from his theatre, and I should
now move on elsewhere. I explained that I had written to Miriam
Warner and that she thought she could find me a job in a touring
company. Charlie quite understood.

'We are sorry to lose you in the middle of a season, Ken,' he
told me. 'The audiences like you. You go down very well up
here.'

I was very gratified by his comment that I was popular with
Byker audiences but, until then, I had no idea of the depth of
their loyalty. When word spread that I was going, the rumour
was that Charlie had given me the sack. To my surprise, I found
people picketing the theatre entrance with placards on poles:
'Ken must stay.' 'We don't want Ken to go.' 'We want More,' and
so on.

Old women with shawls over their heads waited outside the
stage door to offer me chips and butties as I passed them on the
way in, thinking I was without a job.

'Ken, you've got to stay,' one old dear told me earnestly. 'You
can't go. We like you.'

'Thank you,' I replied. 'But Charlie isn't giving me the sack.
Don't blame him for my decision.'

'When do you finish then?' they asked me.

'At the end of next week.'

'Right! We'll give you a party, Ken. That's what we'll do.'

So on the following Saturday night after the show about thirty
or forty people arrived at the stage door. Several men in the party
carried two huge barrels of beer, and two old girls brought plates
of ham and paste sandwiches and sausage rolls they had cooked
themselves. They all streamed into the dressing room and then
on to the stage. Charlie Denville was astonished at this invasion.

'You can't come in here,' he told them. 'This is my theatre. We are cleaning up for the night.'

But they just pushed him on one side. Some carried in trestle tables, others brought glasses and plates – all for a farewell party for me. I was literally in tears at this display of affection, for I knew these people had no money at all. They would bet in tuppences, and if a threepenny treble came up they felt they were millionaires. Many were on the dole, drawing only a few shillings a week. But somehow they had organised a whip-round to give me a party.

We had a marvellous knees-up together. All the company stayed, and in the early hours of Sunday morning the spokesman of all those good people, a huge drayman from a brewery company, made a speech. It was in the broadest Geordie dialect that I could not begin to reproduce here.

'We are making you a little presentation, Ken,' he said. 'It comes to you with all our love and our best wishes for your future. Something to remember us by, as we will always remember you.'

With this, he handed me a seven and sixpenny Ingersoll wrist-watch with a list of the subscribers about a foot-and-a-half long. I read through the names, with the details of the amount they had given. Mrs. Bristow a penny; Mr. Jones, twopence; Mr. McDermott, a penny halfpenny. I could read no more, for my eyes filled with tears. This watch meant more to me than any other gift I had ever received before. It kept perfect time for years. Halfway through the war, when I was in the Navy, I was Officer of the Watch, and leaning over the side of my ship in Grand Harbour, Malta. As I moved, the buckle on the strap came undone. It had not been properly secured, and before I could stop it, the watch fell into the sea. I would rather have lost anything than that watch. But I have never lost the feeling of warmth for the people who gave it to me.

Next morning, I caught a train to London, took a room in Gloucester Terrace and went to see Miriam. I told her that I did not want to play blood-and-thunder melodrama all my life. I wanted to have a go at Shaw and Shakespeare, at the parts actors must play before they can genuinely claim to be actors. Miriam heard me out patiently.

'I'll think about it,' she said. 'At the moment, there is a revival of James Parrish's play, *Distinguished Gathering* at the King's Theatre, Hammersmith. There is the part of an airman which might suit you.'

This was based on the character of Clifford Mollison, the husband of the famous woman pilot, Amy Johnson.

I read for the part, and I got it. We had two weeks run in Hammersmith, and all the time kept telling ourselves that even if Hammersmith might not be quite the West End, it was very nearly West End. A lot nearer than Byker, in any event.

During these two weeks, Miriam persuaded Derek Salberg, the general manager of the Grand Theatre in Wolverhampton, to come and see me in the play. Derek's father was Leon Salberg, a theatrical impresario in the Midlands, who owned the Royal Alexandra Theatre, Birmingham, and had a long lease on the Grand Theatre, Wolverhampton.

Derek Salberg was looking for a juvenile lead for the Grand, and he came backstage and offered me a job for the next season, which would start in a month's time. I was terribly excited, and went to see Miriam to ask her how much money he would pay me.

'A fiver, dear,' she replied shortly.

This was less than I had made nearly a year earlier at the Windmill.

'When am I going to get some more money, for God's sake?' I asked her.

'When you deserve it, you will get it,' she said drily. 'In the meantime, you should thank God you are getting that much. Don't criticise me. Just be thankful you are receiving a fiver a week. Lots of actors aren't and would like to.'

The Grand, Wolverhampton, was everything The Grand, Byker, was not. It was efficient and smoothly run – by Salberg's cousin, Basil Thomas – and we all had proper scripts. We had two performances every evening, as at Byker, but each play ran for a whole week. Every morning and afternoon we rehearsed the following week's play, and in our spare time we learned our lines for the play for the week after next. It was a happy company, although when I started I realised I was at some disadvantage in taking over from a very popular actor, John Harvey.

Like E. Hamilton Jordan, Harvey was an original. One Saturday, he had asked permission to leave Wolverhampton after the last house for his sister's wedding on the Sunday in South London. This was given, and he had such a phenomenal time at the reception, and drank so much, that he overslept badly and did not wake up until two o'clock on Monday afternoon – still in tails and salt-and-pepper trousers. The realisation of his predicament was sobering. He was 120 miles from the theatre, without a car, and curtain up on that evening's first performance was at six. The only possible way he could be back on time was to fly, and this, before the days of London Airport, meant travelling to Croydon aerodrome. He hired a taxi, and found an amateur flier who agreed to ferry him north in a Tiger Moth for seven pounds ten shillings – a whole week's wages.

They set off in an open Tiger – an aircraft in which the pilot sits behind the passenger. When they were airborne, the pilot lifted the voice pipe, which was the only way of communicating, and shouted against the roar of the engine, 'Where will we land?'

'We'll find a field somewhere.'

They circled Wolverhampton several times while John tried to locate the theatre from the air. The time was then half past five. Finally, they landed in a muddy field on the outskirts of the town. John leaped out, ran like a gazelle to the nearest road and waved his arms to stop a car. Many drivers went by, thinking he was drunk or mad or maybe both, and then one driver, who was a regular theatre-goer, recognised him and gave him a lift to the Grand. John arrived breathless, unshaven, feeling and looking ghastly, just in time to go on.

When I heard this I never imagined that I would ever face a similar situation, but I did years later, when I was appearing in *The Deep Blue Sea,* at the Duchess Theatre in London, and filming *Genevieve* out at Pinewood during the day. I aimed to finish at Pinewood by half past five to give me time to drive to London and change. Then I was due to walk on stage, carrying a set of golf clubs, and say to the woman with whom I was having an affair: 'Hello, Hes. I'm just back from Sunningdale. We did 93 m.p.h. in Johnnie's car.'

On this particular evening, the film director had begged for one more shot before I left for the theatre. I did not want to disappoint him, but the extra shot meant that I was late leaving the studios. The driver of the car planned to make up lost time, but half a mile up the road, we ran into thick fog.

The road ahead was nothing but a mass of stationary red tail-lights. I could not bear to look at my watch as the minutes ticked away remorselessly, for the time for me to be at the theatre was already past.

The chauffeur doubled down side streets, through housing estates, across roundabouts, and finally we reached the stage-door. The doorman was outside, looking for me frantically. I raced past him, grabbed my set of golf clubs and went straight on to the stage, without any make-up, without even brushing my hair.

'Hello, Hes. I'm just back from Sunningdale' etcetera, etcetera.

Just before Christmas, the Wolverhampton repertory season

Above: a problem pending; with director Lewis Gilbert on location in Bermuda in 1956 filming *The Admirable Crichton*.

Above: reversed roles – a Christmas tradition: Kenneth More (left) dressed to wait on the ratings at Taranto in 1943.
Below: at the microphone, running a brains' trust on the internal broadcasting system aboard HMS *Victorious* in the Pacific in 1945.

Above: 'Get your shoulder into it! Harder! Harder!' Irate driver Ambrose Claverhouse (Kenneth More) exhorts Rosalind (Kay Kendall) in *Genevieve*.

Below: the cheque that bounced: (left to right) Donald Sinden, Kenneth More, Dirk Bogarde and Donald Houston in *Doctor in the House*.

ended, because the annual pantomime was due to take over the theatre for three months. All of us actors and actresses had therefore to find other work to fill in this season. I went back to London to see Miriam, and within two days she had fixed me up again – but still at five pounds a week. She was a wonderful old girl, growing slightly thinner on top now, I noticed, and sitting more hunched up behind her desk. She had a great reputation in the profession. Managers all trusted her because she would not represent a client who was not prepared to work hard, and she never misrepresented any of their talents or abilities.

Her proposition now was a tour in the play *To Have and to Hold*.
'There's a big star name in it,' she said. 'Phyllis Neilson Terry.'
'Really?'
'Yes,' Miriam went on. 'And the leading man, Heron Carvic, is very fond of her. He plays a cripple in a wheelchair.'
'What am I?' I asked her.
She ignored my question.
'Phyllis Neilson Terry is in love with him, of course. It's a very good play indeed, dear.'
'I am glad to hear it, but what am I?'
'You are a hunting character,' she said. 'You play opposite Jean Webster Brough. You are her brother, her twin brother.'
'But Jean Webster Brough is a lot older than I am. How can we be twins?' I asked her.
She shrugged.
'It doesn't matter, dear. You are her twin brother, and you open the play in hunting pink and a top hat and riding crop.'
'What, both of us?'
'Yes. You both come on and stamp about the stage until Phyllis Neilson Terry enters and says something like, "Tea will be served. How are you, my darlings?" That's how the play starts. It is all very interesting. You'll love it.'
'Well, it doesn't sound very good to me.'
'It is,' she said. 'And you will take the part.'
'How much?' I asked her.
'Five pounds a week.'
We opened at The Theatre Royal at New Brighton, and the most awful thing happened on the first night. Neither Jean nor I could remember the opening lines, or even who had to say them.
I was fairly certain I had to open with something like: 'I hope she won't be long because I want some tea.'
Jean would then reply with a second line, but neither of us could remember these clearly. So, to the amazement and bewilderment of the audience, they saw two idiots banging about

the stage, slapping their thighs with crops, obviously very ill at ease – and neither uttering a word. I could see people look at each other in the stalls, for this went on for nearly five minutes.

Phyllis Neilson Terry was meanwhile in the wings, waiting impatiently for her cue. There was no prompter, and she was sure we must say *something*, but we didn't say anything at all. At last, she came on and announced to us, 'Tea will be served. How are you, my darlings?' Then we were off. Five minutes late.

For the first time in my life I had my name on a poster at the side of the theatre. It wasn't in lights, but it was in big bright red letters. I rushed home to my digs for my little box brownie and took a photograph of it. The only snag was that they had spelled my name wrongly, with two 'o's' instead of one. This misspelling was to dog me for many years.

After New Brighton, we went to the Winter Garden Theatre in Southport, and from there on tour around the country.

The end of this tour coincided with the end of the pantomine season, and I returned to Wolverhampton. I was not too keen about staying in repertory for another season, but I had no other offer. This time I did break the five pounds limit and my salary went up to seven pounds ten shillings a week – quite a considerable sum in those days. But even so, I was conscious that time was passing, and, as at Byker, I felt I had to make a break for bigger things or I might be trapped in repertory for ever. Yet I do not know how long I might not have stayed at Wolverhampton if war had not intervened and solved the problem for me. When it came, in September 1939, I immediately went to the recruiting office in Birmingham to volunteer for the Navy which I chose because it had been my father's service. The petty officer in charge did not give me the answer I expected.

'Go home,' he told me. 'We don't want you yet, thank you very much. We've got all the men we need.'

I returned to the theatre in time to see 'CLOSED' notices being pasted on the front doors. Alongside there was an announcement about Air Raid Precautions – ARP. On the impulse of the moment, I went along to the nearest ARP centre and was accepted for training as an ambulance driver.

When the theatres opened again a month or two later, I rejoined the company. Beryl Johnstone had meanwhile arrived from Byker and joined it too, and the two of us soon became greatly attracted to each other.

Beryl was in digs with a Mrs. Jones about 150 yards up the road from me, and after waiting impatiently for her landlady to go to bed I would walk to her lodgings and climb up the drainpipe to her bedroom. She would leave the window open, and within seconds we would be in bed together. Our great fear was that the air raid siren might sound, as it often did, and Mrs. Jones would then put her head round the door and ask: 'Are you all right, Beryl, dear?'

Sure enough, this happened one night when I was in bed with Beryl. Fortunately, I had folded up my clothes under the bed, and when I heard the siren, I crawled beneath the sheets so far down that Mrs. Jones could not guess Beryl was not alone.

'Are you all right, Beryl, dear?' the old lady enquired through the half open door.

'Yes, I am all right,' replied Beryl sweetly.

Luckily, Mrs. Jones did not see me or my clothes, but such near discoveries are wearing, even when young, and gradually Beryl and I reached the conclusion that it would be a good idea to legitimise our relationship – in other words, to get married.

We came from different backgrounds – hers, cautious and conforming; mine, casual and easy-going. Yet somehow our marriage seemed almost predestined. So many young men were marrying girl friends and then going off to war, and we did not know when or even whether we would see each other again. In addition, there was the prospect of a service marriage allowance which Beryl could claim, and this would help our finances a great deal.

We had the banns called extra quickly because of my imminent call-up.

My mother did not come from Weston-super-Mare for our wedding in the local church. Dear One was ill, and she could not get away. Beryl's father, a chartered accountant in Cheltenham, and her mother did arrive, however.

I walked down the aisle with my new wife on my arm, and as we came out of the church I heard her mother say pointedly to her husband: '*This* is not what I wanted for my daughter.'

Alas, life in Wolverhampton as a married man in digs was not quite the idyllic affair, or even the sexual marathon, I had imagined when I was single. Beryl and I had enjoyed each other's company when we were not forced to endure it day and night, but within a short time we both realised that her mother had been right. Our marriage now seemed a total mistake. We thought at first that we might eventually become a stage partnership like Alfred Lunt and Lynn Fontanne, who appeared as inseparable off stage as they were on, but we very soon realised that this was simply an impossibility.

In the spring of 1940, as a result of having tried to volunteer for the Navy, my name was on their list, and I received a letter asking whether I would be interested in joining DEMS (Defensively Equipped Merchant Ships). Guns were being placed on cargo vessels because of German U-boat and air attacks. Each gun would be in the charge of a naval rating, who would draw his team from the crew. I filled in the form that arrived with this letter and received orders to report for my basic training to naval barracks in Portsmouth.

From Portsmouth I was posted to Tiger Bay, Cardiff, for two weeks training on a four-inch gun. And from Cardiff I was posted to Liverpool to join a merchant ship, the MV *Lobus,* as a naval rating in charge of a four-inch anti-submarine gun set up above her stern.

The strange thing was that as I joined my ship at Liverpool, a mental curtain came down on my past life. I might have had no parents or wife; my experiences in London and Byker and Wolverhampton faded into oblivion. I was a sailor now, proud as a turkey cock of my new bell-bottom trousers, with a badge on my arm that proved I was a gun layer (second class). I felt an important man.

Most of the crew were on leave, and it was explained to me that because *Lobus* was a merchant ship and not a fighting ship, my quarters, by King's Regulations, would be separate from theirs. I was not to be allowed to mingle with them aboard ship. I had to be on my own. I was put into the former sick bay under the gunner's platform on the poop deck, right aft. I had a little bunk, my own bath and my own loo, and felt proud of my quarters despite their vulnerable position under the gun and above the ammunition store.

I unpacked and immediately went up to inspect the gun. It looked an extraordinary weapon to me, as though it had been designed by someone who had heard what a gun looked like but had never actually seen one. It was also very old, but then *Lobus* herself was a venerable vessel which, but for the war, would probably have gone to the scrapyard. I reported my doubts about this ancient weapon to the local Naval Office and asked whether someone could be kind enough to check over this gun for me. I could not understand how it worked.

'I wouldn't worry about that,' the commander told me. 'It's a gun, isn't it?'

'Well, yes, sir,' I agreed. 'It's a gun. But it's a funny-looking thing.'

'It'll bloody well fire though, won't it?'

This is what I felt doubtful about. But the commander changed the subject by telling me that I had been recommended for a commission, and provided all went well when I finished this sea trip, I should expect to be sent to HMS *King Alfred* in Brighton, to train as a potential officer. This cheered me considerably and next morning I was further relieved to see an old salt, a chief gunner's mate wearing first world war medals, arrive on board.

'Now, lad,' he asked me. 'What's up?'

'I am a bit worried about this gun,' I explained. 'We're going to South America and there are an awful lot of U-boats in the Atlantic.'

'Let's have a butcher's,' he said. He examined the gun with the air of someone who had never seen its like before, and perhaps he hadn't. Then his face cleared.

'Now,' he went on, 'you see them hieroglyphics? That Jap writing there? That means it was made for His Imperial Japanese Majesty. This is what is known as a 4.7 Japanese anti-submarine gun. You want to look after this.'

'I am so glad,' I told him. 'But what happens if we have a brush with a submarine? How do I fire it?'

'I'll tell you, mate. If *I* were you *I* wouldn't fire the bloody thing at all.'

And with that, he left me.

Three days later we sailed on the tide. The crew did not reckon me very highly as a gunnery expert, but they discovered that I could read and write better than they could and so commissioned me to compose love letters to their girlfriends and wives back home. For this service, I was paid in cigarettes, which I could never have afforded to buy otherwise. Being an actor, I was full of amazing rhetoric, and since I have a vivid imagination I wrote the most passionate letters for them. They were delighted, and I hope the girls appreciated them, too. But sometimes I wondered how performance could ever match up with the promises I made in the names of their men.

We sailed to Bermuda, through the Panama Canal, then down the West Coast of America, calling at Equador, Peru, and, finally, Valparaiso in Chile. We unloaded our cargo of Sheffield knives and forks and tinware and took on hides and saltpetre and other stores needed in Britain.

Chile was neutral, and it was extraordinary to meet German sailors in the bars. They had been in port when war broke out, and of course, could not leave. We met Nazi sailors in a pub called The Graf Zeppelin, and whenever we had a few beers inside us a free fight would begin. Bottles were thrown, eyes were blacked and insults shouted. I must say I was thankful to crawl under the first available table and watch the footwork and fisticuffs from there. Once, I plucked up enough courage to knock someone on the back of the head with a bottle when he wasn't looking, but to be honest, I was a bit of a coward in those days.

Chile was in a strange position, because the navy was pro-British, indeed built on the British pattern and founded by an Irishman, Bernardo O'Higgins. The army was pro-German and trained by German officers. When a fight broke out and the Chilean naval police arrived, we were escorted back to our ships, and the Germans were put in jug for the night. But if the military police arrived first, we were put in jug while the Germans were escorted back to their ships.

In Chile, so I was told, it was considered rather impolite for men to drink on their own, without a woman. I had very little money, of course, and didn't know any women, but the rate of exchange was then in our favour and for three shillings – fifteen new pence – Scouse sailors from *Lobus* boasted they could buy a pint of beer, ten cigarettes, and a woman for the night – strictly in that order.

I had about three pounds owing to me by then, and with the third engineer, a friend from Liverpool named Bert, I decided to spend this in The Graf Zeppelin. We were sitting there getting steadily drunker and drunker, when some local sitting next to me passed me a note which he had received from someone else. I read this message, written in green ink and very spidery writing: 'I love you very mooch, Eliza Munis.'

I looked hopefully across the crowd of people, through ranks of Germans all glaring at us, and I saw four girls sitting together at a table. Three were talking, and the fourth had her mouth closed and looked rather pretty. She saw me look at her and waved to me. Oh, I thought, *that's* Eliza Munis. I turned to Bert.

'What shall I do?' I asked him, as the experienced mariner.

'Get her over here. She looks a bit of all right to me. Rather fancy her myself.'

So I took his advice and asked her over. Eliza Munis sat down.

'You write-o this note-o to all sailors?' I asked her – not, I realised afterwards, the most tactful of opening remarks. I spoke in this strange way because it was a general belief aboard *Lobus* that we only had to put the word 'o' on the end of a word and we would genuinely be speaking Spanish. We could thus call loudly for fish-o, chips-o, beer-o and were considerably surprised when the locals did not understand and respond immediately.

Eliza smiled and said, 'Yeah, me write.' When she smiled I saw

86

that she had no front teeth. She had two fangs on either side of her mouth, and she reminded me of my wife, Beryl, playing Dracula's daughter. I thought, I am not so sure about this. However, she was young, and apart from her lack of teeth, was quite pretty, and well stacked, so I had another bottle of beer, and then another. With each bottle I drank, she grew another tooth in my imagination. In the end, she had the most beautiful face, like a young Elizabeth Taylor . . .

The next thing I remember was something licking *my* face. This felt like a warm wet sponge being rubbed slowly across my lips.

I dredged through my fuddled memories. I could remember drinking at the bar. I recalled seeing Eliza. Now I opened my eyes, and to my horror saw that a pig was licking my mouth. The pig snorted as he licked me with his tongue. He wasn't a very large pig, but then he wasn't a very small pig. He was a kind of piglet, and around this piglet were chickens, and in the background I heard other farmhouse noises.

I sat up and to my amazement found I had been lying in an old-fashioned iron bedstead in a tin shack, with hay and a horse and all these other animals. Early morning sun was streaming down on me. I turned round, and by my side lay Eliza Munis, still asleep. She was snoring gently with her mouth open and no teeth. Under no circumstances could she be described as a sleeping beauty. She looked, I thought ungallantly, not unlike the piglet.

I must have gone back to bed with her, and now I did not know where I was, or even what part of South America I was in. I had no idea where my ship was. All I knew was that I was in bed with a toothless woman of indeterminate age, surrounded by snorting, crowing, snuffling and truffling animals. This was not an agreeable or pleasing discovery.

I shook Eliza awake.

'Oh, you very nice boy,' she said, sleepily. 'I love you very mooch.' She rolled towards me. I had no time for any of this.

'I have to get back to my ship,' I told her. 'Where my ship? My ship-o?'

'Ah, ship. No ship.'

We were getting nowhere with this ridiculous conversation. I crawled out of bed and picked my way carefully through the animal droppings – shades of the Byker production of *Son of the Sheikh* – and put my head under the farm pump; Eliza came over and pumped the handle and the welcome cold water spurted over my face and shoulders. I felt in a terrible state, ill, feverish, with an awful hangover, soaked by the pump and yet, paradoxically, my mouth was as dry as an oven lid. Fortunately, we were not too far from the docks and Eliza walked me back to the ship. She lived in a kind of shanty town, and had taken me back there, and I suppose made love to me. I didn't remember, and I still don't. What made me absurdly happy was that she handed me back the money I had given to her.

She said: 'You very nice boy – you need the money.'

I thought, my God, I must have been the most marvellous lover in all the world. She has handed me my money back.

I never saw her again, which is probably just as well.

Eventually we set out on our return journey to Liverpool. In the Atlantic the German pocket-battleship *Admiral von Scheer* attacked our convoy, and one of our escort, an armed-merchant vessel, *Jervis Bay*, bravely headed straight for her, with six-inch guns blazing against the eleven-inch guns of the German battleship. *Jervis Bay* did not stand a chance, but by sacrificing his ship and his own life, her commander, Captain Kennedy, the father of Ludovic Kennedy, the TV commentator, saved all of us. While this unequal action was taking place, all ships in the convoy scattered and most came through safely.

One thing that worried us during our return voyage was what we should find when we reached Liverpool. The Press in Chile and Peru was strongly pro-German, and we had read many reports that Liverpool was wiped out, while London had apparently been burning for weeks. We therefore dreaded that we would find the whole country in ruins. In addition to this gloomy prospect, we ran into the most violent storm.

I was at sea a further five years after this, and in all that time never experienced worse weather. A Force 10 blew, a hurricane! Waves twice the size of the ship pursued us. The *Lobus*, thirty-odd years old, kept chugging along gamely, rolling and pitching to such an extent I thought she would never right herself.

'Can the ship take this?' I asked the bo'sn.

'So long as the cargo doesn't shift, yes.'

'Well, is there any danger of the cargo shifting?'

'There's always danger of cargo shifting,' he replied. 'You never know with these old ships. And if it does move, mate, we've had it. We'll turn over.'

So we had to live with this on top of everything else. I wrote rather melodramatically in my diary: 'Oh, Beryl, my darling, I miss you so much. What are you doing in Wolverhampton? Am I ever going to see you again?'

As we drew nearer to England our spirits perked up, and when we finally docked at Liverpool we were all relieved to find the city virtually undamaged, with life going on almost normally. There had been air raids, of course, and the Battle of Britain had been fought and won, and the heavy night raids were still to come.

I had left Beryl in Wolverhampton. The theatre re-opened and she was acting again with the company. She was also receiving two pounds ten shillings a week marriage allowance, which made her financially better off than she had ever been before. Yet when I returned home I found that she was broke. She had literally no money at all – and, of course, neither had I.

I had visualised us having dinner together in the Victoria Grill, a restaurant next to the Grand, but now she said: 'It's impossible, Kenny. We're stony.'

'How *can* we be?' I asked her in amazement. 'What have you been doing, for goodness sake?'

'I have nothing left, Kenny. I needed some new clothes. And then I went and bought Mummy something.'

'Mummy!' I mimicked bitterly. 'You bought Mummy something! That monster! With our money?'

So we had a quarrel. I thought Beryl had let me down in not saving anything at all from our joint earnings. There was, of course, a swift reconciliation. But then there were other quarrels, and other passionate and tearful reconciliations. And each time we grew slightly further apart. I felt that while I had been away fighting for King and Country, and she was at home in a soft job and earning what in comparison was a lot of money, she had been selfish and unthinking. This rankled.

However, more cheeringly, I was now ordered to report to Royal Naval Barracks, Portsmouth, to go before an Officer Selection Board. Another actor, rather better known than me in those days, had preceded me here. This was Robert Newton, then at the height of his fame as a British film star, and with one of his films actually showing in Portsmouth. Newton was a very heavy drinker and an equally amusing raconteur. Every evening, although only an ordinary seaman, he would hold court at The Goat public house, surrounded by officers of all ranks who felt honoured by associating with someone so famous. The Officer Selection Board did not share this view. There had been occasions when Newton would drift off when the pub shut, and carry on drinking elsewhere. Then, rather than pass the sentry in the barrack gates, he would climb over the wall into his quarters. Several times he had been caught and hauled before the

Officer-of-the-Night for his behaviour. At his interview with the Selection Board, Newton also had intimated to the Admiral in charge that he would be doing the Navy a favour if he accepted a commission. He did not wait to be told he might become an officer; Newton said that if asked to accept a commission, he would consider the matter.

Not only was he not asked, but he was thrown out of the Navy. The Admiral explained rather caustically: 'You would be better employed in your chosen vocation – amusing people.'

This news did not cheer me up, for I was the next actor to appear before this board. The candidates just ahead of me were a publisher, a librarian and a coal merchant, all very respectable callings. The chief petty officer on the door ushered me into the boardroom. At a kidney-shaped table sat an Admiral, the head-master of Portsmouth Grammar School, and various other dignitaries. The Admiral read the notes in front of him, which listed my previous job, and then said, 'Oh, God, not *another* bloody actor.'

Facing the table was an empty chair. I should have stood to attention by this chair and waited to be told to sit, but in my anxiety I sat down in it immediately, smiled at the members of the board, folded my arms and crossed my legs, and waited for the questions to begin. The Admiral drummed his fingers angrily on the table. No one said anything. Finally, I did.

'Is something wrong, sir?' I asked him.

'Yes, More. You are not at ease in the Navy until you are told to be at ease. *Stand up!*'

I leaped up and apologised, red-faced. Somehow I bluffed my way through. The headmaster asked me: 'Are you any good at trigonometry, More?'

I had barely heard the name until he mentioned it, but I nodded slowly and sagely, knowing vaguely that this was something to do with mathematics, my worst subject!

'Yes, sir,' I assured him.

'How would you apply your knowledge of trigonometry to a problem, More?'

This was a hard one. I tried to deflect it.

'Well, sir, if I saw a ladder against a wall, and I knew the height of the ladder and the distance from the wall, then I could calculate the length of the ladder.'

He looked at me eye to eye. I began to feel uneasy, a feeling that increased when he glanced out of the window.

'It just so happens that I can see a ladder leaning against a wall over there,' he said at last.

I looked out of the window. I could see the bloody ladder, too. My heart sank.

'Really, sir?'

'*And* I can give you its height from the ground *and* the distance from its base off the wall.'

'Yes, sir.'

He gave me the figures. They meant nothing to me. I looked at the faces of the board members, all staring at me. I wondered what would Nelson have done. He would have failed, no doubt about it. What had a ladder leaning against the wall to do with Trafalgar?

'What's the answer, More?' asked the headmaster. It was no good. I had to give up.

'I haven't a clue, sir,' I admitted honestly. They all laughed. After that, the rest of the interview was easy. I was through. I went back to Wolverhampton for a further brief leave, and Beryl and I did our best to make a go of things together.

Eventually I was commissioned, went to London to buy my uniform, and then, after going to say goodbye to Beryl in Wolverhampton, spent the rest of my two weeks appointment leave with my mother and Dear One in Weston-super-Mare. I felt very pleased with myself as an Acting Sub-Lieutenant (RNVR) with one wavy gold stripe on my arm, wearing the uniform my father had worn all those years before. I was sorry he was not there to see me carry on the tradition.

At the end of my leave, I received a telegram ordering me to report to the Naval-Officer-in-Command, Liverpool. I was very excited, for surely this must mean a posting to a destroyer, a corvette or a cruiser. But when I arrived I found I was not due to go to sea at all. I was to be a gunnery officer, training Merchant Navy officers in light anti-aircraft work. I carried out this job with increasing depression for nearly a year.

During this time, my daughter Susan Jane was born. Beryl had left Wolverhampton and moved to Cheltenham for this event. She stayed with her mother and father. By then it was May, 1941, and the blitz on Liverpool had begun. In one week, the German air force very nearly succeeded in destroying the whole city. The dock area was on fire. Ships blazed uncontrollably in the harbour. Streets were blocked with rubble and overturned buses and trucks. Sewers and gas mains had cracked. Worst of all, the people's morale was beginning to waver. We had little or no sleep for nights on end, for our off-duty hours were spent dragging people out of ruined buildings.

Naval Headquarters were underneath the Liver Building,

buried so deep down they were believed to be virtually bomb-proof. But my barracks, HMS *Mersey,* originally an old hospital, lay naked to every attack. When we were not out in the street helping the ARP people, we lived in the cellars beneath this building.

One Wednesday night, when we were down in these cellars, we heard the most incredible whistle, and a shrieking roar like an approaching express train diving at us from the sky. We looked at each other, faces drained of all emotion. This was it. Nothing could save us. The noise increased, and then the building rocked and trembled. At that moment, the screeching stopped. Dust dropped from the ceiling in clouds, and then – nothing at all. We sat in petrified silence, hearing our hearts beat with fear and relief.

'Looks as though we have an unexploded high explosive bomb somewhere in the building,' the commander said at last. 'Probably on top of us. Anyone volunteer to go out and have a look?'

I said, 'Oh, yes, sir. I'll have a look.'

I could not bear the thought of being buried alive. Any prospect was more attractive than being incarcerated in this dank, dark cellar.

All the lights were out, of course, and I felt my way cautiously up the stairs, and from one ward to the next, until I reached the top ward and walked along it.

Above me, a huge hole gaped in the roof, with an equally large hole directly beneath it through the floor.

From the size of the hole and the glint of metal under the rubble, I thought an aircraft engine must have dropped through the roof, but I had no real idea what it was. I carried a torch and switched this on. Never mind the blackout; the city was blazing with a hundred different fires. I crawled through the debris and saw to my amazement an immense boiler of the type we had used back at the Sentinel works in Shrewsbury. I thought, what the devil are they doing, dropping boilers? I scrabbled away at the dust on the side of this vast cylinder and suddenly saw beneath my hand the letter 'K' printed on the metal. I literally froze with horror, for this was not an English 'K' but a German 'K'.

It had a tall back piece and then a little one, and a 'G' underneath. You can't mistake the sign for kilograms in German. After the 'Kg' came a lot of figures and I thought, it's a landmine. It was the biggest bomb I have ever seen. I flashed the torch around it and saw a metal ring with half a parachute still on it and torn white cords by which it had been suspended. I watched, mesmerised, my bones like water. Then I got a grip on myself, and crawled away, and rushed downstairs to the commander.

'Well?' he asked.

'It's an unexploded landmine, sir, the size of a house. No, the size of a Sentinel boiler.'

'What the devil do you mean, a Sentinel boiler?'

I could not begin to explain.

'You wouldn't know, sir, but that's what it looks like.'

'Someone will have to report to Headquarters personally,' the commander decided. This was because the telephone was out of order.

Liver Building was about 600 yards away.

'I'll go, sir,' I said at once. 'I'll go.'

I knew that if that boiler went up no one would be left alive in HMS *Mersey*. It seemed better to brave falling shrapnel and other bombs than to sit in your tomb just waiting to be buried.

'Good,' said the commander. 'Report to the duty officer and ask him for instructions.'

'Very good, sir.'

I set off. Every five yards or so I heard the shriek of a falling bomb and threw myself flat on the pavement to avoid the blast. It was a slow and terrible journey, with the streets red in the glare of the flames. I eventually reached the Liver Building and went down through sandbagged passages to the door of the duty officer's room, far below ground, and banged on it.

'Come in,' someone called calmly from inside.

I opened the door. Inside, an old grey-haired commodore wearing first world war medal ribbons was sitting quietly behind a desk, stirring a cup of tea.

'Come in, my boy,' he said invitingly. 'You look a bit pale. Have a cup of tea.'

He turned to an orderly.

'Bring this officer a cup of tea,' he told him.

I sat down thankfully.

'Now,' the commodore continued, 'What can I do for you?'

The question and the setting seemed ludicrous; it was as though I had been summoned to the headmaster's study at school to discuss the prospects of the First XV. Here was an isolated oasis of calm, while outside the city was being systematically pounded to pieces.

I said, 'Sir, we've got a landmine on top of us.'

'Here?'

As he asked the question, the commander raised his eyebrows slightly, cup halfway to his mouth.

'No, *there*, sir,' I said. 'Up the road. HMS *Mersey*. Can we have instructions what to do with it?'

He sipped his tea thoughtfully.

'Do you think it will go off?' he asked conversationally.

'I don't know, sir,' I answered. 'I have no idea. But we are all there, sir. In the cellars.'

'Well, to evacuate now wouldn't be very good, would it, eh, with all this going on above? I think you had better all sit tight until the morning. Then we'll send a bomb disposal chappie along. By the way, do you take sugar?'

I took sugar, and ran back through the burning streets.

We bedded down as best we could and lay, some distance from sleep, listening uneasily for any unusual noise on the floor above. The raid passed. Sirens sounded the All Clear, and at first light, to our surprise, we were still alive.

We immediately cleared the entire building, and waited for the bomb disposal expert. He was a young RNVR officer, dark-haired and slightly built, wearing the green stripe on his sleeve that showed he was a specialist. He arrived in a truck, and jumped out, carrying a bag of tools. The truck drove off, and he was on his own. He went inside, all by himself, one young man and a gigantic bomb in a huge empty building.

Air raid wardens had evacuated every house and office and shop for a wide area around the hospital. Buses and cars and trucks still lay on their sides like giant toys in the streets, or upside down in bomb craters. Water streamed from smashed hydrants, and ambulances and salvage teams were carrying out their jobs in the pale spring sunshine. We stood in silence for little over an hour. Then the officer came out of the building, and crossed over to us. He might have been an unusually well-spoken plumber, with his little black bag of tools.

'Well,' he said cheerfully. 'I've disarmed it all right. But there are one or two little innovations I am not too sure about. We are going to move it out to the beach at Southport.'

Here the sands stretched for miles, and unexploded bombs were often examined on them and then exploded. A gang of seamen arrived and set up wooden runways. They rolled this gigantic landmine down these and a crane lifted it up into a truck and it was driven away. We exchanged glances of relief that it had gone.

Later that day, we heard that while he had been trying to discover the purpose of the innovations he mentioned, the mine had exploded. He was killed instantly.

Bomb disposal experts were dying by the dozen then, because

many bombs and mines contained booby traps and other hidden devices which could still set off a bomb which was thought to be harmless.

The Navy was good about these young experts, and fully realised the terrible strain of their job. When a lull came in the air raids in Liverpool, all surviving members of the local bomb disposal squads went to London at the Navy's expense on an extended spree. They booked in at the Savoy Hotel and had two or three nights there with the Navy footing the bill. We were all very pleased with 'The Andrew' (as the Navy was called) for having the imagination to do this.

As the months went on my discontent with my safe job increased.

The Prince of Wales and *Repulse* were lost off Malaya, and Singapore and Hong Kong fell to the Japanese. I wanted to go to sea again to do a real naval officer's job, not to stay strumming around Liverpool with all the tiredness and sweat and dirt of a dockyard in wartime. It seemed wrong for me to be living in a mess, where a Wren brought me early morning tea. I wanted action – which, after all, was why I had joined up in the first place, and I asked my commanding officer for a transfer. He refused to consider this.

'You are too valuable here,' he told me. 'We can't possibly let you go.'

I then asked the unofficial advice of an old chief gunner's mate, a retired petty officer from the first world war, an Irishman who was always full of good counsel.

'Get some sick leave,' he said at once.

'But how can I have sick leave when I'm not sick?' I asked him.

'Easy. Go sick. What's the matter with you?'

'Nothing,' I told him. I was very healthy.

'I can see that,' he said. 'Have you had your appendix out?'

'No.'

'Well, you're going to have it out.'

'How?' I said.

'Simple. Have an attack on duty. Suddenly grasp your side. Fall down in agony. Cry out with the pain. You were an actor, weren't you? They'll have you off to hospital, and whip your appendix out in no time. Then you'll go on sick leave. When you come back you'll be posted somewhere else – to a ship, most likely.'

This seemed a way out, so I read up the symptoms of appendicitis in a medical book in the public library until I knew so much about it I felt I could almost perform the operation myself. Then, choosing my moment during a lecture, I grabbed my side and fell down. I said I had a fierce stabbing pain and felt sick, and all the rest. The local Naval Hospital had just opened a new operating theatre and they hadn't yet had an operation in it. The naval surgeon in charge was therefore keen to have one, so I suppose he wasn't too fussy about what he did.

I was put in a ward full of young submarine officers who had duodenal ulcers, brought on no doubt from the stress they suffered. As I lay in bed here, I felt awful at having faked this operation, but it was too late to back out now, so I gave the best performance I could. Charlie Denville could not have faulted it. Finally, the doctors nodded to each other in the way doctors have and said: 'Yes, it's an appendix all right. No question.'

And so, out it came. The following morning, when I was clear of the anaesthetic, the surgeon came in to see me.

'Nothing wrong with your appendix, More,' he told me. 'The cleanest I have ever seen. However, as you are obviously going back to sea, you might as well have it out now as later, in case anything goes wrong. God bless you, anyhow, More. You have christened the operating theatre. You were our first patient, and everything worked wonderfully.'

I thought, that's fine. At last I've done some good for the nation.

After sick leave, I was sent to HMS *Excellent,* the gunnery school on Whale Island off Portsmouth. Here, in the mess one night I saw a young lieutenant who, I was told, was Prince Philip Mountbatten. Everyone was treating him with awe, because he was someone special, and he was surrounded by our more senior officers, commanders and lieutenant-commanders, all chatting to him rather stiffly. I felt sorry for him, and as I was his own age, I thought I would go over and introduce myself and ask, 'How are you?' I was about to do this when a commander standing by me must have read my mind.

'Where are you going?' he asked coldly.

'To talk to Lieutenant Mountbatten,' I said.

'Over my dead body,' he replied.

'Why not?' I asked him.

'Because you just don't *do* that, that's why. And if you do, I'll have you doubling round that parade ground for two days solidly.'

I realised soon that I was due to be posted to a battleship, which did not please me. A battleship, in my book, was too impersonal. She was the size of a football field, with about 1,500 crew, and battleships seemed to spend most of their time running around buoys in Scapa Flow. I didn't want to do this. I wanted action, with men I could come to know well. I wanted to serve in a light cruiser at the most, or a destroyer or something. The officer in charge of the course was sympathetic.

'Obviously, you are not suited to this course,' he said. 'So we'll take you off it.'

Once more, leave, and back to mother and Dear One. Then the telegram: REPORT TO NAVAL-OFFICER-IN-CHARGE, LIVERPOOL.

'You again,' said the commander cheerfully. 'Well, let's see what we've got for you this time.'

He opened a file.

'Oh, yes. You have been appointed an additional Watch Keeping Officer in *Aurora*.'

I was so pleased, I very nearly jumped up and down.

'Not the *Aurora*?'

This was one of the Navy's crack light-cruisers, and had become a legend during the siege of Malta.

The commander nodded.

'The same,' he said. 'She's in here for a refit. But contain yourself. You may not be jumping up and down in a year's time.'

'When can I join?'

'This morning,' he told me.

I reported to *Aurora* as soon as I left his office. She was lying alongside one of the docks, and I stood for a moment looking at this sleek cruiser, smart in her dazzle paint. I saw her two funnels, her six six-inch and eight four-inch guns, and all the other short-range and anti-aircraft weapons, and I could hardly believe my good luck. This ship was going to be my home for I knew not how long. I had no idea when or where she would sail, but from now on I was to be part of her company, and her destiny would be mine. It was May, 1942.

5

WHEN I THINK back to my years in the Navy, it is as though the incidents I recall must have happened to someone else.

Did I really sail down the Mersey in HMS *Aurora* on a July morning in 1942, as a Watch Keeping Officer, and then up past Northern Ireland where we were escort ship for a fleet of mine-layers?

Did I peer out with aching, red-rimmed eyes through thick fog at icebergs that loomed like floating cliffs in a world of silence and the sea?

I must have done, and yet it all seems so remote now that it could have taken place in another life; and, in a sense, it did.

About one in every ten of the mines laid exploded prematurely, and would pierce the eerie gloom with echo and re-echo, until once more the stillness of fog and empty ocean closed around us.

From this desolate world of ice we thankfully turned south, to be senior escort vessel for a convoy carrying troops bound for North Africa. The route was by way of the Cape, but we only went as far as Freetown on the West Coast of Africa. Every day, the heat grew more intense. Once, our Captain, 'Bill' Agnew, found us at action stations wearing only shorts. This could have been fatal had we needed to fire the guns, because of the danger from flash-burn. We argued that the sun was so hot and the sea seemed so peaceful that no enemy could be in sight. Finally, he said, 'I don't care what you wear, but you must wear *some* proper covering – pyjamas, if you like.'

I took him at his word, and so can claim to be the only naval officer aboard to turn out for duty wearing blue-striped flannel pyjamas.

Like most ship's captains, 'Bill' Agnew hated slovenliness and anything slipshod, but most of all he hated beards. He refused to let any officer 'discontinue shaving', as the Navy phrases the growing of a beard. Possibly he took the view I later heard expressed by Sir Thomas Beecham, that if all the beards in the BBC were placed from end to end they would stretch from Sodom to Gomorrah.

I looked on the captain's refusal as a direct challenge, and at

98

once became determined to grow a beard. Everyone in the wardroom assured me this would never be allowed, but this only increased my determination.

My chance came when I suffered from a prickly heat rash on my face. One baking afternoon, I was on the bridge. The captain was also there sitting in his chair, wearing a panama hat against the glare from the water.

'Sir,' I began. 'I would like your permission to grow a beard.'

I raised my chin and touched some of the spots tenderly.

'It's this rash, sir. Shaving makes it worse. If I stopped shaving for a bit, I'm sure it would clear up.'

'Bill' Agnew gave me an old-fashioned look, as if he suspected I was just trying this on. Then he nodded agreement.

'Permission granted,' he said. 'Just as long as we are in the tropics.'

A few days later, I was again on the bridge as officer of the watch when orders came from the convoy's commodore: 'Follow Zig-zag 11'. This was one of several patterns listed in a book which each ship carried. These patterns were designed to confuse prowling U-boats as to the course the convoy was taking. Zig-zag 11 meant that *Aurora*, with all the other ships in the convoy, would follow a certain bearing for ten minutes, then alter course to another given bearing, and then to a third, and so on.

Captain Agnew was having a cat nap in his chair, and I debated whether to rouse him. I decided against this for I was certain I could cope with the situation. I therefore gave what I considered were the necessary orders, and *Aurora* altered course. Our bows cut great curving furrows of foam as she twisted and turned. I felt totally in command of the situation, and then suddenly I heard an agonising shout from goodness knew who, or where: *'The wheel's to port instead of starboard!'*

Captain Agnew leapt from his seat, immediately awake. His face contorted with horror as he realised what had happened.

'You're heading for the commodore's ship!' he roared.

I stared at him, incapable of speech and not knowing what to say or do to remedy my mistake. Out of the spray ahead, I could see the vast grey bulk of the troop carrier loom up – and we were heading towards her to slice her in half amidships.

Captain Agnew instantly assessed this situation and shouted orders down the voice pipe. Engine telegraph bells rang. The sea boiled around us like a foam bath as *Aurora* went into a 45 degree turn. Only by his absolutely magnificent seamanship was disaster averted with the almost certain loss of two Royal Navy ships and unknown numbers of their crews.

We were all keeping radio silence, but as we drew away from the commodore's ship the flags rippled up her mast in an urgent signal: 'Name of officer-of-the-watch.'

That was me. No one else. I looked at Captain Agnew. He looked at me. He was red in the face with anger and relief. Although I was sorry for myself, I also felt sorrow for him. Since he was captain, he was responsible for what happened aboard his ship and so had to take the responsibility for this near collision. Immediately, he sent a return signal: 'My responsibility. Officer-of-the-watch under training.'

After this episode, I kept what nowadays we call a low profile until we arrived at Freetown. We all went ashore to buy the usual souvenirs – drums, tom-toms, African shields and wooden carvings. One of the crew bought a bunch of bananas – not realising that it was the home of a five foot black mamba. This snake popped out of the bananas and was killed, fortunately, before it could do anyone a mischief.

The man who killed the mamba then wrapped it up in a neat parcel, and left it as a surprise for the chief telegraphist, with whom he was not on speaking terms.

During our stay in Freetown the convoy commodore, whose ship we nearly rammed, invited officers from each escort ship in the convoy to dine with him as a mark of appreciation that the convoy had arrived safely without any loss. At the top table sat the commodore and the captains, and some officers from the troops embarked. The rest of us sat at other tables.

The food was good, the drink abundant.

Finally, through a fog of cigar and cigarette smoke and the fumes of wine in my brain, I heard someone shout: 'Come on, More! Give us a speech!'

I ignored this request. I thought it could not possibly be addressed to me. But I heard it repeated more loudly, and then taken up by others.

'Come on, More! On your feet! Let's have a few words!'

Some officers began to beat time with their feet, and I felt I could no longer ignore their call.

I'd had a good deal to drink by then, and as I looked around, people seemed to be pointing at me, and gesticulating to persuade me to stand up. And so, believing with all the vanity of an actor that because I was an actor they wanted to hear me speak, I did stand up.

Immediately, the noise ceased. I looked confidently across the crowded hall – and saw Captain Agnew's face. At once, my confidence deserted me. He was horrified. I read his thoughts as clearly as if he was making the signal with flags: What the devil is this idiot More going to do now?

I only discovered afterwards that the 'More' everyone had been calling for was not me, but one Colonel Moore, of the Gordon Highlanders. But even though I was ignorant of this at the time, I knew I had made a bish in standing up.

For a second, I stood in silence. My mind raced back to the Windmill, to Byker, to Wolverhampton, seeking desperately for any means of escape from a situation that was excruciatingly embarrassing for my captain, and even worse for me. Then the guardian angel who looks after actors who forget their lines and others, even less fortunate, like me at that moment, who have no lines to forget, mercifully put words in my mouth.

I bowed to the commodore.

'Sir,' I began. 'I am not a great hand at speeches, but I do feel it is time someone said a word in praise of captains. They suffer a great deal, and they usually suffer in silence. Let me give you an instance, sir, of a captain to whom I personally caused much suffering.'

I then went into a completely unexpurgated version of what happened with my near collision. As I continued, amid laughter, I could see Captain Agnew's face going from pink to red to purple. The sight did not bode well for me. I withdrew my gaze and continued to the climax of my story.

'But, sir, there was most fortunately a bright side. For think of the advantage *we* gained. It gave us all a wonderful chance to get closer together than we might ever otherwise have done!'

The commodore laughed loud and long. Captain Agnew also laughed, but not so loud or so long. Slowly, his face resumed its normal colour. I sat down with a silent prayer of gratitude to the actor's guardian angel. But Bill Agnew had his own back on me during our return voyage north. We were on the bridge once more when he turned to me and remarked casually: 'By the way, More, we are now north of the Tropic of Cancer. That mean anything to you?'

'No, sir.'

Until then, the Tropic of Cancer had only meant the name of a book by Henry Miller describing his diverse sexual experiences in Paris. But it had other more nautical connotations in the captain's mind.

'Well, I will tell you. It means we are out of the tropics. Get below and shave off that beard!'

So, unlike all the others who had tanned faces, I was branded by a white ear-to-ear chin mark where my beard had been – and gone.

We continued up the Mediterranean to join the largest convoy I had ever seen. As far as the eye could reach, and beyond, ships dotted the surface of the sea. 'Operation Torch', the invasion of North Africa, was beginning. This was my first experience of life aboard a naval ship as she prepared for action, and it was totally different from the easy-going Dad's Army attitude aboard *Lobus*. She had been but a cargo boat encumbered with a gun; *Aurora* was a ship designed and built solely for the business of war.

I was control officer in charge of the four-inch anti-aircraft guns when I heard to my surprise this brief announcement over the Tannoy: 'Ship's company will see to it that they wear clean underclothes.'

'What's that about?' I asked the ship's surgeon, Lieutenant Sam Balfour, who happened to be passing.

'We're going into action,' he replied. 'If you're wounded, clean clothes give you a better chance of escaping infection.'

Our primary task was to prevent any French warships leaving the disputed port of Oran in Algeria. We arrived off Oran at night in November 1942. I was on the after control platform with the guns. The only sound I could hear was the throb and murmur of *Aurora's* engines, a faint ringing of the telegraph filtering through layers of metal deck, and the slap of the waves. I felt I was living the actor's nightmare I had so often endured when I was in the theatre: I was waiting in the wings for the curtain to go up on Act II – when I did not know what had happened in Act I. And now I had no idea what would happen.

I did not have long to wait. A searchlight blazed from the shore and focused on us. Immediately, our six-inch gun opened fire. The searchlight went out. Then other searchlights came on to illuminate two American ex-coastguard cutters who were bursting through the harbour boom. Guns began to fire down on us from the hilltops. The French artillery used green dye in their explosives so they could check where the shells landed. In the shambles and shouting and thunder of their guns and ours, I saw a big French destroyer, battle ensign at full top, steam out of harbour, determined to make a dash for freedom.

We had no wish to fight her, but we had our orders. We gave chase. Twenty minutes later the French captain, equally with no stomach to fight his former Allies, beached his blazing ship. Two other French destroyers tried to escape. Bursting shells from them exploded in fountains of sea-water all around us. Bill Agnew swung *Aurora* from port to starboard and back to port, as though she were a dodgem – and through his skill she did dodge 'em. We knocked out one of the ships with the help of a British destroyer, *Boadicea*. The other escaped under a thick smoke screen. The battle raged furiously until the French who had been siding with the Axis had a change of heart and came over to the Allied cause. We sailed to Algiers, which then became the chief Allied naval base in that area.

Our orders now were to disrupt supply lines to Field-Marshal Rommel and the Afrika Korps between Sicily and Tripoli. Our advance base was Bone in Algeria, and we led what was known as 'Q Force,' with two other cruisers, *Sirius* and *Argonaut*, and two destroyers now fighting with us, *Quiberon* and *Quentin*.

One night, our force sank two enemy destroyers and four troop ships, and thereafter we were continually dive-bombed. Every night, Bone harbour blazed with burning oil tankers. Incredibly, every ship in that harbour was hit, except ours.

Fortunately, there were compensations. I had been given the job of entertainments officer and organised a ship's concert party. We also played games of soccer and rugger ashore. One of our engine-room artificers, who could not swim very well, put on his Mae West and bravely breast-stroked out into the warm sea. He did not realise that the tide was running against him. He was very lucky to be picked up by a landing craft, but not quite so lucky in that the landing craft was heading for Algiers, 300 miles away. We received a desperate signal to send on his clothes, because, apart from his Mae West, he had been swimming naked.

After the Battle of Alamein, when Rommel began to retreat in North Africa, we returned to Gibraltar, and hoisted the flag of Sir Andrew Cunningham. We took him to Algiers, and then sailed with him and General Eisenhower for the bombardment of Pantelleria, the Axis naval base in the Sicilian Channel.

We opened fire at half past ten one morning and soon the island was completely covered by smoke. A hundred Flying Fortresses attacked it. The blast from all the explosions was so great that, although we were riding three miles out to sea, *Aurora* trembled with the force of the bombardment.

Back to Algiers, then on to Tripoli to pick up King George VI, to carry him to Malta. After he had been piped aboard, the King talked to each of us about our service careers, and then retired to his quarters in the admiral's cabin. It was intended that he would eat there, but none of us thought he could eat very much, because he was suffering from a complaint that had affected every one of us at one time or another – gyppy tummy. His personal doctor was soon visiting him with a bottle of the familiar white stomach mixture the rest of us already knew so very well.

What intrigued me in a theatrical sense was that amid all the Royal luggage taken aboard was one black tin trunk, about five feet long, one foot wide and four feet deep. This lay on the deck in the waist of our ship for everyone to see. There was no Royal crest on it, no cipher, no name. Instead, on the top in white capital letters were simply stencilled two words: THE KING.

When we returned to Tripoli, we discovered that this trunk contained insignia and mementoes which the sovereign always carried when travelling. As he was about to leave *Aurora*, for example, he created our skipper a Commander of the Victorian Order in recognition of the responsibilities he had undertaken in transporting the King, so soon after the siege had been lifted.

We were soon back to normal duty. Following one particularly heavy action during the night, Captain Agnew, taking a walk around the deck, met the ship's surgeon.

'How did you enjoy last night, Sam?' he asked him breezily.

'Well, sir,' Sam Balfour replied. 'Where I was, below decks, I hadn't a clue as to what was happening. The ship could have been sinking for all we knew down there.'

This gave Bill Agnew an idea, for there was obviously nothing more demoralizing than to have to stay below during a battle, possibly deep beneath the surface of the sea, hearing the thunder of the guns, feeling metal tremble all around, but without the slightest idea what was happening, or even who was firing.

As a result, and because I had been an actor and so could speak clearly, I was taken off my job with the anti-aircraft guns and posted to the lower bridge with a microphone connected to the ship's Tannoy system. My new orders were that on all future operations I was to give a running commentary on what was happening. This led to the most bizarre experience – and the luckiest escape – of my life.

From the age of six or seven I had a regularly recurring dream which never altered. In my dream, I was always wearing a naval uniform, and I was lying on the deck of a ship. As I lay, I could hear the sound of engines in the sky, droning like an approaching swarm of bees. The noise made me look up, and I could see an aeroplane right above me. As I watched, a bomb was released from this plane, and began to drop slowly and remorselessly towards me. As it came closer, the bomb grew bigger and bigger until it filled the whole sky. Then, at the moment when it should explode, I would awake, sweating, and with a racing heart.

On board the *Aurora*, and while I was acting as commentator, the exact circumstances of my dream were reproduced. The look-out reported aircraft were approaching on the port quarter.

'How many?' asked the captain.

The look-out began to count.

'Two, four, five, six.'

As the figure grew, our hearts began to sink.

'Seven, eight, ten, twelve.'

'What are they?' I asked him.

'Stukas, sir. Eighty-sevens. Yellownose.'

Hell, I thought. This meant that the pilots were experienced Channel fliers from Battle of Britain days. We should have little chance.

The look-out counted on remorselessly: 'Fourteen, fifteen. I would say, eighteen, sir, making towards us now. Turning.'

We opened up against them with our main armament of six-inch guns – and hit nothing. We had been in the Mediterranean for two years, and I suppose we were a tired ship. Although we filled the sky with hardware the planes still came on totally undamaged.

Speaking into the microphone, so that anyone below decks would know what was happening, I kept nothing back, because I knew instinctively that this was a moment of life or death for many if not all of us.

'Diving now,' I said. 'Fourth plane diving. Third plane's bombs have gone to starboard. Wait . . .!'

Suddenly, my voice left me, for, looking up in the sky, I saw the exact shape of the plane in my dream. There it hung, directly above me, and as I looked I saw the bomb leave the aircraft as I knew it would, and grow larger and larger. And I knew that this one would hit. I lay down on the deck. There was nowhere to go, nowhere to run to and nothing I could do. In front of me was a Paramount News cameraman, who was filming the action. He did not realise his danger.

'Get down, for Christ's sake!' I yelled, and he threw himself down beside me with all his equipment.

'Move up a bit,' I told him, for we were in the narrow side of the bridge and I barely had room to breathe. He moved, and in that second of moving the bomb hit the ship. It landed absolutely square on the four-inch gun deck aft – exactly where I would have been standing had I not been moved to the bridge to do my commentary. By a miracle we were not killed. A piece of the bomb came through the steel protection plates on the lower bridge and gashed the photographer's head. If I hadn't told him to move up he wouldn't have been hit. He took a pretty dim view of this, but he recovered. We both did.

I never had that dream again.

Years later, at various times in my career when nothing seemed to be going well for me, on a professional or personal level, I would think back to this incident and it would give me hope. Surely I had not been saved simply to go down elsewhere before my time? And the belief that I had been spared, largely because I had been an actor, would give me new hope and confidence to continue my struggle in this profession.

We returned to Algiers where in the course of my earlier visit I had made the acquaintance of a pretty French girl whom I nicknamed 'Feathers'. As we lay in bed in her flat one night, I heard the drone of enemy aircraft overhead and then the crump of bombs exploding. I started to reach for my clothes in the darkness.

'What's the matter?' she asked sleepily.

'I've got to get back to the ship.'

'Never mind about your stupid ship,' she said, and proposed an infinitely more agreeable alternative. Nevertheless, I had to mind about my stupid old ship. Full of righteous enthusiasm and red wine, I raced back to my action station. All the ships in the harbour were firing. One gun missed its target and I shouted through the microphone: 'Some silly bastard's shot down a barrage balloon!'

I had forgotten we were in harbour. My commentary was amplified through the deck loudspeakers and echoed round the town.

We sailed to give cover for the Sicily landings, then up the Straits of Messina, and finally to Bizerta in North Africa. Here my concert party gave several shows. We called ourselves The Silver Phantoms, a name chosen because this was the nickname Axis sailors gave our ships, which to them appeared to move as silently as ghosts from one action to another.

When *Sirius* came into port, we had many meetings with the officers, and I remember one especially with a midshipman, Michael Havers. He was a quiet, pleasant-faced young man whose father was a barrister. We would have dinner together, and on one occasion we were discussing our careers after the war.

'I'll tell you what I am going to do, Kenny,' he said. 'I'm going to become Attorney-General.'

In Naval language I expressed the strongest doubts at this determination. After all, the lad was probably not yet nineteen.

'Well, wait and see,' was all Havers would reply.

So I waited. After the war, when I was once more in the theatre, I would sometimes have a note handed into my dressing room. It would inform me that Michael was in the audience and would like to see me back-stage. The first time this happened he was a Cambridge undergraduate. Then he was a young barrister. Soon he was a QC. Next, he was Recorder of Dover, then Norwich, and then Master of the Bench of the Inner Temple. In the meantime he was elected Conservative MP for Wimbledon (now Merton, Wimbledon). Finally, when I was on holiday in the South of France, I saw in the newspaper that he had been knighted and the Conservative Government of the day had appointed him Solicitor-General. He lost this position when the Tories went out of power, but should they be returned at any future election, Sir Michael will be well placed to achieve his ambition and become Attorney-General.

When I remind him of this nowadays in the Garrick, he says, 'Well Kenny, you told me then *you* wanted to be another Spencer Tracy.'

Maybe I did, maybe I didn't. But I tell this story to show that if you set your mind steadfastly enough towards a goal, you can achieve it. Michael did anyway and, incidentally, his son now acts with me in television.

I had now served in *Aurora* for nearly two years. It seemed to me that every other member of the ship's company had changed. My particular chum 'Jock' Offord had left and I was growing restless. But how could I get a posting? Someone suggested I should volunteer to train as a Fighter Direction Officer. They sat in cabins, poring over radar screens called PPI tubes, and guided pilots by radio to within visual range of their targets. This seemed to me a pleasant alternative from being shot at endlessly by enemy ships, and so I applied. I was accepted for the course, and sent back to the Royal Naval Air Station at Yeovilton in Somerset. Knowing the abysmal level of my maths, my friends could never understand how, in a course that involved so much mathematics, I nevertheless passed out near the top. Some suggested that I had achieved this distinction by unfair means – such as becoming friendly with the Wren in charge of the printing room where the examination papers were printed. At this late date, I find such a charge unworthy of a denial. Anyway, who would believe me?

After the course, I was given leave and met my mother in London. We went out to tea together. I was expecting news of my posting and so had left the number of the restaurant where we were going. To my surprise, I was called to the telephone.

The caller was Michael Hordern, then a lieutenant-commander in the office of the Second Sea Lord, who was in charge of naval postings.

'I've news for you, Ken,' he said brightly.

'Good.' I felt it was bound to be some home posting – for preference in a warm part of Cornwall. I could hardly believe my ears when he told me, 'You are going to the Pacific.'

Hell! I'd picked the wrong course. I was now a key man, and while everyone else was celebrating the end of the war in London, I was in a troopship, *New Amsterdam*, in the Red Sea, on my way to the Pacific to join the aircraft carrier *Victorious*.

We worked with the American fleet, and converged for what we believed would be the final air bombardment of Japan. We would refuel at sea, miles from anywhere. In fact, we sailed for 50 days without seeing any land whatever, our aircraft constantly bombing the mainland. Then came the news that the atom bombs had been dropped. For four days we waited, until word of the Japanese acceptance of Allied peace terms came through.

The relief that swept through *Victorious* was tremendous. No more war. We had a hundred Fleet Air Arm pilots on board, and we all drank ourselves silly in a phenomenal party. It was summer, and hot, and we took off our clothes. Finally, from the commander down, we were all stripped stark naked. There were men hanging from the bulkheads, and up among the pipes, all singing uproariously. Such a party had its dangers. When we finished a drink, we merely dropped the bottle or glass on the deck. Next morning we all reported sick with cut feet. And next morning, too, we realised the war was officially over. Our gunnery officer was a regular naval officer and a real stickler. The day after the war ended, he put up a notice: 'All brass on guns will now be polished.' And, with various degrees of enthusiasm, or lack of it, we polished our way back to Britain.

6

ALTHOUGH WE WERE delighted that the war was over, those of us who, like me, had not become established in our careers before it had started so long ago, now felt some murmurs of unease. What would things be like when we got home? Would we be able to pick up the threads of careers we had abandoned so lightheartedly in 1939? Could we still make it?

I was released from the Navy in January 1946, with a gratuity of £146 in a Post Office savings account, a green pork pie hat, a raincoat, a blue and white tie, a utility sports jacket, grey flannels and shoes. I had been twenty-five when I joined up, now I was thirty-one. Six of the most important years in anyone's life had gone; and all I had to show for these years was this small savings account and these grotesque clothes, known then as a demob suit.

In the six years behind me I could have taken my time and moved step by step, gradually, even confidently. But now time was something I could not afford to waste. I must attempt to achieve in months what would otherwise have taken years. And I had to make a come-back on two levels, personal and professional.

I spent part of my demobilisation leave with Dear One, who had moved to Wales. She was delighted to know that I had survived the war, but insisted that I go to see my wife Beryl in the hope that we could sort out our differences, if only for the sake of our young daughter. I was not optimistic, but agreed to go.

Apart from my early leaves in the Navy, I had not seen Beryl for nearly six years. She had left our daughter with her parents to join ENSA (Entertainments National Service Association) and toured Britain and Europe with a concert party, giving shows to troops.

I found she was appearing in a play in Harrogate and went up there to meet her. We spent one night together, in which we discussed our past and any future together from every possible angle. At the end of it all we both knew that we were deceiving ourselves in imagining our marriage could survive. It was just one of many other wartime alliances that had flared with a little brief happiness, and now was best left to die.

Beryl was an attractive woman, and I was certain she would remarry. I therefore felt it fairest not to seek custody or even access to my daughter Susan Jane until at least she was old enough to have some understanding of the forces that can attract people and also divide them. In consequence until Susan Jane was in her teens I only saw her once. She was playing hockey at a boarding school her grandparents suggested she attend in Hereford, and I stood on the touchline and watched the game. We had a shy reunion.

My next concern was my future as an actor. I thought about asking Miriam Warner to act for me again, but decided against it. I felt that to do this would be a backward step. I could not return to provincial rep, for if I did I feared I would never escape.

I sought the advice of Equity, the actors' trade union, and they passed me on to someone who was helping ex-servicemen and women. He suggested that a suitable agent might be Harry Dubens, who had an office in Regent Street.

Before the war, Harry had worked on the production side of the theatre, and among other productions had been largely responsible for launching the Hermione Gingold and Henry Kendall *Sweet and Low* series of revues which had been extremely successful. Now he was running an agency. Two of his earliest clients were Harold Warrender and Andrew Osborn, both of whom became extremely successful and very popular, especially Warrender, who hosted *The Navy Lark*. For my interview with Harry Dubens I had the choice of wearing my naval lieutenant's uniform or my appalling demob suit. I chose the former; it showed that at least I had reached commissioned rank – for what this was worth in 1946. I took the lift to Harry's office on the fifth floor, feeling much as I had felt all those years earlier when I had nervously walked up flights of stairs to see Miriam Warner for the first time.

Harry sat behind his desk, obviously not greatly impressed with me or my record.

'What can you *do*?' he asked simply. He was a small man, with piercing eyes; he spoke with a strong Jewish accent. I told him of my experience at the Windmill and the roles I had played in Byker and Wolverhampton. He nodded as though he had heard all this many times before, as indeed I am sure he had. Then he nodded with more expression, more feeling. 'All right, Kenny,' he said. 'I'll do my best for you.'

Thus began a close association between us, which lasted until his death. I always liked and trusted Harry. We never had a written contract or agreement. We did not even have an exchange of letters between us, only what lawyers like to call 'mutual trust', and the feeling that we could work together and achieve something worthwhile together. When I went down in the lift after our first meeting, I felt more confident of the future than I had ever felt before.

Now started a period of waiting, while Harry tried to sell an unknown to the uninterested. Sometimes I sat in his office and listened as he telephoned sceptical theatrical managers or producers to explain how he had found an actor so talented that others calling themselves Thespians must appear wooden-headed and tongue-tied in comparison. But most of these days of waiting I spent in Lyons Corner House in Coventry Street making a cup of coffee last for an hour. I read and reread the thin newspapers of those austere times until at last I felt I could decently telephone Harry yet again, and ask the question actors all over the world are asking agents, even as you read these words: 'Any news?'

For a long time, there wasn't. Gradually, my lodgings and food and bus fares to Regent Street whittled away the £146, but now at least I knew I was not alone. Someone was working for me. Together we would pull through.

In the years between then and now I have frequently heard actors criticise agents. Sometimes I have done so myself. I suppose we all basically resent paying them ten per cent. Some actors even say they will have a clause in their will so that when they die ten per cent of their ashes are sprinkled over their agent. But without an agent most actors and actresses would never survive.

The agent has to sell his clients to people who, very often, have never heard of them and are not particularly interested in remedying this situation. The agent has also to cheer up his client until he lands a part. And sometimes, ironically, he may have to cut him down to size because he is becoming unreasonable or bigheaded. He helps with advice of all kinds, from tax questions to matrimonial problems, and is a father confessor, when nobody else wants to listen. And remember, the agent makes nothing for himself until he has found work for his client. As the agent likes to tell it, the client then takes ninety per cent of what he has earned for him!

Soon, Harry's telephone calls produced results. He told me that a little theatre, The Gateway, in Westbourne Grove in West London, was holding an audition for a play, *Crimson Harvest*. This dealt with various happenings down on the farm unrelated to tilling the soil, and contained a part which conceivably could

111

be mine. I caught the next bus down the Bayswater Road to the theatre. It was empty and gloomy, and had that stale, shut-in, mortuary-waiting-room kind of atmosphere of all theatres out of performance hours. I had forgotten this peculiar smell and atmosphere, just as I realised I had also forgotten the tingle in my blood as the adrenalin began to pour through my veins at the prospect of a new challenge.

In this mood of almost aggressive optimism, I did my audition, and was told that the part was mine. There was no telephone I could use in the theatre, so I took another bus straight back to Harry's office to ask him what my salary would be.

'Five pounds a week,' he said.

I could hardly believe it.

My sister Kate's marriage, like mine, had also ended. Her husband had left her and sailed for South Africa to begin a new life on his own. Now Kate told me that she intended living and working in London, and since this would also be my base she offered to set up home for me. I agreed, on the understanding that she could find us somewhere to live. After weeks of searching, she discovered a small flat in Westbourne Grove above a photographer's shop only a few minutes' walk from the theatre.

Theatre critics on national newspapers did not usually make the journey out West to cover Gateway performance, but Harry Dubens persuaded representatives from almost every London management to come to see me. One who came to see the play was Michael Barry, later to be head of BBC Television Drama. At that time he was just out of the Royal Marines and trying to pick up the shreds of his prewar career as a television producer.

Television had stopped for the war years and was now about to start again. Michael told Harry he planned to produce four plays on closed circuit for test purposes before TV transmissions reopened. He offered me eight pounds for my first week's work on these, and if I was successful I would get twelve pounds for the next week. I was, of course, delighted to be out of the five pound league but surprised by the casual way in which TV worked. How different from the efficiency we are used to now!

BBC Television operated then from Alexandra Palace in North London. The aerial mast was built on a hill which gave it a range throughout London and the home counties. The BBC ran a green single decker bus which shuttled between Broadcasting House in Langham Place and 'Ally Pally'. The studios we used were very small. By the time scenery and lights and cameras and microphones were crammed in, there was scarcely space for

Above: as Freddie Page, with Peter Illing (centre) and Raymond Francis, in the BBC television production of Terence Rattigan's *The Deep Blue Sea* (1954).

Below: his much acclaimed film portrayal of Douglas Bader in *Reach for the Sky* (1955).

Left: *A Night to Remember*: just so: a much-needed reviver to keep the cold out while on location in icy water in Ruislip Lido, during the making of the film about the sinking of the *Titanic*.

Below: reading the riot act: the stern parent in *Raising a Riot* (1956).

actors and actresses to move or even breathe.

My dressing room had an ancient bath which I never used. This was just as well because a music hall act which involved the use of trained sea lions had kept them in the bath. There was a distinctly fishy odour about it.

I appeared in the first play to be televised after the war. This was *Silence of the Sea*, and it was broadcast on June 7, 1946. I played the part of a German officer. Not a lot of people saw me, however. The BBC then could only claim 1,343 TV licence-holders. Nowadays, the audience for a play can be ten million. If you break this down into the seating capacity of an average theatre – say of 500 – that would mean 20,000 performances. Assume five evening performances and two matinées a week, this means that the show would have to run to full houses for fifty-four years before as many people could see it as now see it on one performance. That is one measure of the difference TV has made to my profession.

Things went wrong during transmissions then that nowadays only happen in amateur dramatics. Most plays went out 'live' and were not prerecorded as they are today. In *Mourning Becomes Electra* I had physically to interrupt a love scene between Andrew Osborn and Marjorie Mars. Andrew was wearing a stage moustache in two pieces – and in their clinch one half had come adrift and was now stuck firmly on Marjorie's upper lip. The two lovers were sharing one moustache between them – and neither had any idea of this until they saw the horror on my face. Both were superb pros. Marjorie simply brushed away her part of the moustache as though this was the most natural action in the world. Andrew Osborn played the rest of the scene with one hand up to his face, covering the bare top side of his lip.

One Sunday evening, Harry took me to the Comedy Theatre for a special performance of a new play *And No Birds Sing*. Sunday performances of this kind, often without scenery, were not aimed at a general audience, but to try out a new play before an audience of potential managements and producers, and to show the abilities of unknown actors and actresses. This play concerned a woman doctor who worked in a slum. Two men were in love with her. I instantly wanted to play one of these men, a clergyman, the Reverend 'Basher' Platt, who was bluff and outspoken and in many ways not unlike me.

'I'd give my right arm to play that,' I told Harry afterwards.

'Don't offer too much,' he replied drily. 'You might have a deal.'

And, in fact, I had.

Harry and Bill O'Bryen – who as an agent years before had interviewed me when I left the Windmill – decided to buy the rights together and put on the play in the West End. Elizabeth Allan, Bill's wife, would play the doctor, Harold Warrender would be the man she eventually married, while I was the well-meaning 'Basher', who lost out.

I was tremendously pleased, for this was my first big chance in the West End. But I was more naive then than I am now, for I was genuinely surprised to run into strong opposition. John Fernald, later director of the Royal Academy of Dramatic Art, had written the play with his wife, Jenny Laird, and he did not want me in his production. He put it more bluntly than that.

'It could be a disaster if you put Kenny More into it,' he told Harry. 'I simply won't have it.'

John was perfectly entitled to this view, but Harry was also entitled to his. And since he was putting up half the money, he was determined that his view would prevail and that I would play the part. Finally, matters came to a head.

'Unless Kenny gets this part, I am not backing the play,' Harry told him. I got the part.

This was the first time I experienced the inner toughness that is essential for success in show business – as, indeed, it is in any other business, too. It was not the last; this toughness is one of the essentials in every actor's survival kit.

Elizabeth Allan and her husband were very friendly and did their utmost to help me, knowing how nervous I felt at the prospect of appearing in the West End. And John and Jenny were now behind me all the way. When I first walked on the stage at The Gateway Theatre I believed I was giving more mature performances than I had done before the war because I was older and had learned more about life and people. I felt that this new play could be my great chance, but now the moment was here, I wondered: Was I really up to it? I had nightmares every night. I would wake up feverish, sweating with fright, wondering at my extraordinary egotism in thinking that, without any qualifications and with really very little experience of acting, I was attempting to succeed on the London stage.

The veteran actress, Helen Haye, who was then in her seventies, gave me the best advice of all.

'Relax,' she told me. 'You are being too brittle. Let yourself go and don't worry. And one day you *will* be at the top. Just wait and see.'

We went on tour before we came to London. In Edinburgh, when I appeared on stage wearing the dog collar of a clergyman, two men in the audience started to roar with laughter. This laughter was repeated whenever I opened my mouth. I couldn't understand it; my part was not meant to be humorous. Afterwards, in my dressing room, there was a knock on the door, and the two men came to see me. Both were old shipmates from *Aurora* days. They apologised for their behaviour.

'The fact of the matter is, Kenny, knowing what we all used to get up to in the Navy, seeing you in a dog collar was just *too* much.'

Between performances on tour, most of us killed time in strange towns by playing golf. Helen Haye, despite her age, would manage a sprightly eighteen holes every morning, and proved to be a formidable opponent.

I had never played golf before and was too hard up to buy any clubs of my own. I usually managed to borrow them, but when this was impossible, I would go round the course with only one club. I became attracted to the game, and a few years later I had cause to thank Helen and all those other people in the cast who had encouraged me to play, for golf helped me to make the real break-through in my career. Let me describe how it happened.

One day in 1951 I was playing golf at Wimbledon Park with Roland Culver. He was an old friend of Terence Rattigan's and told me he was going to be in Rattigan's latest play, *The Deep Blue Sea*. This told the story of a judge's wife who had an affair with a young RAF pilot. Roland was playing the judge.

'You mightn't be bad for the pilot, Kenny,' he said as he played off. He explained that Jimmy Hanley, who had been acting since he won a stick of rock at the age of five in a concert on Clacton Pier, was first choice for the role, but Roly promised to mention me to Terence Rattigan as a possible contender.

A few days later Harry Dubens rang me in a state of some excitement. He had heard that Rattigan had seen me act, and, with Hugh 'Binkie' Beaumont, who ran H. M. Tennent, then London's most successful management company, which was going to stage the play, he was considering me for the part. The producer, Frith Banbury, however, was inclined towards Jimmy. Auditions were therefore arranged at The Globe, rather in the manner of a duel; might the best man win.

Apart from what Roly Culver had already told me, I knew nothing about the play, until Frith Banbury handed me a script.

'Here you are,' he said. 'You are playing a very sexy young man. The older woman is mad about him, not because of his looks or background, but just because he *is* sexy. Now go ahead and read.'

I thought, charming. I looked out into the blackness of the auditorium. Somewhere out there sat Terence, Binkie, Roland, and Peggy Ashcroft, who was to play the wife. I felt nervous and began to read in a heavy, over-dramatic way. Almost immediately I was interrupted by Binkie Beaumont.

'Can't you make it *gayer*?' he asked me. This was before the word had any sexual connotation; then, it simply meant lighthearted.

Hell, I thought, how can anyone feel cheerful in a situation like this? I knew nothing about the character I was meant to play. I read on more and more nervously. I knew I was making a hash of it. At the end, Frith Banbury nodded dismissal.

'Thank you, Mr. More,' he said formally. 'We'll write.'

That's it, I thought. The classic theatrical brush-off. I felt that I had ruined my biggest chance so far, and there was nothing I could do to remedy the situation. But Roly kept me posted on the situation and said that Rattigan was for me, and so, surprisingly, was Binkie Beaumont. It was therefore both of them against Frith Banbury, who still favoured Jimmy Hanley.

For a whole fortnight my future was in the balance. Neither side could sway the other, so a second audition was arranged at Rattigan's chambers in Albany. This time I got hold of a copy of the script in advance and read the whole thing through carefully. I was determined to land this part. It was the best I had ever been offered. I felt I *was* the character. There was no need to act. I just had to live it. Even so, I was very nervous.

Rattigan was sympathetic; he knew how I felt. Years before, when he was down from Oxford and employed in a very humble capacity by a British film studio, he had written a play in his spare time and showed this to the head of production at the studio. This gentleman called Rattigan into his office, and then, in front of him, tore up the manuscript systematically page by page, to show him what he thought of it.

Luckily, Rattigan had kept a second copy. The play was *French Without Tears* which became one of the London theatre's greatest prewar successes and Roland Culver, later Rattigan's friend and mine, played in it. Ironically this particular studio then bid a fortune for the film rights.

Now at a second reading, with the whole cast, in his flat, Terry guided me over to the bar and offered me a large whisky. I accepted it gratefully.

'Another?' he asked. I accepted this with equal gratitude. By the time I was due to read, all nervousness had gone. I was totally confident. As I finished, I turned round to Rattigan triumphantly.

116

'Howzat?' I asked him, like a wicket-keeper in a cricket match appealing to the umpire. I knew I was home. The part was mine, Frith now backed me to the hilt, and all through playing golf with Roland Culver!

7

B UT IN 1946, when I was appearing in *And No Birds Sing* at the Aldwych, all this lay five years ahead and beyond the wilder realms of imagination. Harry Dubens was still trying to shoe-horn me into films and managed to get me, through Irene Howard, the casting director, ten pounds for one day's work in *School for Secrets*. This was a wartime story about radar, and was Peter Ustinov's first film as director.

'This can be a great thing for you, Kenny,' Harry assured me. 'If you make a go of it, we are almost there.'

So off I went before dawn to Denham Studios. I could ill afford any extravagance, but I hired a chauffeur-driven car, for the same reason that I always have travelled first-class on railways, even when such indulgences have left me with only a few shillings in my pocket. There is a good maxim for any young man making his way in life. If you are not rich, act as though you are. Remember, the richer you are, the poorer you can seem. But in my profession, the poorer you are, the more prosperous you must always appear.

So I arrived in my hired car and went through the various departments of reception, wardrobe, make-up. I was secretly very impressed to think that I was going to work in the famous studios that had made such classics as *Things to Come, A Yank at Oxford, Fire Over England,* and *Henry V.*

Here, I told myself, the part I was about to play would be a turning point in my career. Thus agreeably euphoric, I was taken to Stage One which was as chill and impersonal as a vast warehouse. In the centre stood the cut-off front section of a Lancaster bomber, looking like the head of some giant prehistoric fish. I put on my leather flying jacket and trousers, and wobbled aboard the plane and prepared to lie down in the bomb-aimer's position.

'Don't forget these,' Peter Ustinov called up to me. He handed me a pair of service goggles with big rubber edges that completely covered my eyes and most of my face and forehead. Next, I put on an oxygen mask which totally concealed all my features. I lay down on my belly, depressed at my complete anonymity. I felt like the man in the iron mask. Lights flickered and flashed behind the Lancaster, against a black velvet backcloth, to simulate anti-aircraft fire. My lines were simple and few.

'Left a bit . . . Steady, skipper. Right a bit . . . Steady. Hold it . . . Bombs gone. Right skipper, let's go home.'

Time after time I said these words, knowing that for all the good this part would do me, I might as well have stayed at home in bed. I did not tell Harry Dubens of my mortification. He was so convinced this would be my big break that he took his wife and a party of friends to see the première at the Odeon, Leicester Square. Afterwards, he came up to me. I could see he was worried and disappointed.

'A marvellous performance, Kenny,' he said gamely. 'I always knew you could do it.'

Then he lowered his voice conspiratorially, so that no one else could hear.

'But *which one was you?*'

The early months of 1947 were the coldest for years. Snow and ice and fog continued late into March. People were depressed by this vile weather, by food and petrol and clothes rationing, by power cuts and coal shortages, by the feeling that if this was victory, could defeat have been much worse? They were disinclined to go out to the theatre, and so *And No Birds Sing* closed after only three months.

We went off for a second tour, but I was becoming depressed. I had hoped that some other producer would offer me work after my months in the West End, but no one had done so. As I made myself up in one dreary provincial dressing room after another, evening after evening, I began to have doubts about myself and my ability. I was now nearly thirty-three. Perhaps I was simply not as good as I thought I was. Maybe I should not spend (waste?) any more time trying to be an actor, but should attempt some other career? But what else could I do? Answers chased questions in my worried mind.

Harry Dubens meanwhile was still gallantly trying to find work for me. He heard that a freelance producer, Chloe Gibson, was about to cast a new play, and asked her to give me a part in it.

'But I've never seen this Kenny More of yours act,' she protested. 'I missed his play when it was at the Aldwych.'

'No matter,' replied Harry immediately. 'By a lucky chance it's on at Stoke Newington. You can see it there.'

She had no wish to venture so far in bitter weather, possibly to

119

see so little. Harry was allowed a few gallons of petrol a month for business purposes for his car and he persuaded one of his sons, Stanley, now a film producer, to drive Chloe out through the fog.

After the show she came back-stage to see me, and explained she was putting on this play, *Power Without Glory* by a new writer, Michael Clayton Hutton, and could offer me one of the main parts. She was staging it initially at the New Lindsey Theatre, in the hope that some management would bring it into the West End.

'You will be with another unknown,' she said. 'He's just out of the army. A man named Dirk Bogarde.'

'How much?' I asked her.

'Ten pounds a week for a run of three weeks.'

I was never very good at maths, but even I could work out the dismal economics of this proposal. With three weeks unpaid rehearsal, and a three week run, this worked out at five pounds a week. I was back again at this magic figure! However, nothing else was being offered, and this was better than nothing. So I took it.

Half way through rehearsals, Chloe told us that Peter Daubeny, who had recently been demobilised from the Guards, and was beginning to make a name as an impresario, wanted to see a rehearsal. He would then decide whether he would take an option on the play with a view to transferring it to the West End.

This we all felt could be our big chance. How many big chances does an actor feel *must* be his? Probably, if he is honest, and if he is a good actor, every performance represents not only a challenge but also a big chance for a further challenge. One never knows just who is out there in the darkness beyond the footlights; watching, making notes, either to go away without a word – or to arrive back-stage to discuss a future proposition.

On the morning of this particular big chance, there was a power cut. Not a light in the theatre would work. We moved about the stage with torches and candles in jam jars. Chloe did not dare tell Peter Daubeny of the cut in case he cancelled his visit. She therefore went out to a local garage and borrowed four acetylene lamps from them. These were huge roaring contraptions, used at night to light up the scene of a road accident. With two of these hissing in the stalls, and one on each side of the stage, we did a complete run through.

Daubeny liked what he saw and took the option. We opened at the Fortune Theatre to ecstatic notices in February, 1947. Dirk Bogarde received the most tremendous praise from the critics for his part and was immediately offered a long-term film contract by the Rank Organisation. I also received good notices, but was offered nothing more substantial than praise.

In April, at the Fortune, luck – that independent and elusive spirit which uplifts or casts down all human enterprises – played its part in our affairs. After months of cold, April was unexpectedly warm. But people recovering from the miserable weather did not flock into London theatres; they wanted to enjoy the sunshine. As a result, we never played to more than £375 takings in any week. Although we were highly praised, we were still unknown. The play lacked the draw of big names. But unknown to me, our performances had attracted the attention of the biggest name in the theatre – Noël Coward.

One evening I was making myself up when the call boy came into my dressing room.

'Mr. Coward on the telephone for you,' he announced brusquely.

'Mr. Who?'

'Said his name was Coward.'

'Coward? You don't mean Noël Coward?'

'Yes. That's him.'

I followed him out to the stage-door keeper's telephone and picked it up.

'Kenneth More here.'

The Master spoke in his clipped, precise way.

'Is that you Kenny, dear boy?'

Good heavens, I thought. It *is* Noël Coward. And speaking to *me*.

'Yes, sir. Here, sir.'

'Good. Well, I would like you to come and see me in my dressing room after the show tonight. I think I've got something that will interest you.'

Somehow, I survived that evening's performance, then I hurriedly wiped off my make-up, caught a taxi to the Haymarket where he was starring in his own play, *Present Laughter*, with Moira Lister, and timidly knocked on the door of the star dressing room.

Noël Coward was standing in front of his mirror, wearing the blue and white silk polka dot dressing gown he wore so often that it almost became like a trademark.

'Come in, dear boy. Come in and sit down.'

We shook hands. I sat carefully on the edge of the nearest chair. Noël smoothed back his hair and turned sideways, still looking at himself in the mirror.

'Aren't I beautiful?' he asked. 'Absolutely beautiful?'

I was too nervous to know whether he was serious or just pulling my leg, so I replied very earnestly: 'Yes, sir. Of course, you are *very* beautiful.'

A plate of thinly cut smoked salmon sandwiches and a Thermos of tea stood on a table. As we ate and drank, Noël explained that he had written a new play, *Peace in our Time*, which dealt with what might have happened had the Germans won the war and occupied Britain. He had seen me in *Power Without Glory*, and now he offered me the part of the leader of the British Resistance Movement.

I was astonished and delighted. And to think that only days before I had felt sorry for myself because I believed no one had noticed my performance! Such are the switchbacks of fortune in the theatre.

Coward gave me a copy of the script, and invited me to his flat in Chelsea for dinner in a few days time. I accepted with alacrity. We were alone and as before he was wearing his polka dot dressing gown. We had a delightful meal. There were two grand pianos in the room, and, after dinner, Noël sat down at one of them and played, 'I'll see you again', and some of the other lovely melodies he had composed. The atmosphere was very intimate. Subdued lights, a fire burning low, and the tinkling piano in the background.

I sat by the fire feeling rather apprehensive as to how the evening might end. Noël Coward finished playing, and stood up and walked slowly towards me. I lost my nerve and jumped up as he approached.

'Oh, Mr. Coward, sir!' I cried, fearful of what might be about to happen. 'I could *never* have an affair with you, because – because – *you remind me of my father*!'

Noël paused. He looked as enigmatic as a Chinese mandarin. Had I offended him beyond all apology? Then he smiled. 'Hello, son,' he said in his clipped way and roared with laughter!

The air was instantly cleared between us, for I think he appreciated my honesty. Thereafter, until his death, we remained the best of friends. And although he would frequently call me 'son' in front of friends no one ever knew the reason why. In every way he was a most wonderful man.

This was a very fortunate meeting for me, because shortly afterwards *Power Without Glory* closed. The backers lost a lot of money. Although the play was an artistic success it was a commercial failure.

I was sorry for Chloe and for everyone else involved, but most of all I felt sorry for the play's young author, Michael Clayton Hutton. His father had worked for a secret Air Ministry department during the war devising what he called 'escape gadgets' to help Allied aircrews shot down over enemy territory. These included such ingenious items as a compass hidden inside a tunic button on every pilot's uniform. When the crest on this button was unscrewed it revealed a compass so that survivors could establish their position. When the Germans discovered this, 'Clutty' Hutton simply fitted each button with a left-hand thread. The more they tried to undo it, the more they tightened it up. There were other things; pills hidden in pencils, surgeon's trepanning saw blades to cut through steel bars concealed inside boot laces, a fountain pen that fired a deadly dart, and so on. Somehow, Michael felt he could never really live up to his father's wishes for him, and the failure of the play hurt him deeply. A writer is very like an actor; he must expose his dreams and abilities to the public gaze. If the public rejects him, and he is very sensitive, he can take this as a personal rejection, and feel he is a failure. And in the creative arts, from feeling a failure to actually being one can be a very short step indeed.

One day, a senior BBC television executive took Michael out to lunch and commissioned him to write a play for TV. But Michael simply could not believe that this offer was genuine. The BBC executive assured him it was, and promised he would confirm it by letter to arrive the following morning.

Michael told his father what had happened, but expressed his own doubts that he could produce a satisfactory script. Early the following morning his father went round to see him to try and cheer him up, but he arrived too late. During that night of doubt and loneliness, Michael Clayton Hutton had taken his own life. And on the floor, behind the front door of his flat was the letter from the BBC confirming the offer that could have totally changed his luck – and his life.

Rehearsals for *Peace in Our Time* started almost immediately. We had a cast of nearly forty, and Noël, as director, showed himself to be a really terrifying figure. He instilled fear into every member of the cast. If he felt anyone had given a bad reading during rehearsals – and later if he thought they had given a poor performance – he would line us up on the stage in a semi-circle, and address us like naughty children. We would stand in silence, as he stretched out his hand and pointed to one end of the line. Then he would slowly swing his arm until he pointed directly at the offending person.

'How dare you!' he would cry. 'What you've done is

123

unpardonable! Unforgivable! You are a disgrace to the theatre.'

And then he would launch into a fully detailed criticism of that person's faults. The wretched man or woman would stand there, shuffling from foot to foot, while the rest of us stood in silence, thankful not to be in his or her shoes. Fortunately, what we called The Finger never pointed at me.

The play opened at the Lyric in July, 1948. It was not as successful as we had hoped. I still think it is one of The Master's best plays, a view he shared, but looking back, it is easy to see that the timing was wrong. Memories of the war were still too vivid. It had not yet sunk into the mist of agreeable rosy-edged nostalgia which now makes the war years a safe and generally successful setting for drama or comedy. However, I will always have a special memory of this play because it marked so many points of departure for me.

First, I was appearing in the West End as of right, not having been brought in with a play that started elsewhere. Secondly, the play was put on by H. M. Tennent, whom I have already mentioned, and to work for Tennent's was an accolade of a very special kind. They were never associated with anything cheap or shoddy. The best was barely good enough for Binkie Beaumont – in actors and actresses, costumes, settings and the plays themselves.

Next, I became friendly with Elspeth March, who was in the cast, and this helped me enormously in breaking into films. Elspeth was married then to Stewart Grainger, at that time the most successful film actor in Britain. One evening, when Elspeth and I were having supper after the show before going home, she asked me why I didn't go into films.

'I've tried,' I told her. 'Harry Dubens keeps telling producers he's got the most talented film actor in the business, but when they see me they say I'm not good-looking enough. One producer said I had a spot on my cheek. Another thought I was too short.'

'That's rubbish,' said Elspeth. 'I'll speak to Jimmy about it. He'll squeeze you in somehow.'

Jimmy Grainger had been in the army during the war and was very willing to help other ex-service actors. He knew that John Mills was preparing to make a film about Captain Scott of the Antarctic, and suggested that he might give me a part in it.

'There's a bloke called Kenny More in Noël's play with my wife,' he explained. 'I want you to put him in your picture.'

'That's difficult,' Mills replied. 'It's pretty well cast.'

'Never mind that,' Grainger persisted, brushing aside such a feeble excuse. 'You bloody well put him in that picture, Johnny. Give him a break.'

'Well . . .'

Jimmy kept on in this way until finally Johnny Mills passed my name to the casting people at Ealing Studios where *Scott* was to be made. In due course I was asked to report on the set at nine o'clock one morning for a screen test. This meant that, having gone to bed about one o'clock that same morning after coming home from the theatre, I set my alarm for five in order to wake up, cook and eat my breakfast at the kitchen table, then travel out to Ealing, to be dressed and made-up.

The film's director was to be Charles Frend. He was away that day and Henry Cornelius, who was later to play a very big part in my life, was doing the test to help him out.

The man who came in to line up the scene to see that everything was ready and everyone was in position was Alfred Shaughnessy. He was an old Etonian whose step-father was then Comptroller of Windsor Castle, and who had been through the mill in every kind of job on the production side. Freddie stood out from some others in the film business because he was extremely courteous and as polite to unknowns and extras as to established actors. To use an old phrase of Van Damm's about my father, he was 'a white man,' straight and honest and as well liked as he was likeable. Now, of course, he is known throughout the world as the producer and deviser of that enormously successful TV series *Upstairs, Downstairs*. But then, like me, he was still climbing the ladder,

For my test someone had to ask me two questions: 'Is there any mail? Any messages?'

I then replied: 'No, sir. But a request has come through about the dogs and ponies.'

I did this three times and then was told I could go home. To my amazement, there had been so much waiting about, so many postponements for one reason or another – lights wrong, micro-phone not working – that this had occupied nearly all day. I had to race back to London to be in time for my evening's performance at the Lyric. Within a week, a jubilant Harry Dubens was on the telephone to me. My test had been successful, and he had negotiated a contract for me to play Lieutenant Teddy Evans, RN, later Evans of the *Broke*, one of Captain Scott's team.

My pay would be twenty pounds a day, with a guaranteed minimum of £500. A double would be used tor location shots in Norway because of my play. But when the play ended I spent months in a horrible plastic studio imitation of the South Pole constructed in Ealing, W.5. We had to suck pellets, which tasted vile, so that when we spoke vapour would come out of our mouths like breath, so it would seem we really were in a freezing temperature.

What appeared to be hard ice all around us was actually hard, jagged plaster. Lumps and ridges on this cut our hands and knees when we stumbled and fell on them. The 'snow' was a foamed urea-formaldehyde compound. This was brought into the studio in slabs the size of paving stones. They weighed almost nothing, and were chewed up by machines and blown by a fan with blades twenty-two feet across to give the appearance of a blizzard. These flakes also gave us actors a hard time. They were intensively abrasive, and cut into our eyes and beards, and got up our noses, making us sneeze.

Since we were supposed to be in virgin snow, all footprints had to be obliterated between each take. This meant that we would sit sweating, as in a Turkish bath, wearing our furs and windbreakers, while tractors dragged rakes across the floor to flatten the 'snow'. These tractors kept breaking down, and we sat cursing and sweating, our tempers growing shorter with every new delay.

Usually each day's filming is processed overnight, and next morning the director can see what are called the rushes. Here, for technical reasons, the film had to go to Hollywood, and so at least a week would elapse before we knew whether a particular shot had been right, or whether we would have to do it again.

Finally, the film was finished, and now began one of the hardest times of my life; a time of waiting, without work.

My sister had taken a job outside London, and I had moved from Westbourne Grove to a furnished flat in Eaton Terrace Mews, for which I paid five-and-a-half-guineas a week. This was a good address, and if I could stay the course, I felt that when the film was shown I would be deluged with offers. While waiting for this happy day, Harry Dubens felt, quite rightly, that I would be very unwise to accept anything for less money than I had been paid before. Show business is like a one way street. You can go along it to the end. You can also stop, and branch out into some other career. But if you try to go back, you are finished. Word immediately spreads that you are slipping, you've had it, you are desperate for money, you are done. So I had to sit in my Mews and sweat it out.

At that time, six months would usually elapse before the end of shooting until the film was shown to the public. But *Scott* was chosen for the Royal Command Performance and this meant a wait of a further three months, making nine months in all before my work at Ealing could be appraised.

During this time, I was offered a number of small parts, but Harry and I turned them down. I rationed out the money I had saved. When I had spent what I put aside for one week I stayed inside the flat and lived as quietly as I could. I was terrified of sinking into debt, for I remembered how my father had frittered away a fortune. I felt I could not ask my mother for any more money. I was on my own.

Finally, one Friday, with a month still to wait until the première, I was down to the money I had put aside for next month's rent. I telephoned my landlord, and boldly said that I would like to start paying my rent in arrears instead of in advance. Since I had always paid regularly, he agreed, but without much enthusiasm. Next, I paid off some pressing debts and was left with only a few pounds – and four weeks to go. I asked Harry whether he could help with any work – at any price. I realised that this was going against my best long term interests, but I had to eat. Harry had nothing to offer and I came back to my flat very depressed indeed. Behind the front door was a letter which had arrived by the afternoon delivery while I had been out. It was from the Admiralty. The letter explained that they were writing to some wartime naval officers, to offer them permanent commissions if they would care to return to the navy for several years. I read this through a number of times, remembering good days I had enjoyed in the Navy. I compared that free-and-easy existence with my life now; waiting, hoping, eking out my savings. And I wondered once more whether I was being wise in attempting to continue my career as an actor.

I had seen so many others go down, and because, like me, they were qualified for nothing else, they had thankfully accepted any job they were offered. I remembered especially Gerald Cuff in Wolverhampton. Now I could return to the Navy with the rank of lieutenant-commander. I could return to routine and order and security, with a pension at the end of it all. I did not want to accept this alternative – but it certainly had attractions. Was I being stupid in not admitting this?

I lit a cigarette while I considered the matter, and then, on the impulse, I went down on my knees and prayed.

I was holding the cigarette in one hand and the Admiralty's letter in the other, and I prayed aloud: 'Dear God, please help me. Please give me a clear sign so I can know whether I should go on or go back.' I got up from my knees and looked at my watch.

Five o'clock. On a Friday night. Black Friday. Producers' offices would all be shut now, and none of them worked on Saturdays; even the industrious Harry Dubens was not in his office on Saturday mornings.

If I wanted a sign, I would have to hold out until Monday. I could not reasonably expect anything before then. I picked up the telephone and dialled the operator, just to make sure the instrument was still working and connected. It was. I then considered my assets for a siege weekend. I had one full packet of cigarettes, and the remains of a joint of meat in the larder, and some tea and sugar. I would survive.

The telephone did not ring all evening. I went to bed miserable and depressed, and slept badly. In fact, I overslept, and was woken up by the telephone ringing furiously in my ear. I picked it up.

'Hullo? Is that Kenneth More?' asked the caller.

'Yes. Who's that?'

It was Bob Lennard, the casting director of Associated British, the man who selected people for parts in every film his studios produced. But what did he want with me at a quarter past nine on a Saturday morning?

I had never heard of a casting director working on a Saturday, so why was he ringing me so early on this day of all days?

'What are you doing on Monday morning?' he asked.

I couldn't tell him the truth. I couldn't admit that I had nothing remunerative to do in all the world on Monday morning, or indeed any other morning – or afternoon. Being an actor, I played it along.

'Let me look at my book,' I said. I allowed twenty seconds to go by and rustled the pages of the telephone directory. And then I said, 'Here we are, Mr. Lennard. Let's see. No. Nothing firm on Monday morning. What can I do for you?'

'Well, it's like this. An actor has let me down. Badly.'

'Oh, yes?' I said, beginning to perk up a bit.

'So I am ringing to ask if you can possibly help me out and be at Welwyn Garden City on location at seven-thirty on Monday morning?'

'Just let me look at my little book again. See it doesn't clash with anything later.'

I could not admit I was broke.

'Yes, seven-thirty. I think I can manage that all right. What's the deal?'

'It is only one day's work, Ken, but it's worth twenty-five quid.'

I repeated the sum. Twenty-five pounds. A lot of money. A month's rent. And more than I had been paid each day on *Scott*. I

Above: with I. S. Johar, who played Gupta the engine-driver, in *North West Frontier* (1958).

Below: Kenneth More and Lauren Bacall, his co-star in *North West Frontier*, remove their shoes before entering the Taj Mahal.

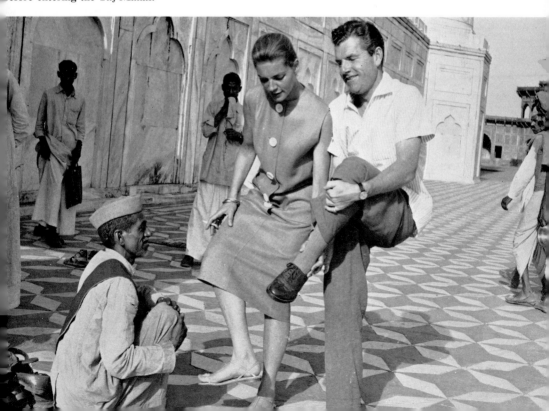

Left: a moment of anguish as Captain Shepherd learns that his son is missing in *Sink the Bismarck*.

Right: tension for a couple on the run: Kenneth More and Taina Elg evade capture in *The Thirty-Nine Steps*.

wasn't lowering my price, I was raising it. Harry would approve. This was the sign I had asked for; this was the green light, the go-ahead.

'What do I have to do, Bob?'

'Nothing, really. You are supposed to say a couple of lines, but I don't think they'll get them in. You're a prison warder in a film, *For Them That Trespass*.'

'Who's the star?' I asked.

'Dickie Todd. Richard Todd. Now, you won't let me down – you're sure you can fill in for this fellow?'

'Yes,' I told him. 'I think I can do that.'

I replaced the telephone and my heart was beating like a drum. My prayer had been answered.

At seven-thirty on Monday morning I was out in Welwyn Garden City. I then discovered that the actor whose place I was taking was six foot three inches tall and built to match. His boots were size tens, and I take eights. His cap fell over my eyes. The uniform sleeves extended two or three inches over each hand and I had to fold up the trouser legs. I didn't look like a prison warder; I looked like a scarecrow.

Cavalcanti, a naturalised Italian who had made his name in documentary films, was directing. As a former documentary man, he was a stickler for accuracy. My appearance appalled him.

'Who is this man?' he asked in amazement.

Bob Lennard explained that I was standing in for someone else at short notice.

'It doesn't matter,' Cavalcanti replied firmly. 'Get him out of my sight. Away. Out of my sight.'

Bob said, 'He has two lines to speak.'

'Not any more, he hasn't. Get him out of my sight. Put him up on the top shelf.'

We were filming in a prison set, where the corridors ran like shelves around a central open space. So I was put away miles out of sight. I didn't care a damn where I was put. I was guaranteed twenty-five pounds, my month's rent for this one day's work. I couldn't care less what I had to do. I would have stood on my head for the money if they asked me. So I stood at the back of the set where no one could see me. The morning drifted on. We broke for lunch.

I climbed down dozens of metal steps from the top of a winding staircase to the canteen, and climbed up again to my position. I did not care whether I was on camera or off. I was being paid; that was sufficient. I could not believe my luck.

During the afternoon, when I had been standing for hours, and was almost soporific, asleep on my feet, I heard a voice shout from what seemed miles away.

'Hey, you!'

A few other extras nearer to whatever action there was looked at me enquiringly. I looked at them. Whoever was shouting must have been calling to someone else. No one could want me; hardly anyone even knew I was there. Still, I peered over the edge just to make sure, and saw Cavalcanti gesticulating towards me.

'Hey, you!' Cavalcanti shouted. 'Big Boots!'

He *must* mean me, I thought.

'Yes, sir?'

'Come down here, Big Boots.'

Several people started to snigger. I drew myself up to my full height. Mr. Cavalcanti had been engaged I knew not how during the war, but I had served as a naval officer for years at sea. I was not prepared to be addressed in these terms by him or by anyone else.

'Mr. Cavalcanti,' I called back coldly. 'You can call me Mr. More, or, 'that actor,' or just 'Hey, You.' But, please do *not* expect me to answer to Big Boots.'

My voice seemed to echo around the set as though I was shouting into a cavern.

'What? What?' Cavalcanti asked, puzzled. Probably his English wasn't too good, but I reckoned it was good enough for him to understand my reply. Someone whispered to him. He nodded.

'Ah, Mr. More,' he said in more conciliatory tones. 'Will you come down here, yes?'

Down the stairs I went, shuffling in my giant boots.

'I want you in the background, here,' he explained. 'I want you to say, "Give this man the keys." '

Cavalcanti turned to a henchman.

'Get him another cap. He can't appear like this. Give him some clothes that fit.'

So they redressed me, and I had a part, even though I had insulted the director. Or was it because I had? What the hell, I thought. I am an independent sort of guy. I don't care if he likes it or if he doesn't. I'm still being paid. At the end of the day, Cavalcanti came over to me.

'Hey, hey,' he said cheerfully.

'Not Big Boots,' I said warningly.

'No, not Big Boots. Not bigga boots. You a funny guy. Funny man, yes?'

'I'm not funny, Mr. Cavalcanti,' I told him. 'I just don't like to be called Big Boots.'

'No. Well, they *are* big – bloody big.'

'Yes, I know. But I don't like being addressed in that manner.'

'Maybe you are right, *Mr.* More,' he agreed. 'Tell me, what are you doing tomorrow?'

'Bugger all,' I said. No need to prevaricate now. 'I've got my month's rent and I'll be grateful to you for the rest of my life.'

'You don't have to be. Anyway, you are working tomorrow. You be here on time – Big Boots!'

So I was paid fifty pounds for two days work in which I really did nothing. And, I firmly believe, simply because I knelt on my knees with a letter in one hand and a dog-end in the other on a Friday afternoon. Now I knew where my future lay; not in the Navy, but as an actor. I had been given a sign; now I would follow where it would lead me. And people ask me, do I believe in prayer?

8

N OW I PREPARED for what I was sure would be a momentous evening in my life, the première of *Scott of the Antarctic* as the Royal Command Film Performance.

Harry Dubens was there in his dinner jacket with a huge tie, walking tall as Nelson's column. He was so proud of me, bless his heart, and – like me – felt convinced that after tonight his early and constant faith in me would be vindicated.

I took my seat in the vast auditorium feeling certain that this was going to be the climactic moment of my whole career. Here I was, ex-Lieutenant Kenneth More appearing as Lieutenant Teddy Evans of the Royal Navy. This was not a part anyone could play concealed by goggles and oxygen mask, speaking lines like, 'Left a bit . . . left a bit. Steady. Steady, skipper. Right a bit . . . right a bit. Steady. Hold it . . . Bombs away!' This was going to lead me forward to bigger things – quickly.

The credits came up and went, and we were into the film. I waited with pleasurable anticipation for the big scene I played with John Mills, which I was sure would make me a star. According to history, Scott told Evans that he was not taking him on his final dash to reach the pole. This decision incidentally saved Evans's life, because Scott and the others died. But, at the time, being left behind was a terrible blow to Evans, and playing him, I was brokenhearted and wept. Charlie Frend, the director, and John Mills both came up to me afterwards and congratulated me on my performance. There was no doubt of their sincerity, and I had gone home happy.

But now, as the familiar scene unfolded on the screen, horror and dismay gripped me. First of all, the camera was mostly on Johnny Mills. True, there was the odd flash of me looking rather like his twin brother, but that was all. Indeed, it was very difficult to tell who was who, except that Johnny Mills had much more to say than I did.

The whole film was really a repetition of my one day's work in *School for Secrets*, when my goggles and mask had completely covered my face.

The only difference was that now we were in windbreakers

and beards – but we all looked alike. You couldn't tell John Mills from James Robertson Justice or me from Harold Warrender. Even differences in our heights were neutralised. Warrender, for instance, was six foot three inches tall, and when he and I played a scene they had dug a pit in the snow for him to stand in so we would appear eyeball to eyeball. My part had gone for nothing. I had made no progress. I was unrecognisable; a bearded male figure in furs. For all the good this would do my career, there was no point in my being on the screen at all.

Afterwards, outside the cinema, Harry Dubens asked me in a tremulous voice: 'What happened, Kenny? What went wrong?'

'Nothing went wrong, Harry,' I replied.

'But it must have done,' he persisted. 'You told me you had a great scene.'

'I did, Harry. I did.'

Then he saw Charlie Frend coming out and dashed up to him. 'What went wrong?' he asked him.

'Nothing,' said Frend shortly. 'It was just the way it came out in the cutting, Harry. I'm sorry, but there it is.'

I felt back where I started. John Mills, by contrast, had taken a great step forward. As star of the Royal Film Performance, he also won the coveted *Daily Mail* award as Film Star of the Year.

One night, shortly after this was announced, I went to see my friend Elspeth March, who was appearing in *Playboy of the Western World*. I happened to go there on the same night as John Mills and his wife, Mary Hayley Bell, who were close friends of Elspeth's.

After the show, when we were all in her dressing room, Johnny said, 'Look, I've just had this wonderful news of the award. Let's all go to the Caprice for supper.'

He leaned over to me in the background, and added magnanimously, 'You can come along, too, Kenny.'

We had a marvellous meal, and I was touched by John's generosity, because at that time I had exactly thirty bob in my pocket – a one-pound note and a ten shilling note.

When the meal was over, someone suggested we should all go on to Al Burnett's night club off Regent Street. They were all talking so busily – they had known each other for years – that they went out, not thinking, and left me alone at the table.

The waiter put a plate down in front of me, and on the plate was a folded bill. I opened this – and realised I hadn't enough money to pay the tip, let alone the bill.

Mario, the director of the Caprice, came up.

'Anything the matter?' he asked solicitously.

'Nothing,' I replied. 'Nothing at all, except that I haven't got any money.'

Mario must have been used to such situations. Not a flicker of annoyance or surprise darkened his face.

'Don't worry, Mr. More,' he said. 'It will be taken care of.'

And, so, like the knight in the fairy story, I got up and slowly walked away.

I tell this story because it illustrates the pitfalls – even the terror – that an actor can feel if, however briefly, he moves out of his level. Generally speaking, in our business, stars can only mix satisfactorily with stars, and money can only mix with money. People will sometimes say about an actor, 'He is aloof, he is standoffish.' The fact is that he has probably learned to conduct himself in this way through an experience not unlike mine.

I was down in the lower echelons of the business then, and had only briefly moved up, through my association with Elspeth, and the fortuitous fact that she was married to Jimmy Grainger.

Nowadays, of course, minimum rates of pay are much higher, and the humblest actor can stand his round. But in those days there seemed to be an even greater gulf fixed between stars and others than there is now. From a theatrical viewpoint you felt you were letting the side down if you moved out of your financial or social bracket.

This had nothing whatever to do with family background or upbringing or education but simply recognised your own position in the galaxy system or the pecking order. Even today, I would not imagine a small part actor going out to dinner with someone like Sir Alec Guinness even though they were in the same play, unless they were personal friends.

I was thus at a rather low point in my fortunes when – as can happen in real life just as it does in TV plays – the telephone rang. Dear old Harry Dubens had some news for me.

'Kenny,' he announced portentously. 'A wonderful opportunity is coming your way.'

I knew Harry's style. He liked to begin conversation with an all-embracing announcement of this sort. He would have made an excellent politician for he was full of optimisim. More important, he genuinely extracted as much pleasure from placing a client in a part as the client did from playing it.

'I am glad to hear that, Harry. What is it?'

But Harry would never be hurried.

'Bernard Miles. You've heard of Bernard Miles?'

'Yes, Harry. I've heard of him.'

'The great hactor, Bernard Miles.'

Harry always gave an 'h' to 'actor'.

'The great *h*actor Bernard Miles wants to see you about a new film he is going to make for Filippo del Giudice. You know him?'

I didn't know Mr. Del, as he was called, but like everyone in the business, I knew of him. He had produced *Henry V*. With Sir Alexander Korda, he was about the biggest wheel of all in Denham Studios.

'It's the chance of a lifetime, Kenny,' Harry went on. 'And funny thing, that's the title of it, *Chance of a Lifetime*. And it could be yours, Kenny, boy.'

'What's the film about?'

'About a factory. I don't understand about factories, but you're the boss, and you've to see Bernard Miles in the Dorchester Hotel at nine o'clock tomorrow morning. So you'd better go there looking like a factory boss.'

'What does a factory boss look like, Harry?'

'I don't know,' replied Harry testily. 'But you know what I mean. Go along looking posh.'

'I've nothing posh to go in, Harry.'

'Why do you always make difficulties, Kenny, boy? You go along and be yourself. You're a good *h*actor, remember. Right?'

'Right.'

I didn't think much of my chances in being chosen to be a factory boss – even though I had once been a factory apprentice. I lacked any formal clothes to wear for the interview, and since it was a hot day in early summer, I walked across the Park to the hotel in shirtsleeves and grey flannel trousers. As I approached Bernard Miles's room along the corridor, I saw other actors coming away from their interviews all soberly dressed with bowler hats, carrying rolled umbrellas, and doing their utmost to look like factory bosses.

Bernard Miles (now Sir Bernard) was, I knew, an unorthodox man, down to earth, the sort of person I felt I could get on with. But I did not expect the reception I received when I walked into his room in my open-necked shirt, clean but shabby. He was sitting behind a table, and as he saw me, he banged both palms of his hands down on the table.

'*That's* the fellow I want! That's my boy. Come on now, read the part. If you can read it, it's yours.'

He handed me a script. I read the part marked for me, and that was that. Fifteen hundred pounds for a summer in the Cotswolds – and all because I dressed in a casual way! Luck – or destiny?

This was a strange film. It was backed by the Socialist

135

Government of the day and was really rather thinly disguised socialist propaganda.

The workers took over a factory because they thought the bosses had made a mess of things. They then discovered there were complications in running a factory, which they had not realised before. An order for a new kind of plough was lost, but despite opposition from some of the older employees, I insisted we made this plough in the hope we could sell it – and we did.

We had a very good cast; Basil Radford, Geoffrey Keene, Patrick Troughton, and Hattie Jacques. It was cheaper to rent an existing factory than to fabricate one in a studio, so we took over a factory in Stroud in Gloucestershire. We were billeted in various hotels, all expenses paid.

I was at the Amberley Arms, on a long winding hill above the factory. Although food was still rationed, we lived like fighting cocks. Eggs, bacon, steaks, ham; you name it, we ate it. Because we were living so well and the summer was warm and we were stuck there for more than three months, we had a fantastic time. I started affairs all over the place. I imagined I was in love with the landlady, with all the girls in the cast, and the very attractive production secretary!

Making this film enabled me to meet John Harvey, the actor I had replaced at Wolverhampton, before the war, for he was also in the cast. One night, after filming, we all went out on a drinking session in Stroud. In the early hours of the morning, someone gave me a lift back to the hotel. John Harvey, who was also billeted there, had an old car of which he was very proud. That night I thought I would play a trick on him. I knew the sound of his car well, and planned to give him a fright by lying down in the middle of the road when I heard him driving up the hill.

It was about two o'clock in the morning, and as I saw the old yellow lights approach, I knew there was no mistake. He was going to have the shock of his life when he saw a body in the roadway.

What I did not know was that John had a secret fear of being mugged or attacked, and so carried a huge, heavy spanner in the door pocket of his car in case he was stopped. His car came slowly up the hill and stopped. I thought at first he was so tight he hadn't seen me, and was going to go right over me. But luckily he stopped about six feet away. My plan was to leap up and shout, loudly, at John. But I barely had the chance, because he jumped out of his car and came at me with this spanner.

I shouted, 'For God's sake, John, it's me! Kenny!'

'You bloody idiot!' he roared in reply. 'I could have killed you.'

I was up on my feet now and we were reeling about, two drunken actors, one waving a large spanner, and shouting at each other. Not a very edifying scene.

Basil Radford was playing the managing director in the film. At that time he was drinking rather heavily, and would sometimes arrive at the factory the worse for wear. Early one morning I had a scene to play with him in which we had to exchange two lines.

He had to say to me, 'Get in touch with our London office. I have just received this telegram from them.' He was then to read the cable and hand it to me. I would then reply, 'Things don't look too good, sir. I'll do it right away.'

In the normal course of events this should be over in a few minutes, even with the delays inherent in filming, but poor old Basil couldn't get the scene right. He shook so much that the sound engineers could not cope with the rustling of the paper telegram. A props man wrote out the words on a piece of white linen which would not rustle, but still Basil could not make out the words distinctly enough to read them. Morning, afternoon, evening, we filmed this scene. Twenty-seven times we went through it and each time I got it right and Basil got it wrong. When he did get his lines right on the twenty-eighth time, I got mine wrong.

'Hell!' said Bernard. 'We'll try again tomorrow.' So next morning we did another ten takes. Poor old Basil kept saying, 'Get in touch . . . Be in touch . . . The office wants.'

Cut! Cut! Cut!

Finally, Bernard decided there was only one solution. He poured out half a tumbler of whisky, gave it to Basil, and said: 'Here, Bas. Have one on the house.'

Basil drank it down in one gulp. We then went through the scene perfectly. He was a lovely man.

When the film was finally released, it lost a fortune. Questions were asked in the House about its cost and its strong political bias. The Board of Trade's Film Selection Committee then took the unprecedented step of ordering the film to be shown on the Rank circuit. But while officials can order a film to be shown or a play to be produced, they cannot order audiences to pay money to see it. People stayed away in their thousands.

But appearing in it was a good shop window for me. I had a number of other offers as a result. One was a part in *The Franchise Affair* with Dulcie Gray, and once more with John Mills in *Morning Departure*, a film about a submarine which, in peacetime, hits a mine left over from the war. I also took various parts on TV. During these stints I came to know 'Tommy' Manderson, the

137

head of make-up at BBC Television. One evening, she asked me to a party in her house in Hampstead, and introduced me to a friend of hers from schooldays.

'Meet Bill Barkby,' she said. I turned, expecting to see a man, and instead was face to face with an elegant woman, slightly older than me.

'Why the boy's name?' I asked her.

'Because my real name is too awful,' Bill explained. 'Anyway, my brother always wanted a boy to play with. He called me Bill. And somehow the name stuck.'

There was something about Bill Barkby, apart from her nickname, that I had never known in any previous woman friend. This was her assurance and her poise. She was not an actress playing a rich woman; she was a rich woman, with the confidence that can only come from solid wealth. And I discovered with some surprise that money doesn't talk, it shouts; and, more important, money is sexy. Bill and I became friends, and eventually rather more than friends.

As my involvement with her progressed, so did my career. In 1950, I became friendly with Anthony Pelissier, Fay Compton's son. He was about to produce Frederick Lonsdale's play, *The Way Things Go*, and thought that I would be right for the part of Lord John. He gave me a copy of the script, and I found that Lord John, the nephew of the Duke of Bristol, was addicted to the bottle. But although his Lordship was always slightly drunk, he never became objectionable. The part called for a delicate touch, and presented a challenge that strongly appealed to me.

The play was still being cast and so Tony suggested that I should meet Freddie Lonsdale. If we got on together, then I would be more than half way home. Someone else's name had already been proposed for the part, but nothing had been firmly agreed. I had a chance – especially if Lonsdale liked me.

Tony took me to the playwright's suite at the Savoy. I felt rather nervous, for Lonsdale was the last of his line, a playwright who lived as people imagine a successful playwright should live – and as many would like to live, but so few ever do. He had made an estimated £1,000,000 out of his plays and musical comedies, which in the twenties and thirties had been wildly popular, and he had spent most of this fortune. Freddie Lonsdale had no permanent home, but booked suites in hotels wherever he wanted to be; usually at the Savoy in London or the Carlton in Cannes.

He was then about seventy, and although he had married several times he was at that time unattached; 'resting', to adopt the theatrical term. Lonsdale had two curious but harmless eccentricities. He always wore a white silk muffler around his neck, and white socks. He believed socks of any other colour would cause blood poisoning. I glanced down at his ankles as he opened the door of his suite to us, and, sure enough, his socks were white as snow. He looked at us without much warmth. Behind him, I could see his sitting room banked up with flowers, like a funeral parlour. Tony introduced me. But before I could even open my mouth and say 'Hello' or 'Pleased to meet you', Lonsdale shook his head.

'Not the right type,' he said firmly. 'Not the type at all.'

I stood there, my mouth open ready to speak, but still saying nothing. Really, I had nothing to say, and Anthony looked amazed, as I was.

This was the shortest audition of my life. Within thirty seconds we were going down in the hotel lift. Tony explained that it was pointless to argue with the old man. Once his mind was made up, he would never change it unless events changed it for him. This was not much comfort to me, for I felt convinced I was right for this part. The director of the production company, Stephen Mitchell, agreed, and he sounded out Harry Dubens as to my possible salary should Freddie Lonsdale change his mind. Harry asked thirty-five pounds a week for me but this was academic because Lonsdale did not want me at any price.

Soon I forgot about the incident. I had several TV and film parts and plenty to occupy my leisure with Bill Barkby, but from time to time I heard on the theatrical grapevine that rehearsals of *The Way Things Go* weren't going too well.

The play opened in Glasgow and on the morning of this first performance, Harry Dubens received a telegram: CAN KENNY COME IMMEDIATELY TO TAKE OVER PART OF JOHN STOP AGREE TO TERMS THIRTY FIVE POUNDS A WEEK.

I was filming at the time and Harry rushed down to the studio to show me this message.

'I don't want to go,' I told him. I had heard of a part in a forthcoming film that I thought I might get, but Harry was much wiser than me. He realised what a good role in a new Lonsdale play could mean to my career.

'You are going to Glasgow tonight,' he told me firmly. 'And I've bought your ticket already, so you can't change your mind.'

I arrived in Glasgow on Tuesday morning, saw the play that night, and agreed to take over the part for the Saturday matinee. Now my experience in rep came in useful for learning the long part presented no problems. I had two rehearsals with understudies, and one with the principals, Glynis Johns, Ronald Squire and Michael Gough.

The young actor I replaced wished me luck, and what seemed at the time to be bad fortune for him proved in fact to be the reverse. He landed a part in *Caesar and Cleopatra* with Laurence Olivier, went to America, and signed a Hollywood contract. He was Edmund Purdom.

Freddie Lonsdale was in Glasgow for the opening run of his play and came on with us on tour to Aberdeen and Edinburgh. Having told me in London that I was not right for the part, he now told me he did not think that Michael Gough, in the lead, was right either, and wanted me to take over from him.

'I couldn't possibly do that,' I replied. 'It's underhand, and, anyway, Michael is playing it splendidly.'

'He is not the type,' retorted Lonsdale stubbornly.

'You told *me* that, and here I am,' I reminded him. 'I am sorry, but you will have to go along with us as we are. We're friends.

And so he did.

As I came to know Lonsdale better, I liked him a lot. He appeared even grander than Noël Coward, but I sensed he had not been born to wealth, and indeed his background was humble.

Like me, he had spent his childhood in Jersey, and money was generally short. One Friday afternoon, when he was a boy, his parents were so hard up that his mother told him they had no meat at all for the weekend. Freddie decided to remedy this in the only way he could – by nipping out to the local butcher's shop and pinching a leg of lamb when the butcher's back was turned.

Years later, in the 1930s, at the height of his fame, when he owned a yacht and two Bentleys, Freddie went back to that shop, because the theft had played on his nonconformist conscience. The butcher was alone behind the counter, cutting up a carcass.

'Good morning,' Lonsdale began. 'Do you know who I am?'

The butcher looked at him blankly.

'No,' he admitted. 'Who are you?'

'I happen to be Mr. Frederick Lonsdale. You may have heard of me? I write plays.'

'Oh, yes?'

'Yes. As a matter of fact I have two plays running in London now, at this very moment.'

'Really?' said the butcher, quite unimpressed. 'So what do you want here, Mr. Frederick Lonsdale? Some meat?'

'Actually, no,' Freddie went on. 'You won't remember, of

course, but twenty-five years ago a small boy came into your shop one Friday afternoon and stole a leg of lamb. Well, I was that boy. I have come to pay for that meat and to apologise.'

'Ahhh!' shouted the butcher. He picked up his cleaver and swung it above his head. 'So *you're* the little bugger? I've waited all these years for this!'

And he chased him out of the shop and down the street.

Now, Lonsdale's great theatre successes were behind him. The tide of public taste had swept on and left him on its bank. He was approaching the end of his creative life, and what worried him even more was that he was also very near the end of his money. And he'd always been incredibly generous.

He kept referring to an unfinished play which was almost ready for production, but Ronnie Squire told me that he knew Freddie would never finish it. He couldn't. He had lost the touch. Creative talent is like a bank account in the mind. There is only so much to anyone's credit, and Freddie had drawn on his without stint, year after year. He had gone back to the till too often, and now the account was all but overdrawn. So while, to the outward view, Freddie lived like a king, and money poured out like water from the fountains of Rome, the façade and the flowers concealed a lonely, worried old man living on borrowed talent from the past.

One day, he walked out of his hotel and along the street. He had little money left, and little hope of earning much more. Then God leant forward, and Freddie Lonsdale died of a heart attack. The curtain came down on his life as cleanly as it had come down on a whole generation of his hits – at the end of a great act. His daughter Frances Donaldson, wrote his biography – far and away the best I have ever read.

My part as Lord John proved, as Harry Dubens had realised, a turning point in my stage career. It also started a friendship with Ronald Squire which enriched my whole life. Many people have influenced my life and career but, of them all, Ronnie's influence was the greatest and the most valuable. As a young man, he had been destined for the Army, but had not quite made it. Before the war, he became an actor playing on stage the parts he would have secretly liked to play in life; aristocrats, gentlemen of independent means, gentlemen of leisure.

Ronnie Squire became like a father to me; a father, moreover, whose vocation was also mine, and who knew its pitfalls.

Ronnie taught me a code of ethics in the theatre, which he summarised in the phrase, 'Throw the ball about a bit.' This

141

meant, that when the scene is not yours but belongs to others, give them their chance, throw them the ball. Never try to upstage them; let them enjoy their moment of glory. There are as many ways of denying them this as there are ways of writing plays. Some of the tricks you can recognise instantly. The TV or film camera is nearly always on the star. Someone else speaking to the star is not even visible; you only hear his or her voice off-screen. Why? Because that is how the star arranges things.

Throw the ball about a bit was always Ronnie's philosophy, and it has been mine throughout my career. But not, I have found, everyone else's.

Ronnie Squire also taught me an enormous amount about playing comedy. His timing was perfect. I had, of course, learned the basic rules of comedy timing from the comics at the Windmill. But now I would stand in the wings and watch Ronnie extract the last nuance of feeling from a line, a gesture or a pause, and then put what I saw into practice myself.

In that play he had the part of my uncle, the Duke of Bristol. He knew it had to be played by an older man.

'When you have learned about timing, about presence, and about style, Kenny, then you are ready for the Duke of Bristol. And one day you must do it. Just for me.'

Finally, twenty-seven years later, in 1977, I honoured that promise and Frith Banbury was my director.

Ronnie was in his mid-sixties when we first met, a warm lovely teddy-bear of a man. I would sit with him until the small hours of the morning listening to his stories of Edwardian days. He was then an up-and-coming actor enjoying the same sort of popularity in London as a television star enjoys throughout the country today, and being paid thirty golden guineas each week – a very high salary indeed. Ronnie as a young man would dine out with high-born ladies – he would always wink when he used that description. One of his favourite places was a private room at Kettner's, in Soho, where he ordered the wines beforehand. The room would be hung with heavy red velvet curtains and lit by candelabra. The waiter served the meal and then withdrew. There was a bell push on one wall. No one would come into that room until host or guest pressed that bell, no matter what happened – fire, flood, or the end of the world. The host was there with the lady of his choice. And then, in Ronnie's evocative Edwardian phrase, 'he pleasured her.'

After *The Way Things Go* ended its run in London, we played for two weeks at Brighton. One afternoon, as I went in to prepare for that evening's performance, the stage-door keeper handed me a telegram from my uncle in Wales: TOPSY DIED PEACEFULLY YESTERDAY AFTERNOON. My mother had felt tired after lunch, had taken a nap, and just not woken up. The doctor diagnosed a cerebral haemorrhage. This was totally unexpected, for Topsy was only sixty. She had never seen me in a West End play, and I had hoped she might come to see me at Brighton. Now, she never would.

I sat in my dressing room, looking at the make-up mirror ringed with bare, bright bulbs, not seeing my face reflected, but hers. I heard her voice in our garden in Richmond; I remembered her enthusiasm for our new life in Jersey, and her help when I wanted to go to Canada. I remembered everything a son remembers about his mother when it is too late for words to tell her how much she meant to him.

More than anything, I wished she could have been spared to see some return on all the love and encouragement she had given to me. And in any and every success I have enjoyed since, I have felt close to her, wishing she was there to enjoy it, to share it, she whose faith in me had never wavered. I told Ronnie and asked him not to tell anyone else in the cast. We were playing a comedy, and such news would only depress them.

Later that week, I went with my sister to Penarth for Topsy's funeral. It was a wet day with a grey sky. For a long time afterwards the memory of that desolate ceremony in the Welsh hills stayed in my mind.

143

9

ALTHOUGH I RECEIVED this bad news at Brighton, there was also good news, which would have warmed my mother's heart. Henry Koster, the American film director, flew over from the States to direct Marlene Dietrich and James Stewart in a film of Nevil Shute's novel, *No Highway*, and came to see our play. As a result, he offered parts in the film to Ronnie, Glynis and me. We were all delighted, but Freddie Lonsdale wasn't. He wanted us to appear in the Broadway run. We could not see such a delicate comedy of manners crossing the Atlantic successfully, and we were right. It folded there after a few nights. Light humour is like light wine; it doesn't always travel.

No Highway was about a scientist, Jimmy Stewart, who calculated that metal fatigue would cause the tail of an aircraft to drop off half way across the Atlantic. Understandably with such a plot no airline would supply us with a plane, so a full scale prototype was built on the tarmac of Blackbushe Airport. It was bitterly cold out on that windswept runway in mid-December. Stewart had an operation for appendicitis, and long before he should have left hospital, he was gamely on duty in these freezing conditions. Marlene Dietrich was a perfectionist, totally conscious of her own looks and her figure. When we were moved to the studios which were only slightly warmer than the airfield, she wore beneath her grey costume a pair of fine gossamer panties made of angora wool. I know this because a regular ritual took place before she would appear in front of the camera.

We would all be ready for our scene, lights set up, camera in place, microphone switched on and then Marlene would say, 'Wait a moment, please.' She would walk behind a piece of scenery and pull off these pants, which she wore to keep warm, bring them back and toss them on one side. Then she smoothed down the skirt of her costume, scrutinising herself carefully in a full length mirror brought in by acolytes, until she was convinced there were no lines or creases whatever.

She would bow in a queenly way and say, '*Now* I am ready.' All this, while the rest of us stood about, beating our hands together with cold.

144

Off to Paris: (left to right) the late Jack Hawkins, Kenneth More and Trevor Howard in high spirits.

Above: sublimely unconcerned in the heat of the pressure chamber, Kenneth More is groomed to be *Man in the Moon*.

Below: Jonathan Tibbs (Kenneth More) shows his patent steam carriage to his screen uncle, Ronald Squire, in *Sheriff of Fractured Jaw* (1958).

The thought occurred to me that this must be the pinnacle of acting success. When you can tell the director and everyone else to wait while you take off your trousers or knickers, according to sex or inclination, then you *know* you have arrived! And with that knowledge, fear goes out of your work and out of your life.

About this time, I was having a fairly heavy affair with a girl I will call Barbara. This was not her real name, but it is far enough away from her real name for no one to be able to identify her. She was married but estranged from her husband, for, true to my rather elastic code, I have never come between a husband and wife who were getting on together. But at that time of my life, when I was technically unattached, any wife who was not in that situation could be classed as fair game.

Anyhow, Barbara and I were conducting this affair, partly in my flat, and partly in hers. One day, she told me she had been invited by a couple of friends in Surrey for the weekend and would like me to join her.

We drove down to a very pleasant house. The host and his wife were a delightful couple with two young children. This weekend they had parked them with a grandmother somewhere, and so the four of us had the house to ourselves. There was no question of my sharing Barbara's bedroom. She had her room at one side of the house and I had mine elsewhere, and our host and hostess had their double bedroom.

I thought, to hell with this. I've not driven all this way to sleep on my own. At three o'clock in the morning I woke up and decided to have a go.

I knew where Barbara's room was, and thought the safest way was to crawl along the floor until I found her door. The corridor was pitch dark and I did not dare to walk upright in case I banged into something or set off a creaking floor board. So I crawled as slowly as a steam roller on my stomach and elbows, pausing now and then to get my breath. I felt like the serpent in the Garden of Eden.

I heard a grandfather clock tick and chime an hour downstairs, but there was no other sound in the whole sleeping household. As I turned on the landing in the pitch darkness towards Barbara's bedroom, I paused and put out one hand to steady myself for the last lap.

To my horror, my fingers touched a human foot. Toes wriggled. My hand moved slowly up a masculine ankle to a pyjama leg. I peered into the darkness and could see nothing. But I knew a man must be standing there. Who was he? If he wasn't a burglar, he could only be my host, and I whispered, 'Where are *you* going?' It was a ridiculous question to ask. My host's voice came back through the darkness equally muted and equally tense.

'The same place as you, you silly bugger.'

Next morning, I came down rather late, hoping my host had finished his breakfast. He hadn't. He glanced up from his newspaper and looked me straight in the eye. I looked back at him straight in the eye. Neither of us referred to the incident. The hostess asked me whether I had slept well.

'Perfectly,' I told her.

After *No Highway* I was offered a part by Betty Box and Ralph Thomas in an adventure comedy, *Appointment with Venus*. While making this picture, I learned two sobering lessons, one about life and the other about show business – which, after all, is only a magnified reflection of life.

The film told the story of a British wartime raid on the Channel Islands, then occupied by the Germans, to bring back Venus, a champion milker pedigree cow. We were in Sark on location for three weeks. My most enduring memory of this time is that the pubs never seemed to shut; I have never drunk so much in all my life. I was also infatuated with Glynis's stand-in, a pretty, delightful girl called Joy. When I was not drinking, I was chasing her all over the island. When I wasn't chasing her, or drinking, I was acting.

David Niven was the star, and he was particularly nice to me, and indeed to everyone else in the film. While all stars will usually sign an autograph willingly and appear pleasant on a TV chat show or when making a public appearance, they are by no means always so pleasant to those with whom they work. And when, as with Niven, they appear to take an interest in you, you feel like a young country curate might feel if the Archbishop of Canterbury paid him a call and told him how well he was doing.

When we arrived in Sark, David came up to me straight away as though I was an old friend.

'Hello,' he said breezily. 'How are you, dear old bird?'

I felt like a million dollars. David Niven had done all the prewar stuff in Hollywood and was an international name. Just then, in the fifties, he had not fully re-established himself after the war. But so far as I was concerned, he was Number One.

After our location work, we all came back to the studios at Pinewood, and at the end of one week's shooting, David asked me casually: 'What are you doing this weekend, Kenny?'

'Nothing,' I told him.

'Like to come back with me?' he suggested. 'We've got a place in the country.'

'Delighted.'

David had taken a little manor house in Wiltshire with his beautiful Swedish wife Hjordis and his two young sons from his first marriage. On that Friday night, after shooting, we were just about to leave the studio when a pushy extra, who had been trying to make his number with David all week, came up and asked him whether he was going anywhere near Marlborough.

'Matter of fact, we're driving through Marlborough,' said David. 'Why?'

'I would like to beg a lift from you,' the extra explained.

'No,' said Niven.

'No? Why not?' asked the extra, obviously put out.

'Because I don't want you,' said Niven. 'That's why. I am taking Kenny home for the weekend and we have things to talk about.'

The extra just stood there in amazement at this truthful reply, and then he pushed off.

I thought, that's *wonderful*. I would have no more have given such an answer than die on the spot. I'd have said, Yes, and the whole journey would have been ruined with this twit in the back chuntering away, saying, 'Ah, well, how are you doing then, David? Tell me about Hollywood,' and all that stuff.

So we set off on a cold winter afternoon. David had a fast car and we reached his house in about an hour and a half. There was a welcome fire burning in the hall, and another in the sitting room on the right. Everything was warm and chintzy and very comfortable.

As we walked through the hall, I noticed a chair near the fireplace. What struck me about it was the material on the seat, which was in a yellow and black harlequin diamond pattern, the like of which I had never seen before and have never seen since.

'Isn't that bloody *awful*?' David remarked, nodding towards the chair.

I had really no views either way, but falling in with the mood of my host, I agreed.

'It does stand out a bit, I suppose,' I admitted.

'It's *terrible*,' he went on, 'We'll have to do something about that, Kenny. No doubt about it. We'll have to deal with it, dear old thing.'

We went into the drawing room. Hjordis came out of the kitchen where she had been preparing dinner. She was a beautiful creature, and chatting to them both in front of a log fire, I began to thaw out. She left us together, and David asked me whether I had ever tasted Campari, which was just beginning to be imported to Britain.

'Good God, no, David,' I replied. 'I'm a mild-and-bitter man. I'm not used to such fancy stuff.'

'You must try some Campari, dear boy,' he said, and poured me half a tumbler. My surprise at the amount he poured showed on my face.

'Don't worry,' he assured me, 'it's not very alcoholic.'

'Are you certain?'

'Positive, old bird. There's nothing in it. Very light stuff. Anyway, I'll keep up with you.'

He handed me this enormous measure and I drank it, without any pain at all. Then I found another equally large glass in my hand, and then a third. David himself had only drunk one small glass, but in the warmth of the room and on an empty stomach, after a tiring day that had begun at about six o'clock that morning, I began to feel unmistakably high.

'I thought you said this wasn't very alcoholic?' I protested.

'Oh, it's nothing much, old bird.'

Hjordis then announced that dinner was ready, and we ate in their beautiful kitchen, and a magnificent meal it was. We had wine during dinner, and afterwards Hjordis said that she was tired, as she had been working all day in the house or the garden, I can't remember which now, maybe it was both – I was now distinctly fuddled – and she went up to bed.

David suggested that he and I went into the drawing room for a nightcap.

'What about another Campari?' he suggested as we settled down in front of the fire.

'No, no, I mustn't have any more.' I thought, if I did, I'd never make it up the stairs to my bedroom.

'You're quite right,' he agreed. 'You shouldn't really drink Campari after dinner. What about a brandy?'

This sounded a most agreeable proposition and so I started on the brandy. In about an hour's time I was over the hill, sitting there with a stupid grin on my face, toasting my toes at the log fire and listening to amusing anecdotes of the film business by my host, a man I admired, almost idolised.

Finally, through drifting mists of alcohol, I heard David say:

'Now – what about that chair?'

'What about it?' I asked stupidly.

'Isn't it terrible?'

'Terrible,' I repeated.

'It's the worst looking chair I've ever seen,' he said.

'I absolutely agree, David. The worst.'

'The colour scheme is appalling. The whole thing is in execrable taste. There is only one thing to do, old boy.'

'What's that, David?'

'Burn it.'

I said, 'What?'

'Break it up and burn it.'

Christ! I thought. Am I hearing him right? Well, it was his chair. If he wanted to burn it, that was up to him.

'If that is all right with you, David,' I declared, as though I was making some momentous statement, 'then it is all right with me.'

'It's absolutely all right with me, old bird,' he replied. 'Go and get it. Bring it in here.'

So I went out into the hall and brought back the chair.

'Come on, then,' he said. 'Get going.'

'How, exactly?'

'Take it to bits and burn it. You can't put it on the fire in one piece, now can you?'

With some difficulty, I pulled off the legs, took out the harlequin seat, and threw the chair bit by bit into the fire. As it began to burn, David did an Indian war dance around me, whooping and shouting, 'Aah! Aah! Aah!'

For some reason, he seemed deliriously happy. I was just delirious with the effects of Campari; wine and brandy, and hardly knew what I was doing. Finally, the chair was reduced to a small pile of charred wood. I staggered off to bed, and slept like a stone. Next morning, when I came down to breakfast, Hjordis was looking worried.

'What has happened to the chair?' she asked me.

'The chair?' I repeated, at first not understanding the reference. And then I remembered. *The chair*!!!

David said to her, po-faced, 'Kenny burned it, darling. He got high and burned it.'

'You burned *my* chair?' cried Hjordis in amazement.

I couldn't deny it. That is exactly what I had done – but on David's instructions – and this I felt I could not tell her. To make such a statement would only increase her annoyance. After all, I was a guest in their house.

What I did not know, was that this was a favourite piece of furniture, with a special place in her affections. She did not speak to me for the rest of the weekend. I was stuck there all Saturday and Sunday with a terrible hangover, laced with guilt and embarrassment at having burned my hostess's favourite chair – at her husband's suggestion! David, of course, had never liked

149

the chair, and this had been one way of getting rid of it. Cunning, of course, but what tactics! Hjordis had to forgive him, but I don't think she ever forgave me. That was lesson number one.

The following week, I learned lesson number two. In *Appointment with Venus*, I was playing a conscientious objector, an artist, who refused to take part in the war, and hated all violence. I was hiding in a cave with others who were trying to remove this valuable cow, Venus, and bring it back to England. Then German troops discovered us and one soldier behaved so badly that I had to hit him and knock him out. This scene was essential for the understanding of the story, and of the character I played. It marked the turning point from being a pacifist to taking an active part in the war. It was also my one big scene. I learned it backwards. I knew it so well, I could have spoken it in Chinese.

The cave was constructed in the studios one Monday, and we were due to film the scene first thing on Tuesday morning. Lights were set up, camera in position. I was so keen and keyed up that I arrived on the set half an hour before anyone else.

To my surprise, the set was totally deserted. No director, no camera man, no continuity girl. An old chippy was sawing a length of wood for some purpose of his own, and a couple of lighting men were dismantling a spot light. I hung about for twenty minutes, and when no one else appeared thought there must be a strike or something. Finally Ralph Thomas, the film's director, came on the set. He was a dear man and I liked him a great deal. This morning he looked upset.

'What's the matter?' I asked him. 'What's the hold up?'
'Kenny,' he said awkwardly. 'Come and walk with me.'
I said, 'All right.'
We walked a few paces in silence. Then he spoke.
'I've some bad news for you.'
'What is it?' I asked him.
'You are going to learn your first unpleasant lesson in show business, Kenny.'
'I've had a few already,' I told him.
'Well,' he said. 'Here's another one. And maybe the most important you'll ever have to learn in our business.'
'Well, what is it, Ralph?'
'This. The star is always more important than anyone else. Because he is more important to the film.'
'What exactly are you trying to tell me?' I asked him.
'I am trying to tell you your scene is out.'
'It can't be out. My part doesn't make any sense without it.'
Ralph shrugged. 'That's the lesson, Kenny. It's out. David is

150

the star, and if anyone's going to be hitting Germans in this picture, it is going to be him – not you. We're all agreed on it.'

Another incident comes to mind which rubbed in the same harsh truth. I had the chance to feature with Clark Gable in *Never Let Me Go*. Harry Dubens was, of course, delighted at the prospect.

'That will get you right into the American market, Kenny,' he assured me. I hoped he was right, but first I had to be approved by Gable. On the afternoon before we were due to meet, I had a telephone call from the casting director at the studio.

'I want you to remember one thing, Kenny,' she told me. 'In this picture, you are supposed to be Gable's friend, not his son. He isn't exactly the youngest man around, and he won't thank you if he looks old enough to be your father.'

'Thanks for the tip,' I said. I stayed up late that night, drinking whisky. When I met Gable the next morning, I didn't feel young enough to be his son, but almost too old to be his father. We got on well. He said almost immediately, 'You're the boy I want,' and the part was mine.

But despite Harry's optimism, it didn't get me into the American market, although I had one very good scene which I felt would do the trick.

I had to give a letter to Gene Tierney, which contained instructions for her to meet Gable at a rendezvous in a North Baltic port, of all places, in the middle of the night. Well, I played this and went on to other things.

Bill saw the finished film before I did.

'It was quite good,' she told me. 'But one thing just didn't make sense. How on earth did Gene Tierney know *where* to meet Gable?'

'Because of that letter I gave her. That scene was the crux of the whole thing.'

'What letter? What scene?'

'My God!' I cried, realising what had happened.

So once more, my one dramatic moment in a film had been removed. There is only one star and in this instance the competition was being cut right down to size. In no way could my scene have affected the career of a man like Clark Gable. But that's show business, I suppose.

151

10

SHORTLY AFTER THIS, I was playing the fateful game of golf with Roly Culver which resulted in my getting my most important part so far, Freddie in *The Deep Blue Sea*. While the play was running to packed houses at every performance, Bill and I decided we should marry. I must admit frankly that I was against this for a long time. The memory of my unsatisfactory marriage with Beryl Johnstone still painful in my mind. I simply did not want to marry again. I enjoyed being free. I enjoyed being able to go out of my flat whenever I wanted, and come home whenever I wanted – and bring home whomever I wanted, without explanation or any need for excuses or subterfuge. The thought of accumulating other commitments, possibly even other in-laws, held no attractions for me. And yet, strong as my instincts were, I felt myself being drawn or pushed or propelled towards marriage and I could do nothing about it, nothing at all.

Why did I not tell Bill that although I liked her very much and greatly enjoyed her company, I did not wish to marry her – or anybody else? We would both have been happier had I done so. But I did not. I enjoyed being with her. I did not want to change things. And so I assured myself that things would work themselves out in some vague and undefined way.

There was another complication. If I married Bill I was going to marry a woman who, like me, had failed once at marriage and who, also like me, had a child by that marriage. We could thus both be repeating an earlier mistake. However, it was just conceivable (although my bachelor friends assured me, most unlikely) that we could both be making the most fortunate decision of our lives.

I had to discuss the situation with someone, and my choice was Ronnie Squire. He heard me out as I admitted frankly: 'I am very fond of her, Ronnie. But I don't think I'm in love with her.'

Ronnie nodded sagely like a stage judge meditating his verdict.

'I think it would be a very good thing if you married her, Kenny. A most admirable decision.'

'But why do you say that, Ronnie?' I asked. 'I'm a bachelor at heart. I have had lots of wonderful affairs. I enjoy life. Why should I marry Bill? I dine with her at least once a week already.'

'Where?' he asked.

'Usually in her flat in Kingston House.'

'Exactly!' said Ronnie instantly. 'Exactly! *You* can't afford a flat in Kingston House on what you make. And I doubt either of us ever will. I think an actor – especially one of taste like you, needs a good address – and a silk shirt or two.'

'I can buy silk shirts myself. I'll earn the money.'

'Rubbish,' he replied. 'You'll never earn the money for silk shirts, Kenny. How many working actors do you know who have silk shirts and live in Kingston House?'

I couldn't think of one.

'There you are,' he said, as though this clinched the matter and ended all discussion. 'Anyhow, so far as I am concerned, I wouldn't mind eating smoked salmon once in a while myself when I come to dinner with you.'

'But *you're* not marrying her,' I replied.

'I don't have to marry the lady surely to be invited to dine once a week? I can see ourselves under silver candelabra, enjoying smoked salmon, plover's eggs, oysters, a bottle of good claret and a decent cigar. You marry the lady! I am very fond of Bill. She's charming. You marry her and settle down. Best thing you could do.'

'But I don't want to settle down,' I said.

But Ronnie wasn't listening.

'It would be a wonderful thing for you, Kenny. The best thing that ever happened to you in your life.'

I thought it over. I weighed the pros and cons, and let me tell every young man, that if he *has* to weigh the pros and cons, then to marry is the wrong decision. Later, when I met Angela, everything was against my marrying her, but I knew that the only decision with which I could live, the only reason indeed for living, was to marry her. But now it was an equivocal situation, with much to say on both sides.

One night, dining with Bill, we discussed the matter.

'I think we ought to get married,' I said hesitantly.

'A very good idea,' she replied briskly.

'But I must tell you, Bill,' I said. 'I am not sure I love you, or whether you love me. We get along well together, the sex works, but I don't know that we *love* each other.'

'That will come later,' she replied.

Women say that too easily. Love never comes later. Love to be real is there before the door is opened. Love is a trembling in the heart and the stomach, a hand on the telephone at the first ring of the bell. It is all these things and many more, but love is also always punctual. Love never comes later. If it's not there at the beginning, it's not there at all.

'Well, Ronnie will be pleased,' I told Bill. 'He likes his smoked salmon, lace tablecloths on the table, and good cigars. All the things I have never had.'

'We'll have them together, Kenny,' Bill promised. And we did.

Someone once said that diamonds are very sexy, and so is money. The cynics say it is better to be miserable in comfort than just miserable, but better by far than either of these depressing alternatives is to be happy with what you have on your own. I know, for I have been all three.

'You must promise me one thing, Bill,' I said. 'If ever I do fall in love – if ever either of us falls in love – I mean physically in love, really in love, if such a thing can ever happen – we will let the other one know. You let me know. And if it happens to me, I'll let you know.'

'All right. If that's what you want.'

We decided to buy a house in Wargrave, on the Thames. I was commanding high fees and could afford to run it; and behind us both lay the solid reassurance of Bill's money. The house was delightful. Closely trimmed lawns sloped down to the river, and tall chestnut trees marched on either side of the drive, trimmed in the shape of enormous bells. Bill furnished the house in style. The dining room had a lime green fitted carpet, pale green and white curtains, with period furniture. Our dining room was in Georgian style, the bedrooms in blue and pink. It was almost too beautiful, rather like a stage or film set, the background for elegant happenings; a lovely house, rather than a home. It was a place to be seen and photographed, but strangely not relaxing to live in. And it proved incredibly expensive to run.

I had been used to a small flat, easy to clean and cheap to maintain. Now, every time I arrived in Wargrave from the theatre or studio, someone seemed to want more money; the gardener, the cook, the housemaid. Then there were repairs to central heating, to relaying the garden, to relaying the relaying of the garden, to all manner of items I had never imagined needed such regular expenditure.

The rich accept these constant demands on their pockets as unimportant; if such trivial things worry you, then clearly you can't afford them. But those of us not born rich, who have had to work hard for our money, find such bills an increasing irritation – and gradually a focus for discontent, especially if

154

other areas of our lives are also a disappointment. Finally Bill and I decided that Wargrave was too far from London. So, after a spell of some years we moved back – to another flat, a large one, in Kingston House.

Ronnie Squire, I am glad to say, often dined with us. We enjoyed his company and he enjoyed his smoked salmon, his hock and claret, and the whole ambience of a good meal served with fine silver on a damask tablecloth. Ronnie and I stayed very close to each other all through the 1950s. My star was rising, and whenever there was a part he could take in any of my films, I made sure he had first offer. We also continued to play a lot of golf together when our free time coincided. Ronnie it was who had introduced me to the game, and so it seems fitting that I should have played golf with him on the day before he died.

We were on the 17th green at Wimbledon Park, Ronnie's favourite course, when, quite unexpectedly, he told me he felt he had had enough of life. He could not understand this new world at all – and don't forget, this was in 1958, so what he would have thought of things today I cannot imagine. He added that his doctor had warned him his blood pressure was high, and he admitted he had difficulty in bending down to put in a tee for the ball.

Then he let me into a secret; he had a great fear of living until he was ninety. Two sisters of his lived to a great age, and they had become so crippled with arthritis that their hands were like elm twigs, gnarled and lumpy. This was what Ronnie feared; a slow decline of the faculties, not death itself. As Swift put it, 'Every man desires to live long, but no man would be old.'

'Kenny,' he said. 'If I can't reach out for a bottle of whisky or a bottle of aspirins, I don't want to live. I want to die on my feet, rather than lingering on like a guest who has outstayed his welcome and won't leave the party.'

He invited me to have dinner with him and his young wife Eysllt, at his house off Queen's Square on the following evening, but something came up and I could not go. So he and his wife dined alone.

Suddenly, half way through the meal, Ronnie put his hand to his left eye, and said in a strange voice, 'I've got a terrible pain over my eye, Pinky.'

Pinky was his name for her. Within seconds, she told me afterwards, he was unconscious. Just around the corner was the famous neurological hospital. They took Ronnie there, but he died without regaining consciousness. He left his life as he had lived it; with dignity, like a gentleman.

155

I was desperately upset. I mourned Ronnie as a father. I wanted to see him once more, to say goodbye to him for the last time, and went to the funeral parlour on the eve of his burial. There he was, with his little moustache all perked up. This was his last appearance, and he looked wonderfully peaceful. He had a slight smile on his face, and I didn't feel sad any more, but happy and grateful that I had known him.

But once more, events are hurrying me ahead of my story. I must go back to my early months of marriage and the success of *The Deep Blue Sea*. Critics hailed me almost as an overnight discovery, conveniently forgetting I was already thirty-eight, and that I had been working in the theatre for nearly twenty years. Nowadays, television and pop can make people stars in their teens, so by the standards of today, I was late to arrive. And while I knew that at last I had reached a certain height in my profession, I still felt like a man on an unstable ladder. I could easily fall. What I needed urgently was to consolidate my good fortune before the ladder slipped. I could only achieve this through an audience wider than the theatre. I had to succeed in films.

It was now that I reached one of the turning points in my career. One evening during the run the film producer Henry Cornelius, whom I have already mentioned briefly in connection with *Scott of the Antarctic*, came round to see me in my dressing room after the show. I did not know him, and was by then a bit blasé about people coming round after the show because the play was such a success. I expected Henry to be one of these. But, no.

'I haven't seen the play,' he admitted.

'So what have you come round here for?' I asked him, a bit put out.

'I want you to read a film script I've brought,' he said. 'I'd like you to play the lead.'

'It can't be done,' I told him. 'I can't work all day in the studios and all night on the stage. I'll be dead.'

Cornelius looked at me closely.

'I don't think you can afford to say "no" to this,' he said, and something in his tone of voice impressed me.

'Thank you very much,' I replied, 'But why me? You admit you haven't seen me in the play. You don't know anything about my work.'

'But I do,' he said. 'Do you remember you played a very small part some time ago in a film of mine, *The Galloping Major*, with Basil Radford?'

I remembered that. But the part was minuscule, literally a spit

156

and a cough. Two days' work, while waiting for something better to turn up. But Corny had remembered it, and so had remembered me, and now he was offering me the chance of a lifetime, for the script he had brought to show me was the script of *Genevieve*.

He offered me the part of Ambrose Claverhouse, an advertising agent whose passion was his veteran Spyker motor car. Ambrose takes part in the London to Brighton run, and a friend who is also an enthusiast has a bet on who will be first back to London in their old cars.

I sensed at once that this film could provide the consolation I needed – but what a schedule of work it would entail! I was only recently married, in a new house, 30 miles from London, and every evening had to take a long and taxing part on the stage. Now I would also have to be at the studio – or worse, on location – by seven o'clock every morning.

I considered the disadvantages, but there was still only one answer; I had to do it. So I signed a contract for a fee of £3,500 which seemed a lot then, but which now is less than a mediocre pop performer can make in a single performance.

My girl friend in the film was Kay Kendall. While this was to be my first bid for film stardom, it was her second. Katie had starred when she was only seventeen in *London Town*, a British musical film generally regarded as the biggest flop in screen history. This had taken her a long time to live down. Now, older and wiser, but beautiful and scatty as ever, Kay was fighting back for the second time around. John Gregson was playing the part of my friend and challenger. Like me, he had served in the Navy, in minesweepers. We had also appeared together in *Scott of the Antarctic*, but he had taken a shorter cut to success through such films as *Whisky Galore* and *The Lavender Hill Mob*. John Gregson had a peculiar problem in the film. He needed to drive this ancient car, but did not hold a driving licence. I don't think he'd ever driven a car in his life. Now he started a frantic course of driving lessons, but learning to drive a modern car is very different from controlling a 1904 model. About all they have in common is an engine and a wheel at each corner. He was unable to take his driving test by the time we started work – so he simply drove without a licence.

His screen wife was Dinah Sheridan, only recently divorced from Jimmy Hanley, who had been first choice for my role in *The Deep Blue Sea*.

Our production schedule was fifty-seven days – from October to February – mostly out of doors, in the bitterest and wettest weather of the year. Since all the action was supposed to take place over a sunny weekend, the unit took mobile generators on location to light arc lamps. Every day, before dawn, a winding caravan of vans and trucks loaded with this equipment, plus portable dressing rooms, lavatories and props of every kind, would set off from Pinewood to wherever we were filming. To cut the distances we did a lot of our shooting in a country lane near Moor Park Golf Club. Motorists were astonished to come across a signpost: *Brighton 6 miles* when they believed (rightly) that they were several miles north of London.

And I still remember the astonishment of a local policeman who looked out of his bedroom window and saw across the road a sign: *Beware: Cattle Crossing*, which had sprung up unknown to him in the night.

Corny was a perfectionist. We would get a scene right after several attempts – but he would still not be satisfied. So we would do it two or three times more to satisfy him. Every evening around five o'clock I began to grow restless, because I had to be in the Duchess Theatre for the evening performance. I look back on those fifty-seven days of hard, cold work on location, with fifty-seven dashes back to London and fifty-seven performances to play before a critical audience, with a sort of amazement that I ever managed to survive such a marathon.

During this time, Charlie Chaplin came over to London, and saw the play. Afterwards, Bill and I were invited to a dinner party in his honour. After dinner, Chaplin began to tell stories of his early days in Hollywood, but my eye kept continually going to my wristwatch. Finally, at midnight, like Cinderella, I had to leave.

'I must be up at six-thirty tomorrow for filming,' I explained. Chaplin was amazed.

'You mean you're playing that part every night on stage *and* filming in the day as well?'

'That's right,' I admitted. 'Every day.'

'Put your hand on your heart,' Chaplin commanded sternly.

I did so. Then he placed his hand over mine and said gravely, 'Promise me solemnly you will never, never do this again. It will take years off your life. This is death to an artiste.'

I was by then beginning to realise what he meant.

The strains of filming showed in other members of the cast. One day, in a drizzle, Kay Kendall and I had to drive towards the camera in our old Spyker. Cornelius was not happy with the shot, so we did it a second time. He was sorry, but a hair had caught in the gate of the camera. We did it a third time, a fourth, and then a fifth time. We were soaked to the skin, but because it was supposed to be a sunny day (an illusion created by the arc lights) we could not wear raincoats. Each time we shot this scene we had to drive down the road for several hundred yards, coax the old asthmatic engine to keep running as I turned the gasping, trembling machine, and then we drove back. After the fifth time, Cornelius shook his head.

'Just once more,' he said.

I was about to reverse, when the whole car rocked on its antique springs. Kay had jumped out. Alongside the passenger seat was a wicker basket to carry a parasol – about the only weather protection drivers in the early 1900s had. She seized the parasol with both hands and began to beat Corny over the head with it. At first, I thought she was just joking. Then I realised she had gone hysterical with the cold and the misery of driving up and down in the rain.

'You miserable little bastard!' Kay cried as she belaboured him. I knew exactly how she felt and sympathised with her.

Having overcome trouble with the weather, we went into the studio – and seven eighths of the way through the film, the company ran out of money. We were well over our budget because of Corny's insistence in repeating each shot so many times. The producer had an insurance policy against such a contingency but insurance companies never like to pay out, and under the terms of the contract they had to pay the producer what was then a large sum, about £20,000.

To cut all possible costs, the insurance company had their men prowling around the studio switching off any lights that were not needed. I felt physically and mentally exhausted, and was glad when *The Deep Blue Sea* ended its run and filming was over, and Bill and I could have a fortnight's holiday in San Moritz.

We returned home to bad news. The chief executives at Pinewood had seen *Genevieve* and decided it was terrible. Some argued that they should have realised this from the beginning, because the film had always been a gamble, with the four chief characters virtually unknown outside London. It had also cost more than had been anticipated, and so all those associated with it were made to feel they must take a major share of the blame for what seemed bound to be a failure.

It was soon made clear to me how much I was held responsible. Peter Rogers, one of Rank's producers, who later made a fortune with the *Carry On* series of films, offered me a part in a comedy he was going to make, and suggested a fee of £3,500.

Harry Dubens, remembering my years at five pounds a week, insisted that I was paid more. After some haggling, Peter agreed to pay £4,500, and we settled on this figure. A few days later, a very embarrassed Peter was on the telephone to Harry. His superiors at Pinewood had decreed that in the light of the loss they were bound to make with *Genevieve*, if they ever even showed it, I was not worth this amount. The most they would pay me was what they had paid me for *Genevieve* – £2,500. I felt I was engaged in a living game of snakes-and-ladders, two steps up and then three steps down.

This blow to my ego was eased when another producer, George Minter, asked me to play in a film he was making, called *Our Girl Friday*. This was based on what in those days was considered a naughty book, *The Cautious Amorist*, by the South African writer, Noel Langley.

The book described what happened when a fussy clergyman, a sharp Cockney, a sophisticated journalist and a rough Irish stoker were shipwrecked on a desert island with Sadie, a beautiful, sexy girl. There was film censorship, of course, in those days, and the story was therefore carefully laundered; and in order to avoid any difficulties over a U-Certificate, the clergyman became a professor. George Minter agreed to pay me £4,500, and Bill and I set off for location in Majorca, which was then an island almost undiscovered by tourists.

We were working in a bay near the village of Paguera. Because the scenery was not considered tropical enough for the film, some trees were sprayed red, two acres of rocks were painted purple and artificial flowers and rubber palm trees were dug in along the beach.

The temperature in the sun was phenomenal. Robertson Hare, who played the part of the professor, had a bald head. The sun on his pate was so hot that he claimed he could literally fry an egg on it. He was nearly scalped with the heat, and George Minter made the rest of us, when we were not working, take turns to hold leaves over 'Bunny' Hare's head.

Joan Collins was cast as Sadie. She was, and of course still is, very beautiful, but sometimes her reactions surprised me. Staying in our hotel was a handsome Swede, who claimed he had a degree in astrology.

'Are you sure you don't mean astronomy?' she asked him.

'No. Astrology. I will answer any question you want to know about the future if you give me twenty-four hours to work it out.'

Joan took this very seriously, and asked him: 'When will I get a mink coat?' The next day we waited breathlessly for his answer.

Above: with Michael Bentine in the BBC television programme *Talking Sport* (1963).

Below: Susannah York and Kenneth More during a break from the filming of *The Battle of Britain*.

Left: Outside the old Windmill Theatre, once famous for its static nudes, where Kenneth More's stage career began.

Below: Heading a line-up of star artists for a Radio Four summer season: (left to right): Kenneth More, Liza Goddard, Cyril Fletcher, Kenneth Williams, Liz Gebhardt, Gyles Brandreth and Nicholas Parsons.

'You're not far away from it, my dear,' he assured. 'In fact, it is very near.' And, indeed, it was. After our film was shown, she went to Hollywood on a lucrative two-year contract.

The script of *Our Girl Friday* called for George Cole, who was playing the journalist, and me, to swim without clothes.

'Come on,' said Noel. 'Let's have a look at you. Get 'em off!'

'Not on your life,' I replied. 'We are only going to be seen on the screen from the waist up, so we'll wear trunks.'

'We must have authenticity,' persisted Noel.

'Rubbish,' I said. 'What about Joan's stand-in?'

'Do her a power of good.'

She was a Spanish lady who had been strictly brought up, and was so religious that if anyone even mentioned men she would cross herself, and lower her eyes demurely.

'We can't walk about nude in front of her.'

'Of course you can. We weren't born with any clothes. *Get 'em off!*'

Others in the unit joined in the general chorus, so Cole and I finally stripped off and ran naked into the breakers. Then we swam back and walked up the beach. The Spanish stand-in was sitting knitting, and suddenly she looked up and saw two naked men approaching from the sea. She fell forwards in a faint, crossing herself as she fell.

When the location work was done, Bill and I returned to Britain – to astonishing news about *Genevieve*. The critics had been sparing with their praise, but what are the contentions of critics against the delight of the general public? People loved the film. It was doing fantastic business all around the country, and since those days, this film, which was so nearly rejected, has become a classic and one of the greatest successes ever made in a British studio.

Its appeal was universal. Two years later, I was in Miami on holiday, watching the curious spectacle of a Red Indian with feathers around his head wrestling with an alligator. While the show was going on, I noticed that the Indian brave kept glancing in my direction. After the show, he approached me.

'You're Kenneth More?' he asked.

I admitted it.

'I saw you in *Genevieve*,' he went on in a strong Brooklyn accent. His dark skin obviously came from a make-up bottle.

'I loved that picture,' he told me.

'I'm very glad.'

'There is one thing I want to ask you. Did Kay Kendall *really* play the trumpet in the nightclub scene?'

So many others have asked me this over the years that I will answer it now, once and for all.

She did, and she didn't. Kay took lessons and mastered the technique of handling the instrument, but the sound was actually produced by a rather more accomplished player, Kenny Baker.

Our Girl Friday was not so successful as we had hoped. We had all enjoyed ourselves making it, but the result was a bit of a disappointment. Again, my guardian angel came to my aid. One morning, I opened a parcel which had come through the post and found that it contained the script of *Doctor in the House*. I read this, and knew immediately that it was for me and it meant working again with Ralph and Betty which was a joy. The success of this film is one of the legends of Wardour Street. It broke all attendance records in London and then throughout Britain, and when it was first shown in America the audience stood up and clapped. And from this first film stemmed more, with books, plays and TV and radio series.

I was playing golf shortly after its première when I had a message from the clubhouse that my wife wanted to speak to me urgently.

'A wonderful surprise,' said Bill, tremendously excited. 'The British Film Academy has just voted you the Best Actor of the Year!'

I was so astonished and elated that for the rest of the round I could hardly see the ball, let alone hit it!

Weeks later, I had a distinction of another kind; Bill went into King's College Hospital to have our baby. I was convinced she would have a son, and slept soundly through the night until woken by the telephone at half-past eight in the morning. Bill's gynaecologist was on the line.

'Congratulations,' he said. 'You have a baby girl.'

'Then you must be speaking to the wrong father,' I replied. 'We are having a boy.'

'Not this time,' he said. And indeed Bill had presented me with a daughter. At first, I was slightly disappointed, but when Sarah Elizabeth began to grow and develop a mind and personality of her own, I was delighted to be the father of a daughter.

One result of the success of *Doctor in the House* was that I received an invitation to visit Sir Alexander Korda at his offices in Piccadilly.

Korda was at that time at the height of his power and influence. He was unlike anyone's idea of a film tycoon. He had round red cheeks and wispy grey hair, and wore thick spectacles. He still spoke with a strong Hungarian accent, and could have acted the part of a foreign professor unversed in English ways.

If an actor had to be under contract to anybody, Korda was the man, for he did things in style. There was nothing petty or mean about him. He lived in a splendid house in Kensington Palace Gardens, 'millionaires' row'. As soon as I signed with him, he said, 'Now you are my new star, Kenny, I must give you a dinner party.' There I was, guest of honour in a party that included Graham Greene, Terence Rattigan, Rex Harrison, Merle Oberon and half a dozen others. Our first course was smoked sturgeon with caviare on top. I thought, this is the life.

Korda offered me a choice of two films. The first was a remake of *The Four Feathers*, which I turned down. The next was *The Deep Blue Sea*. I could play the same part of the pilot which I had played for so long on the stage. I was delighted with this, but not so pleased with the rest of the casting. First of all, Vivien Leigh was cast as the judge's wife, with whom I had an affair. In my opinion, this should have been played by Peggy Ashcroft who had played it superbly in the theatre. There, Roland Culver had been the judge and Peter Illing was the little doctor struck off the register who lived in an adjoining flat. Now instead of these actors we had Eric Portman as the doctor, and Emlyn Williams as the judge.

'I think you are making a dreadful mistake,' I told Korda. 'Can't we stay with the original cast?'

'No,' he replied. 'You must have names around you the public know. Most of the public never go to a theatre in their lives. You must have the best, Kenny, because I am launching you!'

I could not very well argue against this, but the casting of the beautiful Vivien Leigh was absurd. She was supposed to be an outwardly ordinary but secretly highly-sexed woman who meets a young pilot on the golf course and falls for him. My first lines on meeting her were to say: 'My God, Hes, you're beautiful.' She had never been told this before – and understandably it had a remarkable effect on her. But when the part is played by a woman generally held to be one of the most beautiful in the world, the whole meaning is lost.

I told Korda this, but he simply shrugged.

'Never mind, Kenny. The public like to see a beautiful woman. Anyway, what is beauty?' So I lost my argument.

Terence Rattigan, whom I admired tremendously, was a weak man when it came to an argument. He assured Korda that everything would be all right and that the film would work. The director, like Korda, was a Hungarian, Anatole Litvak. A few years earlier, while planning *The Snake Pit* in Hollywood, about madness, Tola Litvak had spent three months in an asylum. His enemies were never quite sure whether this was at his own choice to gain background, or at the wish of others.

I did not greatly take to Tola, and he reciprocated accordingly. He and Terence Rattigan had spent months in Paris working on the screenplay, and because the film was going to be the first British picture made in Cinemascope, which demands action of a wide scale, they had written in extra sequences involving the Farnborough Air Display, ski-ing in Switzerland, and all manner of other things. When my copy was delivered to me, I read it at a sitting. While I had been delighted to read the original stage play, this was something totally different. I felt very disappointed.

Over the months I had played Freddie on the stage, I had come to know the characters as real people, not just shadows from an author's imagination. But now in this script they had lost reality and were simply shadows. I told Korda of my doubts.

'You are totally mistaken. Of *course* they are people. Terry wrote the play and now he has written the script with Tola Litvak, who is the best director in the world for this sort of thing.'

I therefore read the script for a second time to see whether in the light of this I had been mistaken.

A second reading merely confirmed my first opinion. The next morning, I was due to attend a pre-shooting conference with the rest of the cast and the director. Korda was away on some other business, so I confided my doubts to Vivien Leigh.

'If that's what you feel about it, Kenny,' she said. 'You must tell Tola before we start work. Better to let him know how you feel now, than half way through.'

So when my chance came at the meeting to give our views, I gave mine. When I remember now that only a few years earlier I had been on my knees praying to the Almighty for a sign by which I would either continue my acting career or return to the Navy, I am amazed at my temerity. I heard myself speak as though someone else was saying the words.

'Gentlemen,' I said. 'We simply can't start this film.'

'What do you mean, we can't start the film?' asked Litvak in amazement.

'Because the script is no good.'

'No good? The script? What do you mean, Kenny?'

'I mean what I say, Tola. There is too much of you in it and not enough of Terry.'

Litvak stared at everyone in the cast in turn, his mouth opening and shutting, looking, as I recall, remarkably like Kermit the Frog.

'Now, now, Kenny,' said Rattigan soothingly. 'You can't say that.'

But I had said that, and not content with saying that, I added some more.

'If you want to know what I *really* think,' I continued – as though anyone did – 'I'd say, that all Rattigan has come out and all Litvak has gone in.'

'No, *no*,' said Terry protestingly. 'We worked together. We are in entire agreement that it should be done this way.'

'Well,' I said. 'You asked me for my opinion, and that is how I feel. What are you going to do about it?'

No one answered this question. Other members of the cast looked at each other carefully and cautiously but not at me, wondering whether I had taken leave of my senses. The production team, used to temperamental actors, were non-committal, and the meeting ended in a matter of minutes.

Next morning, Korda's office rang me; Sir Alexander wanted to see me immediately. As I knocked on the door of his office, I heard his voice inside shout angrily, 'Come in,' and I knew that this was not going to be the usual sort of friendly discussion I had so far enjoyed with him. I came into his room feeling like a small boy sent for by the headmaster.

'Sit down,' Korda ordered rather than asked. I sat down. He stood up, lit a cigar, and began to walk up and down the room.

'You stupid young idiot,' he began. 'I've spent all this money on you, thousands and thousands of pounds, and months of time and effort to build you into an international star. And what do you do? You insult Litvak, who I consider one of the greatest living film directors.

'You read a script in an evening, and although you've never written a line in your life, you say it's rubbish. You upset the rest of the cast and the whole production team, and you know nothing, nothing, *nothing* at all about it.'

He walked up and down, dealing with other aspects of my temerity, which he clearly took as a personal affront, an intended and deliberate insult. I sat miserably in my chair, watching him walk, listening to his tirade. Finally, he stopped and turned to me.

'Well?' he said. 'What have you to say for yourself?'

'Nothing at all, sir,' I said contritely. 'Only that I am very sorry indeed for the trouble I have caused.'

Korda had not expected this response. He looked at me cautiously, as though suspecting I was not treating the matter with sufficient seriousness.

'I have listened to everything you say, and you are right and I am wrong. I promise you, you won't hear anything more about my views on the script. From now on I'll work with Tola heart and soul.'

'Ah!' said Korda. A smile lit his face.'That's very different, Kenny, dear boy. Have a cigar.'

So he gave me a nine inch Havana which I lit and endeavoured to enjoy.

Vivien Leigh knew I did not think she was right for the part, and so I made an enemy of her from the beginning, which was very foolish of me because I admired her tremendously. And whatever I thought, I still had to act with her. Now, actors working together are either in complete accord or they are not in accord at all. We were never in complete accord. I thought her interpretation was wrong, and so when we played a scene together we had the wrong chemistry between us.

Vivien was a strange woman, never unpleasant and always beautiful, but with the personality of a man. She told funny, risqué stories as a man would tell them. Her personality was like her looks – overpowering. When she walked into a room the whole room would light up.

She was married then to Laurence Olivier, who in my opinion – and in the opinion of most others in my profession – is quite simply the greatest actor in the world. Off-stage, her personality completely smothered his. But then, Vivien would have smothered anybody.

One day when we were filming, Larry came down to see her. He was so much in love with her in those days. He gave her a beautiful aquamarine ring on the set. He pressed this into her hand. I thought, what a gift for a girl to have. But she hardly looked at it. She just said, 'Oh, darling, how lovely,' and put it into her handbag.

She was born beautiful and had been spoiled all her life. That was the key to Vivien. I said as much in a book Alan Dent edited after her death. Dent, the film critic, had written the screenplay for Laurence Olivier's film, *Henry V*. He asked whether I would contribute something to this book he was producing in memory of Vivien Leigh.

'Do you want it sweet or sour? True, or sugar-icing?' I asked him bluntly.

'I want the truth, of course, Kenny.'

'Then I'll give you the truth.'

And I gave my opinion. I thought she was brilliant, with a lovely personality, but not the world's greatest actress. When the book was published this was the only critical viewpoint. I had letters from people all over the country asking me how I dared write such things about such a brilliant actress; I should not criticise the dead, who could not speak for themselves, and so on.

But to return to the film of *The Deep Blue Sea*. Despite what Korda said, I still felt the script was wrong. Expanding the story had destroyed the essential intensity of a drama between three people. And when the film was shown, the critics agreed with me.

Bill and I crossed to New York in the *Queen Mary* for the American première. Every night we had a cable from Alex Korda giving us his news of plans for promoting the film. He had instructed the chief steward to serve us with champagne. He ordered flowers for us every day by radio telephone, and when we arrived in our hotel suite, the rooms were full of flowers. He believed in looking after people who worked for him. He spent a fortune, often of other people's money. I adored him.

After this, Bill and I took a brief holiday in the South of France. We rented rooms in a *pension* and spent most of our time swimming or lazing on the beach. One of several books I took with me was *Reach for the Sky*, Paul Brickhill's biography of Douglas Bader. I was immediately impressed by its possibilities for a film. Bader was a man who never gave up, who adamantly refused to be beaten. He was an athlete of renown, due to play rugby for England, and then he broke his legs in a stupid foolhardy dare, flying a plane too low. Both legs had to be amputated above the knees.

He learned to walk with tin legs and refused to use a stick. He taught himself to dance on tin legs; he even flew again – and became one of the great pilots of the second world war. He was shot down and captured, damaging both his artificial legs. When the Germans sportingly allowed a spare set of tin legs to be dropped by parachute, Bader immediately and impudently used them to try to escape.

Here was a story of humour, pathos and that most rare and rewarding of all human virtues, personal courage. The book moved me so deeply that I was convinced I was the only actor who could play this part properly. This sounds very boastful now, but I believed it. Most parts that can be played by one actor can equally well be played by another; but not this. Bader's philosophy was my philosophy. His whole attitude to life was mine. I wanted this part, not just because I felt I could do full justice to it, but because it was an embodiment of my own belief that courage, faith and determination can overcome all obstacles. But at that particular moment I had to admit I could not quite see how these qualities could overcome one seemingly unsurmountable obstacle: the part had already been promised to Richard Burton.

Very few other British people were staying in our *pension*, but among the few was an RAF wing-commander and his wife. We all nodded to each other when we came in for meals, in the careful, cautious way the British adopt abroad, when they do not want to get involved with their compatriots. I knew he had recognised me, and I was grateful he did not come up, anxious to make conversation, with queries about parts I played and what I really thought of this or that star, and so on.

But towards the end of the holiday, when I was bathing alone, he did come over to speak to me.

'I hope you don't mind me introducing myself,' he began. 'But my wife and I have just finished reading *Reach for the Sky*. We both know Douglas Bader, and I have been watching you closely for some days, and thought I should tell you that if any film is made, we feel you should play the part.'

As soon as I read the book, I telephoned Harry Dubens and said how interested I was. Harry contacted Danny Angel, who had bought the film rights, and was told that Richard Burton was first choice. Danny was the son of Morris Angel, a well known theatrical costumier in London. He had a peculiarly personal interest in this film because while serving in the army in India during the war, he had contracted polio and lost the use of his own legs. Like Bader, Danny refused to accept the limitations on his life that this disability could have caused him, and branched out from the family business to make a number of successful films. When he was invalided out of the army his total assets were a gratuity of £125. He rented an office for two pounds a week in Regent Street, managed to borrow £2,000, and made a documentary, *All the King's Horses*. He invested the proceeds from this in another picture, and with Lewis Gilbert as the director had recently made a successful war subject, *The Sea Shall Not Have Them*.

Danny's faith in *Reach for the Sky* was such that he paid £15,000 for the rights without even reading the book, because he was convinced that the story of one man overcoming what seemed insuperable odds would have universal appeal.

When I returned to London, I was in a club one day with a friend and told him how much I wanted this part. Someone else, whom I did not even know, overheard me. He happened to be a close friend of Danny Angel, and immediately telephoned him, because my obvious sincerity had impressed him. When Danny went home from his office that night he mentioned me to his wife. Now, by one of those curious chances that happen in real life, and which cannot be countenanced in fiction, Danny's wife was Betty Van Damm, with whom I had been friendly so many years before when her father, Vivian, had given me my first job in the theatre. She put in a good word for me. I was in Harry Dubens' office a few days later and the telephone rang. Harry picked it up and held his hand over the mouthpiece as he whispered to me, 'It's Danny Angel.'

I knew instinctively that my luck was in, and indeed it was. I don't know why Burton dropped out, but his decision or somebody else's was my incredible good fortune, for the part was mine.

Danny and Harry worked out a deal together. I was to receive a flat fee of £25,000, the highest I had ever been paid.

Alexander Korda released me from my contract to play the part, but with grave misgivings.

'This is hopeless, Kenny. You are a young man with legs, and you want to play a man with no legs. Why? It just won't do.'

Laurence Olivier held similar views.

'How can you *hope* to play a legless man convincingly?' he asked.

Ignoring these opinions, I resolved to meet Bader. He invited me to play golf at Gleneagles. I didn't know whether he would accept me, because it must be difficult for anybody to meet a stranger who is about to impersonate him before an enormous worldwide audience. I also felt embarrassed about playing golf with a legless man. I needn't have worried. Bader had a handicap of six, while mine was fifteen. He beat me hands down. We played two rounds on the Queen's Course, and he licked me five and six, without a single false shot. It was a warm day, and I was glad when we finished the second round, but Bader appeared as fresh as when we started.

He was most anxious there shouldn't be what he called any 'clangers' over technical details. His last words to me as I left to return to London were: 'Good Luck, Ken. I know you can do a good job. What I worry about are the other people in the film business. I don't trust them an inch.'

On the train south, I practised walking along the corridor, locking my knees to try to reproduce Bader's walk. But I knew the movements were not quite right. I visited Roehampton, where they specialised in rehabilitating limbless patients. The

169

experts there devised a contraption of steel plates and straps to lock the joints in my feet and hold my knees rigid. This gave me a rolling gait like an old-time sailor, but I still felt I was an actor playing a legless man. I did not really know how a legless man felt, so I asked Danny for his advice.

'You've got to remember,' he explained, 'that there is no *pain* in your legs. You haven't *got* any legs. Imagine each time you want to bring your left foot up to your right foot, there is the weight of a million tons pressing down on you. Every step is a production. This shows in a man's eyes. You've got to act the part with your eyes.'

And that is what I did.

At the première I was asked to make a personal appearance on the stage before the film began. The thinking behind this was that everyone would be scrambling for their hats and coats when the film ended. But I decided to take the risk and appear after it had been shown. The audience, I was pleased to see, were still in their seats. As I began to speak, they stood up and cheered in a spontaneous tribute to Douglas Bader's courage.

This picture gave all of us associated with it an unexpected bonus: the encouragement it offered people who had lost one leg or both legs through injury or accident. I received hundreds of letters from these people and from their relations, explaining how at first the loss had seemed insuperable. But Bader's example was of immense help in regaining their faith and confidence. Bader to them was like the hero in the ballad of Chevy Chase, who 'when his legs were smitten off, he fought upon his stumps'. Bader gave them courage to fight on, and never to accept defeat by disability.

As a result of *Reach for the Sky*, Danny Angel and Harry Dubens worked out a deal whereby my services as an actor were available to the Rank Organisation and 20th Century-Fox at the rate of two films a year. This meant that for the first time in my life I was financially independent. I also had the choice of scripts and the right to choose my co-stars. At last it seemed that all the years of professional frustration and worry were behind me.

How misplaced such optimism proved, and how this agreement was to have a calamitous and totally unimagined effect on my career was brought home to me very soon. However, at the time I signed it, my future could hardly have seemed more rosy.

My next film, *The Admirable Crichton*, made after Korda's death, received bad notices. But by the time they appeared I was in America, publicising *Reach for the Sky*, and then I received a visit from Roy Baker, the film director, who had flown out from Pinewood to see if I would play Franz von Werra in the film of *The One That Got Away*. This was a story by Kendal Burt and James Leasor about the only German prisoner in the second world war who succeeded in escaping from a British prisoner-of-war camp and returning to Germany. I did not feel I could possibly accept the part, because I had just played Bader. Roy accepted this and then explained that Pinewood had also bought the rights in the book, *A Night to Remember*, a reconstruction of the *Titanic* disaster, which he planned to direct after the German film. Would I be interested in this? Indeed, yes.

The sinking of a so-called unsinkable liner; third-class passengers staying below while first-class passengers had access to the boats; the band playing as the ship went down; engineers trapped beneath the surface of the sea, calmly preparing to die because there was no escape from the engine room . . . all this intrigued me. So did the blows of chance. There was the telegraph message that was never received – and the knowledge that if only the *Titanic* had gone forwards instead of backwards when she hit the iceberg, passengers and crew could have sheltered safely all night on the floe and been picked up next morning. Then why did the captain of the *Birma*, a Russian steamer, take a roundabout course to the scene, when he could have come directly and saved so many of those who perished?

All the coincidences of life which have fascinated me from boyhood were here incapsuled in one story.

Although the *Titanic* would obviously be the star, I felt a part of this ship, and agreed to play the part of Second Officer Charles Lightoller. Again, people thought I was mad. This would be the fourth *Titanic* film, including one that Hitler had ordered to be made in 1941 for propaganda purposes.

The producer was Bill MacQuitty, who had a belief in numerology. He felt that five was his lucky number: the film would be the fifth he had made: so it was certain to be successful.

When I asked him for further proof he said that, for a start, being a film producer was his fifth career. He had worked in a bank in China, in an office in London, then had been a soldier in India and a farmer in Ireland before he landed up at Pinewood. He had been born on the 5th month of 1905 at No. 5, St. John's Avenue, Belfast. He was married on the 15th. His wife was born on the 15th of the month, and so were his son and two daughters.

'I'll tell you another thing,' he said. 'I once rode in a horse race in Lahore. I was drawn fifth in the fifth race, and I put everything I had on the horse.'

'And did you win?' I asked.

Bill shook his head.

'I came in fifth,' he admitted.

Part of the *Titanic* was built in a field near Pinewood Studios. This section was 300 feet long, about half the size of a real ship. Cranes lifted funnels, ventilators and deck rails, until the superstructure was forty feet high. To bear the weight of this landlocked vessel, four acres of concrete had to be laid as a base. This section was so large that it called for one-and-a-half tons of paint and two tons of nails and screws.

Because the real *Titanic* ran into an iceberg, in the middle of the night, we worked at night and in bitter weather, so that our breath would show. The decks were so slippery with frost that we had to scatter sand on them to prevent ourselves slipping head first on to the concrete below.

A curious phenomenon by day was the attraction this vessel in the middle of the countryside had for seagulls. There are always some seagulls inland in the home counties, probably coming off the Thames. The sight of this ship, funnels, masts and all, must have made them feel they were still at sea. Flocks of them wheeled above us every day.

We had no tank at Pinewood large enough to show survivors in the sea trying to climb on lifeboats, so these shots were to be taken at Ruislip Lido. This is a pleasant enough stretch of water in the summer, but the view from the shore, at two o'clock in the morning in mid-November, of a chill infinity of dark icy water presented a totally different aspect. We stood miserably on the bank while lifeboats were pushed out.

'Right!' cried Bill. 'Everybody ready? In you jump.'

Not a man or woman moved. We stood, fully clothed, and still feeling the cold. What it would be like in the lido was beyond imagination. The water lapped at our feet. The nearest lifeboat bobbed thirty yards away under the lights.

'Come on!' shouted Bill anxiously. 'We haven't got all night.'

I thought I'd jump when the man next to me went. He looked to his left, where a woman in a fur coat was standing.

'She's waiting for the extras to go,' someone else explained. None of us fancied the prospect of being chilled in this murky water.

'Hurry up,' said Bill.

'Why don't *you* bloody well jump in then?' asked someone from the safety of the dark.

'That's not my job,' retorted Bill. I could see worry on his face. A long delay would cost him a fortune in overtime and other costs. If someone didn't give a lead, no one would jump and the whole night would be a total waste. Worse, we would only have to come back and do it on the following night. I swallowed. It had to be me.

'Come on!' I shouted with a bravado I did not feel. 'Last one in's a cissy!'

I leaped. Never have I experienced such cold in all my life. It was like jumping into a deep freeze. The shock forced the breath out of my body. My heart seemed to stop beating. I felt crushed, unable to think. I had *rigor mortis*, without the *mortis*. And then I surfaced, spat out the dirty water and, gasping for breath, found my voice.

'Stop!' I shouted. 'Don't listen to me! It's bloody awful! Stay where you are!'

But it was too late. The rest were in, swimming around me, shouting and cursing with the agony of coldness. We struck out for the boats as though we really were shipwrecked, struggling and kicking anyone who got in our way. We weren't acting. We were desperate to be rescued. There were eight lifeboats, which would carry about sixty-four each. This meant that more than 500 men and women in overcoats and fur coats, were threshing about in the lido for quite a long time before they could all haul themselves aboard the boats.

Bill MacQuitty had brought along a caravan fitted with machines that blew out a hot blast of air. These dried our clothes on us within seconds. Then we stood ready to jump in for a second time for further takes.

After my experience on the stage at Byker I never drank alcohol when working, but Bill had brought along a bottle of rum and now I took a tot after each take for medicinal purposes. Without it, I think I would have perished. I was so cold that I found I could drink half a tumbler of neat rum without its having any effect on me whatever.

Finally, the film was finished, and we all felt that this was something of which we could be proud: this time I was sure I had made the right choice.

My next film was *North West Frontier*, in which I took the part of a British Army captain in India at the turn of the century who fell in love with the governess of a young prince whose state was threatened by rebels.

Lauren Bacall came over from New York to play the governess. We met in London and Betty Bacall and my wife Bill struck up an immediate rapport. Having a keen eye for the girls I thought that if she grew too friendly with my wife, then I wouldn't have too much chance of any 'how's your father' in India, which would be most agreeable after hours of filming in the sun.

I had then been married for several years and had been a faithful husband. But faithfulness in marriage – for a man at least – is like a hand-made silk shirt; it can wear thin, and I certainly took a shine to Betty, and hoped she did to me. We had our costume fittings, and after doing several scenes in the studio, we flew out to India. Bill stayed at home, and I must say, ungallant as it may sound now, this arrangement suited my book. I thought, now Betty and I are on our own, and I indulged in all manner of romantic fantasies, as men in their forties and fifties are prone to do.

One of the scenes involved the use of an old-fashioned train in Jaipur. The Maharajah's former palace had been turned into a hotel, and we drove out every day to the Sind desert. The temperature was 120 degrees in the shade, if you could find any shade. The crew dropped like flies with dysentery and fever and malaria and goodness knows what else.

In those days I had a stand-in, and my stand-in, Jack Mandeville, was one of the first to fall. His job was to 'stand in' the position where I would stand while lights and camera and microphone were set up correctly. Then he would leave and I would take over. Now I found myself waiting on him instead of him waiting on me!

All in all, the trip was a great adventure, and half way through came an unexpected three-day break. I told Lee Thompson, the director, that Betty and I would like to see the Taj Mahal. He agreed and we flew down to Agra.

I always remember that first evening, as we walked through the formal gardens past the long ornamental pools of the Taj Mahal, the monument a Mogul emperor raised in memory of his wife, the only woman he had truly loved. It is one of the most beautiful settings in all the world, literally a temple of love. Fireflies the size of grapes fluttered all about us as we walked by the light of the full moon. There was a sound of distant music from some village. The night was warm and made for you-know-what.

Betty and I strolled hand in hand along the marble approach-way to the Taj Mahal, and finally I felt moved to speak.

'You know something, Betty, love,' I said. 'This is the most romantic setting I have ever seen in all my life, you're one of the most desirable women in the world, but – I don't know how it is – I just don't *feel* romantic.'

'Neither do I,' she said. 'Isn't it *awful*?'

'Terrible,' I agreed. 'Here we are, walking hand in hand, and the thoughts of both of us are elsewhere. I'm thinking about food, and you've probably got something else on your mind.'

'That's life,' she said.

Too true, I thought, and why does it have to be mine? But there it was. We went back to our respective bedrooms and nothing happened at all. Whenever I meet Betty now, she always calls me 'My gallant captain,' which is better, I suppose, than saying, 'My romantic captain.'

Our producer was Marcel Hellman, a veteran film maker, whom I love dearly. But in this film he developed or increased an unfortunate habit. He would take out his watch, look at it and then at the director and the actors in a pointed manner. It was his way of saying: Get on with it.

Every moment wasted in making a film on location costs an enormous amount of money, in fees for technicians as well as for the cast. And when, in his view, things were going a bit slowly, Marcel would stand behind the camera, take out his watch, and shake his head. This used to worry me, but not so much as it annoyed Lee Thompson.

One day we had been filming since sun-up in the heat of the Sind desert, and finally finished a big scene where the rebels had tried to attack a fort. There had been a lot of watch-watching by Marcel Hellman that day. The cameras kept turning in the last rays of the sun because Marcel was anxious to get as many shots as he could in the can and so avoid another day's filming there. Everyone was tired and edgy: the prospect of a bath and an iced beer seemed infinitely attractive.

At last the sun was too far down the sky for any more work. We climbed thankfully in our cars to drive twenty miles over the dusty desert plain to our hotel. Lee and I were already in the back of the car when we saw Marcel running towards us, unfortunately for him with his watch in his hand.

Lee had taken a lot of watch-pulling that day and this was too much. As Marcel pushed his head through the car window to speak to Lee, Lee deliberately wound up the glass. Marcel's head was trapped between the window and the top of the car.

Lee tapped the driver on the shoulder.

'Drive on,' he ordered, and poor Marcel had to do a side-step for about ten yards by the side of the car. They weren't on speaking terms that night. All ambassadors were withdrawn, but the next day, of course, things got better again. They had to. We all had to carry on working together.

The film was a great success. I seemed now to be the golden

boy or the middle-aged man who could do no wrong. Offers poured in. I was wanted in this play, that film, the other TV series. One paper even carried a headline 'MORE magnificent'.

I was riding on the crest of the wave. But soon that wave would break.

11

Two of my closest friends throughout the 1950s were Jack Hawkins and Trevor Howard. Trevor was married to Helen Cherry, and Jack to Doreen.

We were all asked by Otto Preminger to attend the première of his film *St. Joan* at the Paris Opera House, which he had taken over especially for this occasion. He invited us to stay in Paris at his expense, and so we put on our white ties and war medals for this première, and our wives bought new dresses for the visit.

It was an evening of some social significance. The President of France was there; so were Jean Seberg and Richard Widmark, the stars, and goodness knows how many other men and women of fame and renown in their different professions. As representatives of the British film community, the six of us had a box to ourselves.

Now this box was of curious construction, long and narrow, with the door at one end and the opening on to the theatre at the other. The seats were arranged in rows, rather like a tube train, so that only two or three people could sit at the front and watch the show, while the rest sat in this tunnel. We arranged things so that our wives sat at the front in their finery and we men sat at the back. It was so dark that our wives couldn't even see us. They were up front, all dressed up, eyes on the screen.

As actors, we did not hold the highest opinion of this film and in a very few minutes we decided that the agonies of Joan of Arc on screen were as nothing to the agonies of watching the film from the audience.

I said to Jack Hawkins, 'Let's slip out across the square and have a few drinks at the Café de L'Opéra. No one will even know we've gone.'

Jack was a bit anxious about this and frowned at the idea. The film droned on without improvement. As an entertainment it was a disaster.

Finally, Trevor agreed with me.

'I can't stand this any longer,' he said. 'Let's get out of it.'

So we all tiptoed out, closed the door of the box very quietly behind us, crept down the stairs and crossed the road to the café. Here we ordered large whiskies and sodas and sat in the open air, very pleased with ourselves at our escape. Our wives wouldn't even know we had gone, and were, apparently enjoying the spectacle on the screen.

We ordered a third round and noticed an Englishman walk past us. Then he paused and did a double take. After all, we must have looked odd, three men in white ties and tails and decorations, sipping whisky in a pavement café. He turned towards us.

'Hullo! Hullo!' he said. 'Who have we here?'

He knew damned well who he had here, because he then went through our names: Mr. Howard, Mr. Hawkins and Mr. More.

'Aren't you guests at the première?' he asked.

We began to hum and haw and look at each other in an awkward way. Finally, Trevor asked him: 'Why are you interested in the fact that we are not in the Opera House?'

'It is a professional interest, gentlemen. I am a reporter from the *Daily Mail*.'

'What?'

'Yes. I am doing a story over here. I understood you were the guests of honour. So why are you not in your places, instead of drinking whisky out here?'

For a moment none of us could think of an acceptable explanation. Then Trevor and Jack exchanged glances and one said in a conspiratorial way:

'The fact is, old man, Kenny fainted, and we had to carry him out.'

'Thank you very much,' I said. With friends like these, who needed enemies?

I turned to the reporter.

'Give us a break,' I asked him. 'The film was as boring as hell, so we just slipped out for a quick one.'

The reporter assured us of his best intentions, but next morning the paper printed the news that the three of us had skipped Otto Preminger's latest film. Preminger was livid. He said he would never employ us again. Since he had never employed us before, this did not worry us unduly.

We had crept back into the box without our wives even knowing. When they saw the paper next day, they said, 'That's *impossible*. Why, you were in the box right behind us.'

We shrugged our shoulders.

'Well, you know how it is with newspapers.'

Now to a more serious matter – the death of a friend. One

morning on the set of *The Thirty-Nine Steps*, which I was making for Betty Box and Ralph Thomas, Ralph, who was directing the picture, took me on one side.

'I have some bad news for you, Kenny,' he said. 'Harry Dubens died this morning.'

I was heartbroken. Apparently, he had hailed a taxi in Regent Street, and as he sat down inside, had suffered a fatal heart attack. Here was one man who had always expressed his faith in me, right from my first meeting when I went to see him in 1946, still wearing my naval uniform. He had guided me well and loyally through all kinds of disappointments and achievements. And whenever I sought advice, no matter at what hour of the day or night, he would always give his wise counsel.

I then took as my agent, Laurence Evans, with whom I soon developed a close and friendly relationship.

One day, John Brabourne rang me up.

'Kenny,' he said. 'Lewis Gilbert is going to direct a film for me called *Sink the Bismarck*. We would both like you to play the lead, Captain Shepherd.'

Now Captain Shepherd had fought that battle without going to sea. He had controlled it from the underground Operations Room beneath the Admiralty in London. I was delighted to have this chance to portray a naval commander who, probably for the first time in history, had directed a major sea action by radio and other electronic means thousands of miles from the ships concerned. I accepted immediately. 'I don't want any naval advisers,' I told John. 'The Navy has been my life. I will be my own naval adviser.' Even so, John Brabourne's father-in-law, Admiral of the Fleet Earl Mountbatten of Burma, gave us the benefit of his immense knowledge and experience throughout the making of this film.

An exact duplicate of the Operations Room was built in Pinewood Studios, and we began work. During the war, *Aurora*, in which I served, became the flag ship of the 12th Cruiser Squadron under Rear Admiral Sir Cecil Harcourt, who had earlier played an important part in the search for *Bismarck*. He was retired and living in London and I thought it would be a nice gesture to ask him, as my old admiral, to come and see the filming. This was arranged and we laid on a bit of a show for him. Before I moved a ship on the operations board, I would ask him, 'Is that all right, sir? is that correct?'

He was delighted. As he left, he shook us all by the hand.

'This has made my day, More,' he said.

A few days later, his wife wrote to tell me that the Admiral had died. He had driven home and as he turned off the ignition in his car, his heart turned off too, and he died at the wheel. I like to think that his last memory of the Navy he served so well was with us.

My next film was *Greengage Summer*, adapted from Rumer Godden's beautiful novel.

Bill and I were again on holiday in the South of France where we had bought a flat in Monte Carlo, when I was called to the telephone. Lewis Gilbert was on the line.

'Kenny,' he asked me. 'Can you lose some weight?'

'What do you mean? I'm pretty slim.'

'In your body, yes,' he agreed. 'But not your face. You have always had a face like a full moon. Can you lose some weight from your face?'

'What the hell do you mean? I've been a film star with a full moon face for years.'

'But you've never played a romantic part before, with young love. You need a slim face for that. Am I making myself clear?'

'You'd better ask Dirk Bogarde or Donald Sinden for romantic stuff. Not me.'

'I'm not asking them, Ken. I *am* asking you. We want you to play opposite Susannah York in *Greengage Summer*.' There was only one part I could play; the gentleman crook with whom Susannah York, as a very young girl, falls in love.

'That's right,' agreed Lewis. 'But he is supposed to be romantic. So it would be better if she fell in love with someone who hadn't a face like a full moon. Do you follow me?'

'All the way. I'll see what I can do.'

So I went on a diet, for this was a film I dearly wanted to make. I cut out patisseries, cream sauces and chocolate mousses, and the delicious croissants and honey and coffee and cream the French serve for breakfast. I must have lost ounces off my face, because when I reported back to England they decided my face was thin enough.

Susannah York had only played in one film before – *Tunes of Glory*, with Alec Guinness. She was just twenty-one and an adorable creature. The part of her younger sister was taken by Jane Asher who seemed like a child, just in her teens.

We made this film around Epernay, in the champagne district of France, and it was one of the happiest films on which I have ever worked. There wasn't a nasty word spoken between any of us and much of the credit for this belongs to Gilbert. He is a very simple person with no side or pretence, and a great technician. He is also extremely efficient, and so extracts efficiency from others. This is not a gift in the possession of all directors.

Bill and I returned to London, and the future seemed set fair to magnificent, because here was Carl Foreman offering me my greatest chance so far – a part specially tailored for me in *The Guns of Navarone*. I had met Foreman many times during my years in films. He lived in London, having left Hollywood after the McCarthy witch hunt in the United States. As a producer who also writes screen plays he had written this new script with me in mind as the sergeant in the team that undertakes to destroy these guns.

'Who else is in it?' I asked him.

'Anthony Quinn. Gregory Peck. Lee Thompson is directing. Columbia will put up the money. We'll have full American distribution, of course.'

'Carl,' I replied. 'Say no more. I'm on.'

This film would consolidate all my years of work. With a story and a team like this, it could not be less than an international blockbuster.

I felt an extraordinary feeling of peace, laced with relief, as I had often enough experienced during the war when *Aurora* was sailing into a safe harbour after a rough passage. I had been poor before; after this film I would never be poor again. This was quite simply the chance of my lifetime, for to succeed in America meant international success. Although I was a major star in Britain all through the 1950s, I was not so well known in the United States. This was because the films in which I appeared were made in Britain, largely with British capital. Many British films were successful in the United States in an artistic sense, but only a few in a commercial way, which was where success really mattered.

When *Reach for the Sky* was acclaimed in Britain, John Davis, the chairman of Rank, sent me over to the States in the *Queen Mary* with an unlimited budget to advertise and promote it. He hired the Sutton Theatre in New York to present his film, but the Americans did not want to know about British war heroes. At the time Bader was flying a plane over Germany without legs, the United States was not even involved in the war.

I went on every radio show I could find. I gave Press conferences, lunches, dinners, from East to the West Coast, to promote the film. We received good coverage, but not good distribution.

The same thing happened with *A Night to Remember*. Critics praised it, but because it had been made in Britain, with British capital, that was sufficient to damn it. *Sink the Bismarck* made a

181

considerable profit in the United States, largely because American money was behind it.

So Carl Foreman's offer was the chance for which I had been waiting since I first appeared in *School for Secrets*. Every creative artist needs his big chance. This I knew, instinctively, was mine.

Films were still very big business, but television was already beginning to make discernible inroads into cinema audiences and its influence was steadily increasing. A film had to be very good, or on an epic scale, to make a large profit. In an effort at self-protection, British film production companies had each paid a sum of money into a kitty. The purpose of this was to buy up British films to prevent them from being sold to television companies. They wanted to stop this because they rightly feared that if people could see films on TV in their own homes, they would not go out and pay money to see them in their local cinema. Film producers in this country therefore agreed that if a TV company made an offer for any of these old films, they were honour-bound to offer them first to this consortium for whatever fee the TV company had offered.

I knew nothing about this, and there was no reason why I should. I was an actor. What arrangement the producers came to among themselves did not affect me. In fact, this agreement, then totally unknown to me, was to change my whole life.

Carl Foreman went to see John Davis, who agreed to my making *The Guns of Navarone*, and they settled on a figure for my services. I was fitted for my costumes, and a seat was booked for me on a plane to Greece, where the unit would be on location. I felt tremendously excited.

A few days before I was due to leave, after the distribution of the British Film Academy Awards, the film companies held a big dinner and dance at the Dorchester. Bill and I sat at the top table with John Davis and all around sat other leading film stars and producers. We were having a thoroughly enjoyable evening.

I was so excited at the prospect before me that I drank far too much. In the warmth of the room, surrounded by people I had known and worked with for years, I relaxed to such an extent that I behaved very badly. John Davis stood up to make a speech and I heckled him continually. Bill tried to restrain me – so I heckled even more. Whatever Davis said, I capped with a remark that seemed witty and indeed aroused laughter from the hundreds of people in the ballroom. But in my fuddled state I did not fully appreciate the danger of what I was doing. I was unknowingly and unintentionally humiliating the head of the company which for years had employed me, before an audience of his employees and rivals. I thought the audience were laughing with me; I did not imagine they might possibly be laughing at me.

Finally, John Davis, who had seemed to take my behaviour in good part, finished his speech and sat down. There was a silence at our table. Then a woman half way down it, turned to me.

'What are you going to do next, Kenny?' she asked me brightly.

'I'm very excited,' I told her. 'I'm going to play in *The Guns of Navarone* for Carl Foreman. Next week I'm off to Greece.'

Suddenly, like a man in a dream hearing someone speak beyond the frontiers of sleep, I heard John Davis say quietly: 'Oh, no, you're not.'

I looked at him, thinking he must be joking. But I had been the joker; John's face was serious.

'What do you mean?' I asked him. 'Carl's seen you, and you've agreed.'

'I have changed my mind,' he said. 'If you think I'm going to have anything to do with Danny Angel, you're mistaken.'

I sat for a moment, lost for words. What could he mean?

'What's Danny done?' I said.

'Haven't you heard?'

Davis explained that Danny Angel, for reasons of his own, had either sold, or was contemplating the sale, of a number of his old films direct to TV without apparently giving this consortium the chance to buy them.

'What about it?' I asked. 'That's nothing to do with me.'

I did not know why Davis took such a serious view of this.

'He's broken the code,' Davis explained. 'And you have a contract with him, haven't you?'

He then explained about the agreement between the film producers.

'But I assure you, John, this has nothing whatever to do with me. You can't take this out on me.'

'I am not doing so, Ken. I'm just saying that we as a company are not hiring you out to Carl Foreman for his picture. And that's final.'

As Davis spoke, I remembered my idiocy in heckling him during his speech. How false the laughter of sycophants sounded now! In my frustration and disappointment and anger at my own behaviour, I committed another unforgivable folly. I lost my temper.

I should have controlled myself, but I was now beyond control. So in front of all John Davis's fellow directors, all his lieutenants, all his rivals in the industry, I called him every name to which I could lay my tongue. I still remember the look of amazement and horror on the faces of everyone. John Davis remained impassive. Finally, I had nothing left to say. I was still high with drink and indignation, and I stood up, took Bill's arm and guided her out between the tables to the door.

Next morning, when I was sober, I realised with horror and disgust what I had done. I telephoned John immediately and apologised profusely, and said I still could not believe he would make me suffer for what he considered was someone else's impropriety.

'I'm afraid that's how it's got to be.'

'Can't we forgive and forget? I apologise for my behaviour.'

'And of course I accept your apology,' he said.

'Well, can I do the film?'

'No,' he said. 'That's off so far as we are concerned.'

I explained the situation to my solicitor, for I had still two films to make for Rank. He proposed a meeting with John Davis and Rank's lawyer. This took place in their main office in Mayfair. John and I shook hands formally, but I felt cold and bitter inside, and my heart was thumping as I told him in front of our lawyers that I felt it was unfair that I should be penalised for something someone else had done which was quite unknown to me.

I can see John Davis's point of view now, and certainly his decision was not made through personal pique. Today we are the best of friends, but not then. By the way, he is now, 'Sir John'.

Our meeting solved nothing and changed nothing. Carl Foreman was told I was not available. The American distributors had agreed I should play the part, even though I was not well known in the United States, but as soon as I dropped out, they pressed strongly for David Niven, who was, of course, a bigger name in the United States.

I was compensated for the films I did not make, but what was important to me was not the money, but the fact that from then on Pinewood Studios were virtually closed to me.

I was still offered plays and TV roles, of course, but films were where my heart lay.

For more than a year, I lived on my past success, and pretended that I had no wish or need to make more films. Every day this pretence became harder to sustain, and I was both glad and relieved when in 1962 I was approached by a producer, James Archibald, who was making a film in Bristol in aid of the Duke of Edinburgh's Award Scheme and the National Playing Fields Association.

This film, *Some People*, was to be a musical, entirely shot on location, and while the rest of the company would be paid their usual fees, he asked me if I would play the lead for nothing, apart from my expenses. No one else had offered me even this much of a deal, and since this was for a good cause, and could conceivably lead to other film work, I accepted.

I was to play a welfare worker, who helped to put on the right path a gang of teenage tearaways in Bristol. In those days, I had a Rolls-Royce which I had bought a year or two earlier, because I thought of this as one of the trappings of a film star. I could either spend the money in tax or on a Rolls, so I chose the Rolls. And because you need a chauffeur when you run a Rolls, I had a chauffeur, too. I also owned an MGB two-seater, and it was in this open car that I drove down to Bristol to meet Archibald and Clive Donner, the director.

We were staying in a hotel on the Avon Gorge and I met all the cast, and noticed among them a very pretty young girl, Angela Douglas. She was a fair-haired, blue-eyed Irish girl and just twenty-one. She had been filming in *Cleopatra* with Richard Burton and Elizabeth Taylor in Rome and had been a member of what they called 'the rep company'. This involved about twenty-five actors and actresses who were each paid a flat £50 a week plus expenses, and had to be ready to play any small part at short notice – if they wanted another gladiator, or a maidservant or slave or whatever. Angela had had a rather hit-and-miss love affair in Rome, and so was still a bit tearful, which intrigued me. Some of the younger members of the cast were rather in awe of me, simply because there is always some glamour attached to the star, but we all got on well together and they soon lost their reservations about me.

After two or three days, I lost some reservations, too, and realised I was falling rather madly for this pretty girl. I'm not someone who can keep his feelings or emotions tightly buttoned down. If I fancy someone, I don't make any untoward move, but I do make it quite clear that I am attracted – and this was the situation then. She reacted to me, but outwardly we still behaved formally to each other.

Events came to a head one night when I was dining with James Archibald and some others at the hotel. Angela came over to our table, carrying a bottle of wine, which she unexpectedly presented to me. I felt that her message was, tonight's the night, and indeed it was. We all went upstairs to our various bedrooms and, quite by accident, Angela and I met along the corridor. I manoeuvred her into my room, and that was the beginning of it all.

185

There were two single beds in my room, both extremely narrow, and between them a telephone on a small bedside table. This telephone had a very short lead and could not be moved out of the way. I went into the bathroom to clean my teeth, and when I came back Angela had ripped the whole telephone right off the wall, thus enabling us to move the table and push the beds together. Only an Irish girl would do that, I thought! So our affair began.

Every Friday evening, while I was filming, I would go home and spend the weekend with Bill and my daughter, and then drive back to Bristol early on Monday morning. We were on location in Bristol for about ten weeks. Sometimes, on my own, I would work out a kind of profit and loss account in my mind. On one side, I had been a star in every film I had made in the 1950s. I had trodden very carefully, and had never been linked in any scandal, which made me all the more vulnerable if news of my affair should now leak out. I had no doubt that the Press and public opinion would crucify me. Here was a man, who had appeared as the true-blue Britisher for years, carrying on with a young girl twenty-six years younger than himself. I was determined that no one would discover this secret. I thought it would be wonderful to keep Angela as a kind of hidden friend in a flat no one knew anything about; a princess in an ivory tower, to which I alone held the key.

One evening, Angela said, 'Kenny, darling, I am an Irish Catholic and very funny about one night stands. I don't like them.'

My heart began to sink. Was this to be the end of our meetings?

'So that we won't just have a succession of one night stands, could we have an affair?' she went on.

'What do you mean? Say that again,' I asked her, unable to believe my ears.

She said it again. This was exactly what I wanted. We decided that in case our relationship like the one in the song, 'One of those things,' was too hot not to cool down, we would not tell Bill about it. It might all explode and end and then we would have hurt her for no reason. I bought Angela a gold shamrock on a gold chain, because St. Patrick's Day, March 17, was the day we first met. From then on, this day would always be our special anniversary.

While making this film, I had a call from Lady Astor, the daughter of Earl Haig, a charming woman who did a great deal of work for charity. Bill and I had been involved with one of her organisations, Sunshine Homes for Blind Babies. Now she invited us both to a private dinner party to meet the Queen, in her town house near Lowndes Square.

She swore me to secrecy, because if news leaked out to the Press that I was to be a guest, the whole point of a private evening would be lost. I explained to James Archibald that I had to go to London for some unexpected business and arranged to take a day away from filming.

When Bill and I arrived at Lady Astor's house, it was clear that the host and hostess were both rather concerned about me because I am an extrovert. They were afraid that after a few drinks I might embarrass them, so they warned me: 'For God's sake, Kenny, remember, if you don't behave tonight you will be in the Tower. And not only you – maybe we'll all be in the Tower.'

This was said jokingly, of course, but I noted the hint of apprehension behind the remark.

The Queen arrived with her lady-in-waiting, and the atmosphere before dinner was rather formal with everyone on edge and each of us waiting for someone else to begin the conversation. I had been presented to the Queen at first nights and at several Royal Film Performances, but this was quite a different thing. She knew who I was, and, of course, I knew who *she* was, but that was about it. After dinner, when I had been able to drink a little, I thought, to hell with this, I can't stifle myself more. I must be who I am. The result was that this turned out to be one of the most delightful evenings I have ever spent in my life.

I knew from others that the Queen could become quiet if she did not like someone, but if she is interested and being entertained, then she can relax completely. She stayed until half past one in the morning, and I sat on the floor swapping stories with her.

Both of us spend a lot of time on our feet in our respective careers, and I wondered whether she had any bunions. She took her shoes off and showed me that she hadn't! It was a marvellous and relaxed evening, but afterwards I knew that my host and hostess breathed a sigh of relief because I could either have gone too far or not far enough. As it happened, I had been as frank and as unembarrassed as I could be, and the result had been successful.

We completed the film in Bristol on schedule, and returned to London where the cast and crew dispersed. I am always sorry on these occasions. A group of strangers have worked closely for three months and become friends. Then they all go their separate ways, and everything starts again. It's a bit like leaving school; all the goodbyes and the promises to keep in touch. I hate goodbyes; I don't die a little over them, I die a lot.

Angela and I decided we would still not say anything to Bill. Angela was living with her mother, father, sister and brother in a flat in Upper Berkeley Street, and I was still with Bill at Kingston House. Angela and I would have secret meetings. I would tell my wife I was going to play golf on a Wednesday or Sunday afternoon, and, of course, I would spend an hour or two with Angela. But this was not a very satisfactory arrangement, and I decided I would have to set her up in a flat. Before I could do so, I had the offer of a film from Danny Angel, who would distribute it through British Lion, the rival to Rank. This was a comedy, *We Joined the Navy*, to be made in Villefranche, near Cannes, with Wendy Toye as the director.

Bill and I stayed in our flat in Monte Carlo. Angela wrote to me several times a week, so I gave her the address of my bank in Nice because I could not very well have her writing letters to me at the flat. I used to go to the bank every morning on my way to the location, collect these letters, read them and then tear them up. It was a life of pretence, which I did not like. I felt lonely and unhappy, living a lie; worse, living with one woman and loving another.

One day, I opened Angela's envelope in the bank and out dropped a carrot. It wasn't the usual sort of carrot, but a strange freak vegetable in the exact shape of a woman's lower torso and legs. The bank clerk looked at me with amused Gallic understanding.

'She must be very beautiful, sir,' he said, 'if she looks like that.'

I told Angela in a letter that if she wanted to break our association then my return to London would give her an ideal opportunity. We had been apart for some months and she had no doubt met other men, and might feel differently towards me. I knew that my feelings for her had not changed and would not change, but I did not want to persuade her against her will to continue a relationship that for her might be already dying.

I told her that I would be at the River Club in London, alone, on a certain evening. A Variety Club Dinner was being held there and I knew she had also been invited. If either of us decided not to continue our association, that person would simply not turn up. But, of course, I was there, and so was she. Nothing had changed. Nothing would change.

Angela now found a flat in a mews off Marylebone High Street. It consisted of a bedroom, sitting room, bathroom, and she needed £1,000 to buy the lease. I went to my bank, drew out the money in cash and gave it to her. Now she had a flat and I still had my home. Her parents, Peter and Marjorie MacDonagh, were understanding, and lovely people.

I was beginning to feel the pinch with regard to film work. There was simply nothing being offered to me. The scripts were not coming in, and I did not know what to do. I could return to the theatre easily enough, and I was offered roles in TV plays, but my aim was to keep my position, so hardly won, as a star in films.

Then an independent American producer, Hal Chester, offered me a film, *The Comedy Man*. I read the script and was profoundly struck by its relevance to my own life, and to the lives of so many actors I had known. It described the experiences of a middle-aged repertory actor who comes to London in a last bid to find the success that has eluded him all his life in the provinces. He has an affair with a young actress, but the fame he dreams of only comes when he makes an advertising commercial for a product that combats bad breath! And what kind of fame is that?

Angela was cast as the young girl, and we started work. The character she played was called 'Shrimp', and this nickname stuck. From then on, my special name for Angela was Shrimp.

My association with Hal Chester was not the happiest of my professional life. He had been a child actor in *Our Gang* and in that tough school had learned lessons he still remembered. He was the money man and cut scenes ruthlessly, regardless whether they were necessary to the story or not. Also, he was not the fastest man in the film business to part with a dollar – and believe me, he had some competition!

All this time, Angela and I were conducting what was now a very hectic affair. She used to drive to and from the studio with me in my Rolls. My chauffeur would drop her off first on the way home and then take me on to Kingston House. He was very discreet and never mentioned this arrangement to anyone. I paid him, as I paid all the rest of the staff, while Bill dealt with the food and the rent of the flat.

When the film was shown, the critics were unsparing in their praise. Elspeth Grant, writing in *The Tatler* on November 2, 1964, declared: 'This is (Kenneth More's) best performance to date, and it is a mystery to me why the film has been kept in cold storage for eighteen months.'

Rank had contracted to distribute the film; they eventually sent it out as a double bill with *Lord of the Flies*.

At this rather unhappy period in my career I realised I could not go on with any further deception. I had to be with Shrimp all the time. I had to marry her, if she would have me. So I told Bill that I had fallen in love with another woman, and reminded her of the agreement we had made when we became engaged, that if either of us should fall in love, the other would allow them their freedom. She understandably denied there had been any such arrangement, and was certain that this was just an infatuation.

I did not agree. I felt about Shrimp as I had never felt about any other woman. I needed her not only physically, but mentally and morally. I enjoyed her company; she made me feel young again. A day without her was like a summer without the sun.

There followed a terrible time for Bill. Looking back, I am ashamed at the way I handled things with her. I should have cleared out immediately and gone away from home and lived with Angela, or lived in a hotel or a flat on my own. But I didn't. Men are like that. They want to have their cake and eat it – and still have some for tomorrow. But I did tell Bill I was in love with another woman. She persisted that it was probably only an infatuation, a sign of the Indian summer of the ductless glands.

Finally, I told her that I would go away on holiday with Angela to find out whether this really was infatuation or something deeper. Bill naturally fought against this plan, but I was adamant. I told her that until I had been alone with Angela, away from the pressures of filming or other work, I could not be absolutely certain we had as much in common as I thought.

'You can't go,' Bill said. 'You mustn't go.'

'But I *must*. If it does work,' I promised, 'then I'll move out of our flat here as soon as I return.'

'And if it doesn't?' she asked.

'Then I'll come home and we'll go on together.'

I decided to go to Cyprus for this holiday because it seemed unlikely we would meet any of my friends there. I booked both of us into the Dome hotel in Kyrenia. We would fly separately, for some of Bill's friends might be at London airport flying somewhere else. I also knew that reporters watched all arrivals and departures, and the last thing I could afford at this delicate stage was a photograph of Angela and me flying off together.

There were two flights every day to Cyprus, one in the early morning, the other after lunch. I arranged that Angela would take the morning plane and I would follow in the afternoon. To cover ourselves even further, we booked on separate airlines.

'I am travelling first-class,' I told Angela. 'And I'll buy a tourist ticket for you.'

'You bastard,' she said.

'Well, you don't *really* mind, do you? I'm a bit of a film star still, and so can't go economy, otherwise I might be pestered a bit. And, anyway, you're always saying how you *like* to save money. So here's a good chance.'

'Of course, *I* don't mind, darling,' she said. 'It's just typical you.'

I arrived at the airport and was very relieved we had taken precautions, for two friends of Bill's were sitting in the lounge, just as I had feared. They were off on holiday somewhere, and immediately waved to me.

'Hello, Ken.'

'Hello, darlings,' I said as naturally as could be. I didn't mind. I was on my own. They had nothing on me. Then suddenly, out of the corner of my eye, I saw a little, blue-eyed Irish girl waving frantically to me from across the lounge. I thought, my God! It *can't* be! She's supposed to have gone hours ago.

My friends saw me look, and one of them asked, in that flat expressionless voice much used by married women when they ask one question but mean another: 'Who's that, Kenny, dear?'

'Who do you mean, darlings?'

'That little girl there. The pretty, blonde one.'

'Oh, *her*. Nobody, I know. Must be a fan who's recognised me!' Inside, my stomach was churning like a mill-race as I made idiotic conversation. Luckily, their plane was soon called, and I could cross over to see Angela.

'I missed my plane,' she explained in a piteous voice.

'But you should have been in Cyprus by now,' I told her. 'And you're not even booked on my plane.'

'I know, I know,' she said. 'I'm such a fool! I'm so excited, I didn't hear my flight called.'

'Well, there's nothing else for it now,' I told her. 'You'll have to come with me. But for goodness sake, let's sit apart. We've only just missed being seen by two friends of Bill's. We don't want the whole world to know we are going away together.'

So Angela had her ticket transferred to my flight, economy class, and I told her that once we were airborne I would arrange for her to come up to the first-class section with me, and pay the extra when we reached Cyprus.

'But keep away from me now, for God's sake, darling. We have only to be seen once together and that's it.'

So Angela went off to the other side of the lounge, and I bought some magazines and sat reading them as I waited impatiently for the flight to be called.

I went through customs first to minimise the risk that we might bump into each other. I took my seat in the first-class section in the front of the plane and when we were over the Channel, I beckoned to the steward.

'Do me a favour,' I asked him. 'Back aft you'll find a pretty Irish girl with blue eyes and blonde hair, about twenty-two. Please ask her to come up here and I'll pay the difference on the flight.'

He disappeared. Moments later, he was back.

'Sorry, Mr. More, but there's no passenger answering to that description on the plane.'

'What?'

I couldn't believe him. I walked right down the aisle to the tail and he was quite right. Angela just wasn't there. So she must have missed that plane as well.

We reached the airport at Nicosia, and sure enough, on the message board a telegram was waiting for me.

TERRIBLY SORRY, DARLING, MISSED THAT PLANE TOO. AREN'T I A SILLY IDIOT? LOVE ANGELA.

I tore the telegram into pieces. I must be mad, I thought. I'm a raving idiot. And this is the person I am leaving home for; the girl I'm wrecking my life for – who misses not one plane, but *two*!

My hotel was approximately fourteen miles away over the hills in Kyrenia, in the north of the island. I hired a car and drove there. Next morning, I drove back to the airport to meet the morning plane. When I arrived I was told it was delayed until late afternoon, so back to the hotel again to wait for the late afternoon flight. Then back to the airport to find that the plane had come in early after all, and Angela had left for the hotel in a taxi. We must have passed each other on the road.

No, I can't believe it, I thought. We are destined not to meet. These are all signposts to stay away. I drove back to the hotel – and found Angela in bed and in tears.

'Never mind, you are here at last,' I said, for now we were together we could laugh about the incident. I was so exhausted with the nervous strain, the waiting and wondering, that I just collapsed into bed and fell asleep.

Minutes later, it seemed to me, someone was shaking my arm.

'Get up, darling,' I heard Angela say, 'the day's started. We must go on the beach.'

I crawled reluctantly out of my cocoon of sleep to look at my watch.

'But it's barely dawn,' I protested.

'I don't care. Can't waste a moment of that wonderful sunshine.'

I groaned. What was I doing? I had left my home for a woman

Left: Best man's privilege: Roger Moore salutes Kenneth More's bride, Angela Douglas, to the groom's mock outrage.

Right: Angela and Kenneth in ATV's 'Father Brown' series.

Left: 'Argyle', his beloved cat, gives Kenneth More a good send-off from Victoria Station en route for Brazil in February 1976.

Below: with friends and fellow-actors John Bennett and Angela Thorne, Kenneth More reads his own choice for the programme *With Great Pleasure*.

who had missed two planes, then missed me at the airport, and now wakes me up at five in the morning! But instead of being annoyed and put out, I felt incredibly and unbelievably delighted. We had a wonderful time sunbathing on deserted beaches, for we were out of the holiday season. There were few guests in the hotel and the only other Britisher was a woman who always ate on her own. We never saw her on the beach.

'I feel sorry for that woman,' I told Shrimp after dinner one evening. 'Let's ask her over for a brandy.'

I asked the waiter if he could invite the lady to join us. She came to our table.

'Good evening, Mr. More.'

Hello, I thought. So she knows who I am. She went on: 'You do know why I am here, don't you?'

'No. I have no idea. I assume you are on holiday and a bit lonely and would like a chat.'

She sat down.

'I am a reporter. My newspaper sent me here to find out what you are up to.'

'Oh, my God!' I cried. 'Please. *Please.* We throw ourselves on your mercy.'

'Mr. More,' she said. 'I promise you I haven't found you.'

She kept her word. We had an idyllic three weeks holiday in Cyprus, and nothing appeared in any newspaper. Our time here decided us that from now on we would live together. There would be no more deception. We flew back together, in the same plane side by side. We were together, for better or worse. There was no point in doing anything in any other way now.

I had wired the Mandeville Hotel in Baker Street from Cyprus for a single room, but they had no room available and foolishly I thought I would go home just for one night to collect my belongings. I could then book into some other hotel and move out.

I had reckoned without Bill.

'This is your home,' she said. 'Why waste money on a hotel?'

So one night became two or three weeks of misery for both of us. Before we were married, she had told me that love would come, and I think possibly she was a little in love with me, and even if she was not I was doing a terrible thing to a middle-aged wife, leaving her for a young girl. She was bitter and jealous as, of course, she had every right to be. When I telephoned Angela, Bill would come into the room and make sarcastic remarks about both of us.

Odd as this may sound, one of my major concerns about

breaking my marriage with Bill had been how I would tell her brother Cyril who was – and is – with his charming wife Pat, a very dear and valued friend. One night, a mutual friend, Leslie Dawson, a director of Partridges, the antique firm in Bond Street, asked us both to a dinner party. I behaved really disgracefully because I had made up my mind to tell Cyril after dinner, and as a result felt agitated and tight inside as a violin string. Everyone was ashamed of me. After dinner, I manoeuvred my brother-in-law into a side room.

'Brother Cyril,' I began – I have always called him that – 'I have something terrible to tell you. It's so bad I don't know how to start.'

'What's the matter?' he asked.

'I am going to leave your sister. I am sorry, but our marriage is over.'

'Don't worry, Kenny,' he replied. 'Your friends have been wondering how you, a born bachelor, could remain married for so long.' He was, of course, easing my predicament, but it did help!

I summoned up my decision and bought a mews house off Queensborough Terrace in Bayswater. I did not mess about with searches and deposits, subject to contract and all that jargon, so beloved of lawyers and estate agents. I simply wrote out a cheque for the £25,000 the owner asked and the house was mine.

'Darling,' I said to Shrimp, 'this is our new home. I know you have had no chance to decorate it or make it as you want it, but we've got to be together now, and this is our chance.'

She agreed, and we moved in.

I was in a mood for burning boats, for erasing all memory of the past. From now on, we would have no backward glances; the way lay ahead, wherever the road might lead. So, for a start, I sold my Rolls and paid off Bint, my loyal chauffeur. The last few weeks had been very embarrassing, because while it was my car and I paid his wages, Bill still had the use of the Rolls. I would ask the chauffeur to collect Miss Douglas and take her shopping, and he would say, 'I am sorry, but Mrs. More has already asked me to take *her* shopping this morning.'

With the departure of this beautiful and very expensive car – a symbol of my past stardom – I felt that at last I had cut free of my life as it had been. From now on, Angela and I would be together, making a new life. Whether it succeeded was up to us. Certainly, we were to enjoy little help from any others around us.

12

S O BEGAN A CHAPTER in my life which in one sense was the happiest I had ever experienced and in another a time of loneliness and isolation from nearly everyone I had known previously. To put it bluntly, Angela and I found ourselves in a social wilderness. I had committed the crime which, for a man in my position, was said by everyone to be unforgivable. I had left my wife and daughter for a young 'bit of skirt'. Consequently, the wives of other actors of my age and standing, with whom I had been friendly for years, were not at all eager to have me – and certainly Shrimp – in their homes. What I had done might be contagious; as with leprosy, their husbands could become infected by the wish to do likewise.

We were thus better avoided. No one asked us out to lunch or dinner. We invited people ourselves, people I had thought of as my friends, but they always made some excuse. Given a second or even a third choice of dates, they would still find other more important engagements. We were ostracised.

I was invited by a film company on one occasion to attend a première at the Columbia Cinema in Shaftesbury Avenue. Shrimp and I decided we would accept and make a first public appearance together. In the foyer, I saw actors, actresses, writers and directors I had known for years, but as I approached them they literally drew away from us. We were surrounded in that theatre by people I had known intimately for years and most would not even turn to look at us. One or two allowed themselves a brief, 'Hello', but that was the extent of their conversation. After this, I felt too proud to accept any other public invitations one humiliation was enough.

Bill, as the wronged party, had adopted what I considered to be a foolish line. She had been treated badly, which I freely admit; she reacted by telling everyone just *how* badly. She wanted all our friends on her side, and because many of them feared for their own, often equally shaky, marriages they rallied behind her flag.

Our daughter was only eleven and I could see her whenever I wanted. But Bill did not particularly encourage my visits, and I was so disgusted with the whole situation that unfortunately I saw Sarah far too rarely. When I look back, I have a conscience about this. Only in more recent years have we developed the warm relationship which is so important between father and daughter.

One of my best friends in the old days had been Paul Gallico, the novelist. We used to go fishing together for sea bass from his home in Salcombe in Devon, and Bill and I had been guests at his house in Antibes. We were on the warmest terms. One day, after I set up house with Angela, I was in a shop in Queensway, near my home, and bumped into him in the doorway. He went scarlet with embarrassment and could not escape quickly enough. I see Paul's widow now and her daughter, and we are all friends, but then such treatment was heartbreaking.

Angela took an Irish view of the situation. She retreated in fury into her shell, and said we should have nothing to do with such people if they behaved like that.

I realised that my life now was an unequal equation. I was trying to make my relationship with Angela take the place of my previous relationship with literally scores of other people. I retreated into myself. So far as I was concerned, it was obvious that films were now out. I decided to return to the theatre, if I could find a suitable play. And until I could find the right play, I would do TV.

Here, my guardian angel again looked after me, and Ted Kotcheff, the TV director, sent me a play which had been written by John Mortimer. I have known John for years and his plays always have two themes; sex, and a middle-aged man chasing his youth. I like his work, and understand it – especially as this was my own situation at the time.

He had written a TV play called *Collect Your Hand Baggage*, and this was to be my first real impact on the small screen. At that time other actors of my standing were rather afraid of TV. And they thought that it was somehow beneath them to transfer from the big screen to the small. I did not have much option.

The play was about a middle-aged Lothario who wanted to fly to Paris with a young girl in search of his own youth, but the girl let him down and left him at the airport; he was twenty-five years too late for such a romantic expedition.

We did a lot of filming on the road to Heathrow, and the story involved me speeding in an open vintage car with several young girls in the back, frequently breaking the speed limit. Kotcheff had no permission to film on the Great West Road, and during one of our screen shots a police car stopped us and the officer in charge asked him to show his form of permission.

'Permission?' replied Kotcheff. 'Why, I've a letter from the Chief of the Metropolitan Police, another from the Duke of Edinburgh, and a third from the Archbishop of Canterbury, who are all interested in this project.'

The police officer was so astonished that he said, 'Carry on, sir! Carry on!'

A further few miles up the road, we were stopped by a second police car. The policeman inside again asked to see our permission to film in fast-moving traffic. Kotcheff listened patiently to his request, and then shook his head.

'Just ring up Room 247a at Scotland Yard and you will find it's all in order. Now, if you will be so good . . .'

The policeman again took his word for it, and we continued.

The critics were as kind to this play as they were to *The Comedy Man*. Once more, I was playing the eternal juvenile, the man who could not face the thought of growing old. Was I playing myself? A lot of people thought so. There is a saying in the acting profession that if a man can keep his hair on and his stomach in, he can go on playing juveniles for ever. Nevertheless, to play the part of an ageing Peter Pan in two productions, one after the other, having regard to the crisis in my own private and professional life, rather touched the bone.

Through all this Angela and I lived a very quiet life. Most evenings we stayed at home. Sometimes Wendy Toye would come round to see us, and Lloyd and 'Mel' Nolan. Lloyd had appeared with me in *We Joined the Navy* and we were now close friends. Angela had friends of her own age and they would call in for a drink or a meal, but none of my contemporaries.

I remember that Christmas so well, for Shrimp and I spent it on our own. The only friend who came to see us was the loyal Wendy Toye who brought us each a present. I could not tell her then, but I hope she knows now, just how much this meant to us. Also Angela's parents, Peter and Marjorie, were sympathetic and immensely loyal and understanding.

After Wendy left, I sat by the TV set watching *Till Death Do Us Part*, the Alf Garnett show with Dandy Nichols. Years previously, Dandy had been a girl friend of mine, and now I sat roaring with laughter at her antics on the screen. I could hear Shrimp singing away in the kitchen as she cooked the turkey. I felt relaxed and at ease, and then, WHAM! A half-cooked turkey, weighing about 20 lbs, caught me full on the face, bounced off and landed in the fire. I looked up in amazement, and saw Shrimp standing red-faced at the kitchen door.

'You *bastard*!' she shouted.

'What's the matter?' I cried in bewilderment. 'Are you mad?'

She did not answer me. She just slammed the door and went out.

197

We had no Christmas dinner, for the turkey was in the fire, sizzling away, all burnt and black. I scraped the fat off my eyes and face and had a whisky to steady my nerves. An hour went by. Then Shrimp came back.

'What's the matter, love?' I asked her.

'You were laughing at Dandy Nichols. You told me you had a bit of a thing about her years ago when you were doing *Without Power Glory*. How *dare* you laugh at her?'

'Because she's funny. That's why.'

'I don't think that's the reason. You're laughing at the thought of one of your old love affairs. How you can sit there and laugh is beyond me.'

'Darling,' I assured her, 'You're utterly wrong.'

But this gave me an inkling of the sort of extraordinary jealousy I was liable to provoke now I had become involved with an Irish girl. Or maybe the strain of our predicament was also affecting her. For this was a period for me of scripts that did not arrive; of former friends who turned away from me in the street; of women who cut me dead.

Looking back now I don't know how we stood it, but at the time Angela and I were so close that we had utter and complete faith in ourselves, and these insults did not really matter.

In 1963, Darryl Zanuck threw me a lifeline. He was casting his film about the D-Day landings, *The Longest Day*, and he wanted me to play the part of the beach-master. I was offered a salary of £1,000 a day, with a guarantee of five days on location in La Rochelle in France. I did my five days, but then the whole sequence had to be reshot in a different way, so I went back for a further three days and collected another £3,000. This put my finances in order, and also did much for my self-esteem.

With me at La Rochelle were two other actors, each with only one line to say as they came up the beach from the landing-craft. One was Michael Medwin and the other, Sean Connery.

Shortly after this, Angela and I were spending a few days as guests of my ex-brother-in-law, Cyril Porter, at the Bear Hotel in Woodstock. I remember that she and I were in bed in the early hours of April 1 when the telephone rang. The operator said it was a call from Hollywood. Her agent out there came on to say that he had agreed terms for her to appear with Shirley MacLaine in the film *John Goldfarb, Please Come Home*. She was very excited, and I listened, and said, 'Oh, yes. Happy April the First,' and went to sleep and forgot about it. Four hours later, the telephone rang again. Her agent now told her she had to collect a visa and be over there in twenty-four hours. So much for an April Fool's Day prank.

'It's *true*! It's *true*!' Angela kept shouting .

I must say I greeted this wonderful news with rather a long face. 'What about *me*?' I asked. 'What about *me*?'

Angela was delighted, not least because at twenty-three she was going to do something I had not then done at twice her age. It gave her a bit of one-up-womanship to be asked to go to Hollywood first.

'Never mind, Kenny,' she said. 'I *must* go.'

'I'll miss you terribly, darling,' I told her.

'I'll come back and tell you all about it,' she promised.

To hell with that, I thought. I had visions of her being leapt upon by every male film star, and was actually sobbing when I put her on the plane.

I suppose really it was jealousy, but I thought it was love. Anyhow, I was most unhappy at home. We spent a lot of money on telephone calls. An Englishman now working out there said a lot of nasty things about me, and this hurt Angela and she got very upset.

One night she phoned me and told me about this.

'Don't be silly, darling,' I said. 'He's only trying to undermine our relationship, and get you into bed. I'll be out right away.'

I thought, as I wasn't doing any work here, I might as well go out and do nothing there. I flew out first-class and was delighted to see Shrimp at the airport with a huge black limousine she had organised. Bless her heart, she had overcome a problem of a kind that would not arise now. She was staying at the Beverly Wilshire hotel and had heard rumours that in the States there was some law that forbade unmarried people to occupy the same room. She was wearing short socks and had her hair in a pony tail, and looked about thirteen and a half years old. She could just about reach the top of the hotel reception desk. She wanted no embarrassment when I arrived, and so she asked the man behind the desk if there *was* any state law to this effect. He looked at her in amazement, and assured her there wasn't. He was obviously embarrassed, and it was soon all over the hotel that her boy friend was arriving.

Actually, Wilfred Hyde White, an old and dear friend, who was filming in Hollywood, found us a flat. She had gone to great trouble to prepare this flat so that it was more like home. There was a bunch of red roses, a bottle of champagne in the fridge, and yet the whole thing was an illusion. I felt that underneath this façade of first-class air-fare, hired car and driver, flowers and champagne, we were still a couple of outcasts. Or, at least, I was an outcast, and because of her association with me the contagion had passed to Angela.

Once, we went out to the famous Brown Derby restaurant and

199

they wouldn't serve her with a drink. They thought she was under age.

'What about my wife?' I asked them. 'Can't she have a drink?'

And the waiter said, 'You're not married. She's not old enough.' He said he wanted to see the back of Angela's hand, so we stormed out. I thought, he'd be looking at her teeth next, to calculate her age, like a horse.

When out in Hollywood I met Mike Frankovitch, who had been the head of Columbia in Britain and was running Columbia Studios over there. He introduced me to William Wyler. He was making *The Collector* with Samantha Eggar and Terence Stamp. This told the story of a young man who kidnapped a girl (Samantha) and kept her his prisoner. Now, the collector had a confidant, an older man, known as J.B., and William Wyler was very anxious that I should play this character. I was flattered, for Willie Wyler is one of Hollywood's greatest directors, whose career has spanned more than forty years.

Vivien Leigh had told me years before that her idea of paradise was Tobago, so Shrimp and I flew off together, island-hopping on Pan Am from Hollywood over Cuba by way of the Virgin Islands, to test Vivien's opinion. We stayed in Tobago for three weeks. It was the wrong time of year and terribly hot, but we enjoyed ourselves. I realised, and I am certain that Shrimp did, too, that we were both putting off the evil day when we had to return to England – and what? More ostracism, more evenings and week-ends in the mews cottage alone, waiting for telephone calls that never came? More pretence that we didn't care?

Finally, we could delay our departure no longer, and we flew home. Some good news awaited me. My agent told me that Giles Cooper, who was one of TV's most gifted dramatists, had written a stage play, *Out of the Crocodile*. This was about a couple, Celia Johnson and Hugh Williams, who lived in a flat in London. Into their lives comes a mysterious character, Peter Pounce. This was the part I was being offered.

I thought the first act was very funny, the second act less so. However, the three of us were pretty experienced, and we believed we should be able to carry the whole thing through.

Unfortunately, in the second week of rehearsal, Hugh Williams, a gentle person I had admired all my working life, lost his voice. He had a bad prognosis on this, just as Jack Hawkins was to have soon afterwards. It was said to be cancer of the throat, and he could not work. The part was then offered to Cyril Raymond.

We were still confident that we could make a go of it, although I had some doubts about certain parts of the play. In Act Two, I was pretending to be a matador, using my jacket as a cape, while a girl pretended to be a bull. This was meaningless to me. I asked the writer bluntly: 'Why am I doing this?' He couldn't tell me.

'I know what it means,' Cooper replied. 'But I can't explain.'

The director said he couldn't explain it either, but it should work. I felt it *had* to work, for I was desperate for some success, and this would mark my return to the straight theatre for the first time since *The Deep Blue Sea*.

This fact drew some publicity before the play opened, and with any luck we felt we should be over the hump. But luck just then was elsewhere for all of us, especially for me.

There is a custom in the London theatre that the leading man gives a party in his dressing room after the opening night. I went to a caterer, hired a butler and ordered three cases of champagne, canapés and smoked salmon sandwiches, because I felt that this night must really be one to remember.

The final curtain came down to a good deal of applause, though I felt inside me that a lot of this enthusiasm was probably just loyalty on the part of a first night audience to a cast they knew, and unrepresentative of other audiences. However, it was very agreeable to bow once more in front of the curtains, and to be applauded.

I knew I had about five minutes before the first guests were due to appear in my dressing room, so I removed my make-up and had everything ready to receive them.

Angela and Laurie, my agent, and I waited in the dressing room with the butler, full of anticipation. Five minutes passed. Then ten. Then fifteen.

'Shall I open the champagne now?' the butler asked.

'No, wait a minute.'

Five more minutes. Ten. Still no one arrived.

'A bottle now, sir?'

'Well,' I said. 'There's not much point, is there?'

I tried to laugh it off, but Angela was scarlet in the face. She was ashamed of my so-called friends, and so was I. This to me was the cruellest blow of all. And in the background, like a gramophone record, the butler kept asking: 'Shall I open the champagne now, sir?'

We drove home in silence. In my depressed state I realised that the play would not run; there was something wrong with its construction. I had given the best performance I could – we all had – but the show would die. I also knew that if it had been a hit, calculated to run for years, all my so-called friends would have come crowding in the dressing room. And if they hadn't then, it wouldn't have mattered. But because the play would not succeed and because I had flopped socially, my mood was bleak indeed.

Bernard Delfont and Arthur Lewis now approached me to take the part of Crichton in a musical version of *The Admirable Crichton*, to be called *Our Man Crichton*. My first reaction was that I couldn't sing, but Bernard talked me into it.

'Have I got to sing much?' I asked him.

'No,' he said. 'You take a few lessons and you'll be all right. So long as you can put a number over.'

'I can put a number over, if I can speak it,' I told him.

'Fine. Speak it to music. I'll get Millicent Martin to play Tweeny. Have a go.'

I had a word with my agent, Laurence Evans, and asked his opinion.

'Before you decide, let's see what we can get for you, Kenny.'

What he got for me was £1,000 a week for the run of the show in lieu of ten per cent of the gross takings; a lot of money.

'But Laurie,' I protested. 'I can't sing.'

'Well,' he said, 'for a thousand a week, anybody can!'

Before the show opened I had three weeks of lessons with a singing teacher. As a result of these, I could cope with the point numbers, which don't require much of a voice, but simply a personality and a manner, but I had a serious ballad I had to sing to Lady Mary, who was played by Patricia Lambert. This was a love ballad and I was so terrible that I asked the producer to take it out of the show. It was essential for the action, however, so it had to remain. I got away with it on most nights, I think, but only just. Pat has a beautiful voice and she covered me so well that I would just come in now and then with a word or a line or a gesture.

On the week of Churchill's funeral, business was very bad. People stayed away from the theatre because their thoughts were about the death of a man who had for so long symbolised so much that was fine in our country. But the show had to go on, although on the Wednesday matinée I saw I was singing this ballad to a house three-quarters empty.

I looked across the orchestra pit to the front row of the stalls and was about to warble, 'And I love you' or words to that effect, when I saw, to my horror, Noël Coward in the circle with Graham Payn on one side and Cole Lesley on the other. Noël's eyes met mine. He shook his head slowly from side to side as though to say, 'Dear boy, that is absolutely *terrible*. Don't *ever* do it again.'

I immediately dried up. I could no more finish the song than I could have flown. Pat took up my lines and finished it for me. Afterwards, Noël came round to see me in my dressing room.

'Dear boy,' he said gravely. 'That was absolutely terrible. Don't *ever* do it again.'

Despite this, we ran for six months. But I took Noël's advice. I never have done it again.

But *Our Man Crichton* was just a shaft of light in the gloom. Some time later, my bedside telephone rang at half past three in the morning. William Wyler was on the line from Hollywood. As soon as I heard his voice, I perked up immediately. At last my luck must be turning.

'Kenny,' he began. 'I have just cut the film.'

'Yes?' I said, thinking he was going to congratulate me on my performance.

'Yes,' he went on. 'And I have cut you out.'

'You've done *what*?'

'You're out. The part doesn't work. It did in the book, but for the film we must have all the action with the collector and the girl in the cellar. You played it beautifully, but it doesn't work.'

My mouth was dry with disappointment.

'What about my name on the bill?'

'We'll remove all that, Kenny, don't worry. Just thought I'd be the first to tell you.'

'Thank you very much,' I said, and lay back, in a mood of near despair. Such high hopes, such a cruel disappointment.

The strange part about this was that my contract stipulated that if I appeared in the film, I had to have equal billing with Terence Stamp and Samantha Eggar, because on paper at least I was still a star. My agent, therefore, insisted, quite rightly, that they remove every trace of me from the film. If they showed one shot where I could be recognised, they would be liable for heavy damages, having removed my name.

They cut me out completely, except for one scene where the camera held a close-up of Sam Eggar in an English pub and I, for a split second, was seen in the background. The scene was essential for the action of the film, and they had forgotten that I appeared in it. I could have taken them for thousands of dollars, but Willie Wyler was such a lovely man I hadn't the heart to do anything about it. This was just another blow I had to bear, and the most dignified thing was to accept my misfortune in silence.

13

O N A FEBRUARY Saturday morning in 1966, I reached the lowest ebb of my career. I was actually passing time by weeding the small garden outside my mews house. When Angela called from the window to say that Donald Wilson of the BBC wanted to speak to me I wondered, what on earth for? I had known him slightly since 1946 when I appeared in the first TV play to broadcast after the war, *The Silence of the Sea*. He was then working at Alexandra Palace. Later he moved to Pinewood, and occasionally we had bumped into each other in corridors going to and from the studios, and we had shared the services of Harry Dubens. I couldn't imagine what he wanted to ring me about now on a Saturday morning. But then I remembered that other Saturday call, all those years ago from Bob Lennard, and how it had changed my life. I came in and picked up the phone.

'Kenny,' said Wilson,' I want to see you for lunch. I want to offer you a part which I think will be the best thing that either you or I have ever done in our professional lives.'

So began my connection with John Galsworthy's *The Forsyte Saga*, which Donald intended to dramatise for BBC TV in twenty-six parts. This would take a year out of our lives, maybe longer. The part he offered me was young Jolyon, who told the story, a character the author was said to have based on himself.

'I intend to make young Jolyon a key figure,' Donald assured me. 'The whole series will be seen through his eyes – your eyes. You will appear in fifteen or sixteen episodes, from a young man until your death on the screen. More than that, you will head the cast, and we'll work out a deal to give you enough money so that you won't mind turning down any film offers.'

I remembered that MGM had once made a poor film of *The Forsyte Story* with Errol Flynn as Soames and Greer Garson as Irene. They still held the rights. It had taken the BBC twelve months of argument before MGM agreed to allow this TV series to be made. This determination on Donald Wilson's part showed his enormous faith in the project, but I still had reservations.

'Listen,' Donald said at last. 'I am going to spend a quarter of a million pounds of the BBC's money, which is an enormous sum for them. I need your name, Kenny, before I can get this off the ground, because, believe it or not, it's still a very important name in this country.'

He saw I was looking at him sceptically.

'You want proof that you are still a pull?' he asked me. 'Well, here it is. A poll was printed recently in the *Evening Standard*. You were chosen as the film star most people would like to see in a war film. You are just behind Charlton Heston, Richard Burton and Elizabeth Taylor as their choice for an epic. And The *Sunday Times* has just published another chart in which you are listed as one of the twenty most exciting men of the twentieth-century, in this country, of course!'

'Have you written anything?' I asked him.

'I've done two scripts,' he said, and he handed them to me. I went home and read them. They were written from the heart and I realised that Wilson was a man who had found his métier. To produce this series had been a consuming ambition for years; I could not afford to ignore its importance to him – and to me.

At fifty, a man must come to terms with himself, and look back on what he has done and consider what he can hope to do. He must equate practicalities with dreams. At fifty, I had begun to wonder privately whether my star was indeed on the wane. Socially and professionally I had been almost passed by, and I could see no way in which I could fight back. Worse, the will to fight back was itself diminishing. I had taken the popular image of Kenneth More, the extrovert, the perennial beer-drinker and good fellow, as far as it could go. Peter Pan was always young, but I had the mind, and – sometimes more dangerous for an actor – the face of maturity.

I could have tried to make a niche for myself by playing character parts of ageing officers or men-about-town or ambassadors, as so many other actors have done in middle life and beyond. But this would only be a treading of already well-trodden ground. Each performance would, of necessity, have been a diminished success, and as success dwindles, so does one's income, and, more important, one's horizons.

I was not seeking to build a reputation, only to hold what I had already achieved – and, if possible, to consolidate my gains. I needed a role which would be a shop window for my talents. I wanted people to see for themselves what I could do, that I was not limited by a sports jacket and a laugh or by the confines of a uniform in a studio ship. Jolyon would give me the chance of ageing from early thirties to mid-seventies. It is usually easy for a young actor to play an old man, but it is the mark of the professional when an older actor plays someone half his age. This was the challenge I knew I must accept. In a sense, what Donald Wilson was offering me was the longest audition in the world. Well, I had undergone auditions before, and although here the audience would be in tens and finally hundreds of millions, it was still an audience of individuals. The chips were down. This was my chance – perhaps my last chance – to pick them up and play on.

The BBC worked out a scheme whereby I was guaranteed £15,500 for six or seven months' work, with a share in any world sales that might or might not materialise later. This was very fair payment indeed, but by then I was so enthusiastic that money was of secondary consequence.

Sometimes, when one does a TV production, the cast is sent along to Morris Angel or Monty Berman, the theatrical costumiers, and they can if necessary be issued with clothes off the peg. There was nothing of that sort here. I was measured for four suits before we even started.

When we travelled on location we did not have a caravan to change in; we changed into our costumes in cars, and sometimes even knocked on the front doors of houses nearby and asked if we could use their lavatory, but everyone showed a rare and genuine enthusiasm for the whole project. Because of the cost, most of the exterior work and filming country backgrounds was done in Richmond Park, and had to be compressed into three weeks in June when it was calculated that the weather would be as good as it ever is in Britain. In fifteen working days therefore we had to shoot all the background exteriors for the first fifteen episodes.

Some of the later scripts were not even written, so Donald Wilson had to keep in the back of his mind ideas for backgrounds which could be filmed in advance.

We rehearsed the interiors in a drill hall in Ealing, week after week; two weeks of rehearsals and then three days in the studio to record. We were expected to know all our lines by the tenth day of rehearsal. Lines were chalked on the floor to represent wardrobes, sideboards and beds until props arrived about the sixth day. These were not the final props we would have in the studio, but a big box would represent a chest of drawers and a smaller one a chair and so on, to give the cast a sense of the size of the real furniture.

I would arrive at the drill hall at ten o'clock each morning. Work would begin immediately. We would break at one o'clock for lunch in a café or pub, then would work through the afternoon until 5.30. The drill hall had a room which had been the sergeants' mess and here we could have a drink and manipulate the fruit machine. We did not all rehearse at the same time, and those of us working out a scene would hear our off-duty colleagues playing this machine and listen for the peculiar clank it gave when it paid out the jackpot. Whenever this happened – which it did several times during each week's rehearsals – we would all rush out and congratulate the winner. Usually he or she would buy a round of drinks to celebrate.

Eric Porter, who was playing Soames magnificently, was known for a disinclination to spend two pennies when one penny would do. We all said that if he won the jackpot we'd stop everything for a round of drinks. Sure enough, just before lunch one day we heard the clank of coins pouring out. We stopped work at once and ran into the bar. There he was, counting out his sixpences and shillings into a funny little hat he always wore, like a Dutch engine-driver's cap. We grouped about him waiting for him to buy a round. But this was not to be.

'Thank goodness, I won't have to go to the bank this afternoon,' was all he said, and gave us a beaming smile. The laugh was on us.

After Episode 15 I was free, while the rest still had several more months of work. I had no immediate financial problems, but equally, I had no idea how *The Forsyte Saga* would go, because it would not be shown for some months.

I wrote to John Davis in an attempt to thaw the coolness between us. He replied with a very pleasant letter, but nothing more happened. I therefore decided I had better forget about films and look for another play. Then quite unexpectedly I was offered a role in the film, *The Mercenaries*, with Rod Taylor and James Brown. This was about white mercenaries fighting in Africa, and I was to play a drunken doctor. It would largely be shot in location in Jamaica. I read the script, and mine was a 'nothing' part. Anyone who could remember his lines and pretend to be drunk could have played it, but anyone wasn't being offered the chance. I was. I had nothing else, so I signed up for this. It was one of my less happy acting experiences.

Rod Taylor was the star opposite Yvette Mimieux. Jimmy Brown, a once famous American football player was playing second fiddle to him and not greatly relishing this situation. I was fourth on the totem pole, a long way beneath both of them.

Rod Taylor told me proudly: 'I had Johnny Mills in my last film,' not, as someone might have said, 'I have been filming with Johnny Mills.' After *The Mercenaries* I had a feeling he would tell the cast of his next picture, 'I had Kenneth More in my last film.' I felt I just didn't belong.

Jack Cardiff, the director, was rather lax about starting each day. If Rod or James weren't quite ready, we would all wait about until they were. This meant that some mornings we started at eight or nine, or even ten o'clock. This sort of casual indiscipline spread through the whole unit. It was not a good atmosphere in which to work, and encouraged tensions.

Rod Taylor had been an amateur boxing champion before he became an actor, and he and James Brown threatened to settle disputes with their fists. Taylor fancied his chance of knocking out Brown, which was more than I did, because Brown was six foot four inches, and built like a solid brick privy. They appeared to hate each other. Maybe they were only acting. If so, they must have been better actors than I thought. And all the time the rain teemed down like something out of a Somerset Maugham short story. We were soaked all day on location, and at night we only had each other's company in our hotel.

Everyone's opinion was asked about different shots, except mine. And yet I had appeared in more films than the rest of the cast put together. If I had a good line in the script, it was cut down, and then pruned, and finally it would disappear altogether. But I consoled myself with the fact that I was being paid. This was a job. I had to accept that the wheel of fortune turns, and whereas I had been lucky in being at the top for years, now I was underneath. The secret of survival was to hang on, and not fall off the wheel altogether, which had happened to several of my contemporaries. This was my state of mind, depressed and yet determined. I would wake up, unwilling to face another day, and yet forcing myself to do so. I wasn't only acting in front of the cameras, I was acting all the time, displaying a confidence I did not feel.

Then, early one morning, while Angela and I were still asleep, the telephone rang. It was a person-to-person long distance call from London.

'Who is it?' I asked, for the atmospherics were bad. It was the *Daily Mail* TV correspondent.

'I want to ask you how you feel about your enormous success,' he said.

'What?' I replied. 'I don't know what you are talking about.'

'Haven't you heard about it, then? The effect of *The Forsyte Saga?*'

'No, I haven't heard a thing. Tell me.'

'It's fantastic,' he went on. 'You're all the toast of the country. Churches are empty on Sunday evenings, when the show is on. The series is the most successful ever to be shown. It will be sold all over the world. You're very big, Mr. More. Much bigger than you've ever been in films. There's never been a series like this.'

I went back to sleep a happy man. Metaphorically, I could raise two fingers at anyone, and everyone who belittled me. I knew that if I really made the grade on TV, I would be seen by more people in one

208

Left: with Angela in Kew Gardens.

Right: in Terence Rattigan's *In Praise of Love* (1975) with Claire Bloom.

Above: Kenneth More as Young Jolyon in the BBC television production of *The Forsyte Saga.*

Left: with Irene (Nyree Dawn Porter) in *The Forsyte Saga.*

night than would ever gather together to see the greatest film ever made, in the longest run on record.

The wheel was still turning. I was on my way back. From then on, nothing changed in my attitude towards them. I had gone through the valley and at last I was out into the sunshine beyond.

When Angela and I returned to London a cohort of reporters waited to interview me at the airport. Once more I was a household name. Now we found that many of the people who had run away from me for years were coming back. They would ring me and say, 'Hello, Kenny. How are you? What are you doing?' Or: 'Just a call to congratulate you on *The Forsyte Saga.*'

Angela and I had decided earlier on that if the day should ever come that these people wished to be accepted by us, we would pick and choose the ones we wanted, and so we did. We left the others out in the cold where they had put us. We accepted their calls, but we did not return them.

It was an extraordinary feeling to be at the centre of all the publicity and excitement about the series. I had discovered with amazement that Nyree Dawn Porter, Eric Porter and Susan Hampshire and I were being talked about in nearly every home in the land. Very soon, we would be talked about in nearly every home in the world.

Two stories show how extraordinarily popular this series was, not only in this country, but everywhere. Its appeal was truly international. Harold Wilson was Prime Minister then, and his government had invited a Yugoslav trade delegation to London. He held a reception for them at No. 10 Downing Street.

Usually, at such functions, the guests meet their opposite numbers in Britain, so one has merchant talking to merchant, trade union leader to trade union leader, and so on, but Harold Wilson realised that in this instance such an evening would be pretty heavy going, and many of his guests would stand like a pork chop at a Jewish wedding. He decided instead to invite the cast of *The Forsyte Saga* to meet this delegation, for the series had recently been screened in Yugoslavia. Eric Porter couldn't go, but Nyree Dawn Porter accepted and so did I.

The evening was an unbelievable success. We were ushered into the room, and immediately saw the Yugoslavs standing round the walls looking like wooden dummies in their rather quaintly old-fashioned Iron Curtain suits. Wilson's private secretary explained to me that they were the guests of honour.

'They don't look very happy,' I remarked.

'Well, what can we do? Not many of us speak Serbo-Croat, so it is very difficult.'

Then suddenly, one of the guests looked up, saw Nyree Dawn Porter and did a double-take. Then he saw me and did a second double-take. He nudged the man next door and we heard the words, whispered excitedly: 'Forsyte Saga, Forsyte Saga!' At once the whole evening became alive. The interpreter had never worked so hard in his life as he translated their questions and our answers.

Two or three years later, Shrimp and I decided we would spend Christmas in Madrid. Our flight was delayed, and we arrived at the hotel at about half past nine in the evening, and checked in at the desk. Because we were tired, we decided to have a light meal in the hotel instead of going out to a restaurant. As we passed through the main lounge to the lift, I saw a large TV screen had been set up, with a number of people watching it. About fifty men and women in armchairs, eyes on the screen. The women wore diamonds and furs, and many of the men had grey hair and seemed the type who pass in advertisements as men of distinction. They were a pretty wealthy audience and all absolutely absorbed by the action on the screen.

I looked at the set to see what was holding their interest so closely. There I was, as Jolyon, speaking the most superb Spanish. I was grasping the curtains in Jolyon's fatal heart attack, and died in front of an audience of fifty Spaniards in a Spanish hotel. A woman in one of the front seats, a middle-aged, dark-haired, diamond ear-ringed and fox-furred lady, was practically having hysterics.

'Es muerte. . . ! Es muerte. . . !' she cried in anguish. A friend in the next seat to her was fanning her and held smelling salts under her nose, and all because I had died on the screen. It was an extraordinary sensation for me. I had not realised the impact of *The Forsyte Saga* in Spain, and remember, this was the second showing! Shrimp and I exchanged glances.

'This is too good to miss,' I said. 'I'm going to tap her on the shoulder to prove I am still alive.'

'Go on,' agreed Shrimp. 'Give her a laugh. She won't believe it.'

On screen my eyes were closed for the last scene, as I began to pick my way through the chairs.

'Es muerte. . . !' cried the woman again.

I tapped her on her shoulder gently and said, 'No, madam. He's not. He's *here*.'

Pandemonium! The woman screamed and leaped out of her chair. The smelling salts were spilled and the glass bottle smashed. Everyone shouted in amazement.

Until then I had not realised we were the toast of Spain. Now, I was not allowed to forget it. Magazines displayed our pictures on their covers. The hotel proprietor insisted that everything we wanted must be on the house, and during our stay, when we went out to dine in a restaurant, someone at another table would invariably recognise us and insist on paying our bills. Whenever we waited for a taxi at a taxi-stand, we were immediately passed up to the front of the queue. I would protest, 'No, *please.*' But a Spaniard would reply in perfect English, with a smile: 'No. No. Senor, please. After all, dead men do not argue.' The whole experience was extraordinary, like a royal progress.

On Christmas Day, we decided to attend Mass in the oldest and most famous church in Madrid. We deliberately arrived slightly late because I did not want to be noticed.

We crept up a side aisle to one of the small chapels, because Shrimp wanted to light a candle to St. Teresa. No one saw us. Everyone was looking at the priest. Then a woman from the main body of the church turned and her eyes met mine. I thought, Please, God, not here! St. Teresa, please. Not *here.*

The woman immediately nudged someone next to her, who also turned to look at us.

'Jolyon Forsyte. Jolyon Forsyte,' she whispered. Within seconds, the nudging went around the whole congregation and a kind of sigh ascended to the roof of the cathedral: ' . . . 'Jolyon Forsyte . . . Jolyon Forsyte . . .'

The old priest was about to chant when he saw me and went, 'Ahhhh!' The whole service stopped. People now began to call from the back of the cathedral: 'Jolyon! Jolyon!'

I panicked. There could be no Mass for us that morning. Shrimp and I literally ran out of the cathedral, and we did not stop running until we reached the seclusion of our hotel.

While I was in Jamaica I had read a book, *The White Rabbit*, the story of Wing-Commander Yeo-Thomas, who was a Resistance hero in France during the war. The book impressed me because it was about personal courage, and, as Churchill declared, courage is rightly esteemed the first of human qualities because it is the one which guarantees all others.

When I returned to England after the success of *Forsyte*, I went to see David Attenborough, who was then in charge of Features at the BBC, and told him how much I would like to play Yeo-Thomas in a four-part TV series.

Attenborough discovered that the rights were held by Hal Chester. He would not give permission for the series in case he decided to make a film of the book himself, and so the idea seemed a non-starter. But the BBC by law can by-pass this obstacle. They can make one transmission of a particular subject, but they cannot repeat this or sell the programme elsewhere. This is an extraordinary fact, but Attenborough said he was still willing to make the series.

'That's very kind of you,' I replied. 'But what's in it for you?'

'Nothing, really, Kenny, except that it will make a damned good series and we are all so thrilled with your work in *The Forsyte Saga* that this is my way of repaying the BBC's debt to you. We'll do *The White Rabbit* and show it once, and then we'll have to destroy the tapes.'

So we started work. What impressed me about Yeo-Thomas, in addition to his courage, was his humility, and what angered me was the terrible way in which the British Government had treated him at the end of the war. He was not even awarded a pension for disabilities caused by his work with the Resistance. When he died, an autopsy revealed that his skull had been cracked in thirty-six places from beatings he had received from the Gestapo.

He had suffered terribly in concentration camps and prisons, but everyone who ever met him remarked on his strong character, and the inner peace he radiated.

I could not slim down to a prison camp skeleton, but my hair was shaved off, and I wore a bald bladder wig. In addition, I was dragged with shackles on my feet through a bath of water which nearly drowned me – as it had nearly drowned Yeo-Thomas in real life. The worst moment of the film came when I was in solitary confinement in a damp cellar. Here Yeo-Thomas had been incarcerated for weeks, while rats walked over him, night and day.

'You're not going to do that to me, surely?' I asked Peter Hammond, the director.

'Oh, yes. We must have the rats, Ken.'

'Have you got a proper rat trainer?' I asked, hoping this would confound them.

'Oh, yes. We know a chap who trains rats, all right. We use him a lot, for all kinds of animals.'

I have a horror of rats, and I was shaking for a week before we did the scene, which was in a mock-up cellar with water running. It was cold and miserable lying there for hours, and when they released four rats and I saw them come out of their cage, I whispered: 'Are you *sure* they're tame?'

'Yes, Mr. More,' said the trainer. 'Never had any trouble with these little fellows. They've walked over dozens of actors.'

They should belong to Equity, I thought, and at that moment shut my eyes for they were crawling over my face, their little claws tickling my flesh, their sharp noses sniffing at mine.

'You *sure* they're tame?' I repeated through clenched teeth.

'Yes, Mr. More.'

'Well, one has just bitten my ear.'

'They're all tame enough, Mr. More. I've had no complaints before. Maybe that one's just a wee bit hungrier than the others.'

After this production, an Italian director asked me to make a film for an Italian company in Yugoslavia with Suzy Kendall and James Booth. This was called *Fraulein Doktor*, and was a movie in the old-fashioned, red-blooded manner. It was set in the first world war, with poison gas attacks, Kitchener going down in the *Hampshire*, German spies landing on the Norfolk coast *und so weiter*.

I was cast as a British Secret Service Colonel and my task was to capture the notorious Suzy Kendall, who was having it off with Germans and British alike. The plot was so complicated that none of us had any clear idea of what was going on, but we all had a hell of a good time in Yugoslavia, although I never managed to see the film afterwards and so cannot say whether our pleasure in making it was shared by the audiences who saw it.

Halfway through the filming Shrimp came out to see me, and one weekend we visited Novisad, an old Yugoslavian garrison town. Here, as elsewhere in the country, the custom was that when you have drunk from a glass you should break that glass. They actually have factories to manufacture glasses so thin and cheap that they cost almost nothing. This means that in a tavern that has seen a lot of drinking the night before, you are literally ankle deep in broken glass the following morning. The locals in Novisad also have the habit of throwing plates about when excited.

Now Angela, as you must know by now, is very Irish, and so can become excited very easily. I had further proof of that – as though I needed any – when we visited a restaurant in Novisad which had little alcoves with small tables. I was sitting in one alcove with James Booth and the camera man, and she was sitting in another with Suzy and two other people. Suddenly, from an alcove behind her, a plate flew over the partition, a big dinner plate. It came through the air like a flying saucer. *Wham!* It smashed on the table in front of her. This was too much for Angela. She immediately threw a plate back. Then two more came from where one had come before – and then we were all in on it. Plates were flying through the air with the greatest of ease and by this time Angela was standing on the table! The floor was soon white with broken china. The double bass player in the band was so keen to join in that he made frantic signs to me.

'You play double bass, and I play throwing plates. Yes?'

'Yes!' I shouted, and picked up his double bass and strummed it while he joined in the game.

When I was back home, John Gale, who controls one of London's leading managements, sent me a play, *The Secretary Bird*, written by William Douglas Home. The play is about a man who has lost the affection of his wife. She admits she has had an affair with another man, and he tries to win her back by inviting his secretary down for the weekend, claiming he is having an affair with her. It is simple and straightforward, and has some witty dialogue.

It turned out to be the biggest stage success of my career. From the opening night we played to fantastic business at the Savoy. I also claim that we put the Savoy Grill back on the map as a smart place to eat. We had an upper class, black tie audience, for people largely like to see plays about their own kind, in situations they find familiar, and after the theatre many went into the Grill next door for dinner.

I played in *The Secretary Bird* for a year, which was twice my original contract. The prices for seats were low then – thirty shillings top whack – and I have a weekly return, framed, which shows that the takings for every show that week, except for the Wednesday matinée, were in four figures, and that matinée was only a few pounds below the £1,000 level, a West End record.

David Shipman has recorded in his book on movie stars, in which he deals with anyone who has any claim to this distinction, that I got personal notices which must be among the best accorded to any light comedian during this century. Sir Harold Hobson wrote in The *Sunday Times* the week after our opening: 'Mr. More's performance is not only irresistibly amusing, it is morally beautiful . . . All his jokes succeed. He is the delight of the entire theatre.' This made me feel very good indeed!

By this time Bill and I had been apart for several years, and now she agreed to give me a divorce. A settlement was amicably arranged, and I was free to marry Shrimp.

We were married on St. Patrick's Day, March 17, 1968. Shrimp's family come from Galway, and although she is not now a practising Catholic, she takes religious matters seriously and she wanted to be married in church. Our trouble was to find a church that would marry a man like me who has already been divorced twice.

No one seemed able to help until I heard that the minister of the Kensington Congregational Church had been known to do this. I went along to see him, and explained the reason for my visit.

'I don't suppose you will marry us, but I just called in the hope that you might consider it.'

He heard my story and made his decision.

'I will marry you both, Mr. More. You obviously love this girl, and I am sure that when you take your vows you will both mean them sincerely.'

So we were married in church and held a reception at the Royal Garden Hotel. Roger Moore was my best man and he made the first speech. Then it was my turn. I can't remember all I said, but I do know how I began.

'This morning,' I said, 'my wife nudged me in bed and said, "Wake up, darling, we're getting married today." '

In September of that year we both attended the première of *The Battle of Britain*, in which I played the part of a group captain who was a station commander. Having played Bader – whom I met again during the making of this film – they could not contemplate an RAF film of this size without my taking *some* part! But now, of course, I was too old to play an active pilot.

What I remember most about the film was publicising it afterwards. We were each allocated various territories which we had to visit for promotional purposes.

Peter Townsend, who was living in Belgium, had, of course, been a famous Battle of Britain pilot and he advised on some aspects of the film. He and I were assigned to Brussels together, and I was told I must cover Amsterdam and Oslo on my own.

In Amsterdam, at the première, I presented a model Spitfire to Prince Bernhard, who had been a Spitfire pilot, and Queen Juliana took a great shine to Angela, like a mother to a daughter, and told her all about the Occupation years.

Our final promotional trip was to Oslo, where Angela and I were to attend the royal première. We were booked to fly out on the Wednesday morning, attend the première that night, spend Thursday sightseeing and giving interviews on TV and to the Press, and then return. We packed enough luggage for two nights, with Angela's evening dress and my black tie, and we travelled, as we always did, in casual clothes.

It was very pleasant flying first-class, drinking champagne, and looking forward to meeting the King and Queen of Norway, with every expense paid by the film company. Half way through our journey, the cabin steward approached me.

'Mr. More,' he began awkwardly, 'I have a message for you from the captain that has just come through on the radio telephone. There has been a mistake. Your luggage has been sent to Rome.'

'What?' I cried in horror and disbelief.

'Yes, sir. Your luggage has been sent in error to Rome. The girl on the checking-in desk made a mistake. We thought we should tell you, in case you might need something for tonight.'

'Might need something?' I repeated. 'Well, tonight we are

215

meeting the King and Queen of Norway as guests at the royal première of *The Battle of Britain*. I have nothing to wear except this pair of flannels and sports jacket. And my wife here is in jeans. How can we possibly go like this?'

'We'll do what we can, sir,' the steward assured me. 'But we can hardly get your luggage back from Rome in time. When is this première?'

'Seven o'clock. This very night as ever is.'

The steward scuttled off to see the captain, who came back to explain that he had spoken by radio to his colleagues in Oslo, and an airline executive would meet us and take us to the best shops, and of course, British Airways would foot the bill for a new dinner jacket for me and an evening dress, shoes and handbag for Angela, and for anything else she wanted.

We landed in Oslo only hours before the première. The British Airways man was waiting and took us to one store after another. But the dresses were awful, mostly silver lamé in dreadful colours. Angela finally chose one in shot-gold and azure blue, which was frightful, but at least better than jeans, and she bought shoes and a handbag to go with it.

I could not find a ready-made suit to fit me so easily. The trousers were all too long. I took the one that was the least bad fit, and the manager of the shop promised that a tailor would alter the trousers immediately and bring them to our hotel. But when the suit arrived, the trousers had not been altered at all, so I had to leave for the première with trousers three inches too long. This meant that they slipped under the heels of my shoes at every step.

Because of this frantic search for clothes, we were late for the première – an appalling social gaffe, because we should have been there first, to receive all the guests. The King and Queen of Norway had already established themselves in their seats when we arrived, and, by etiquette, they should be the last to arrive. The royal anthem was being played and the lights were about to dim when we came pounding through the doors. We had to pass the King and Queen in their box and hoped that they wouldn't notice us. But this was not to be. As we tip-toed in front of the Royal Box, my ridiculous trousers caught under one heel and I went flat on my face. The King roared with laughter. So did the audience. Then they all began to applaud. Clearly, they thought I was drunk. This was one of the most embarrassing moments of my life.

Afterwards, Angela and I were presented to the King and Queen, and I explained the reason for our lateness. They thought the whole story very funny.

Nineteen-sixty-nine was also the year of an unfortunate law suit involving Dorothy Squires. I had been asked to be a commentator at the British Film Academy Awards reception which was to be held in the Hilton Hotel in London. They were making a TV programme of this, and my job was to introduce each guest as they arrived, and say a few words about them.

The evening started off as a great success. I stood at the top of a long staircase from the entrance hall and made my spiel.

'Now here we have Sir Ralph Richardson. Hello, Ralph, darling boy. How are you?'

'Hello, Kenny. Nice to be here.'

'Now here is Sir John Gielgud. How are you, Johnny? Hope you enjoy this evening . . . '

'Here comes my old friend Roger Moore and his charming wife, Luisa . . . '

And they all passed by on their way into the reception.

Then someone came up the stairs I had never seen before. A man with a bald head, with not one hair on it, like a gigantic Easter egg.

'Here we have, umm-umm-um.'

The journalist whispered, 'Telly Savalas.'

'Who?' I asked him. I had never heard the name before. This was years before the success of *Kojak*.

'Telly Savalas,' he repeated.

I still could not hear him properly. People were crowding around on every side, laughing and talking. By this time, Savalas was right up next to me.

'Here we have . . . '

Whisper from the side.

' . . . a famous American star, Telly Savalas.'

'Here we have that famous American star, *Smelly Tavalas*.'

'That's great, buster,' said Savalas, much amused. 'I must say, that's the best introduction I have ever had.'

Apart from this *faux pas*, the evening appeared to pass off splendidly. But within a few weeks, I received a letter from a firm of solicitors claiming that I had slandered their client, Miss Dorothy Squires, who was, in fact, Mrs. Roger Moore, in that I had called another woman his wife. At that time, Luisa was not married to Roger, although she had borne him two children. I knew that he had been married to Dorothy Squires, but so far as the world was concerned, he was living with Luisa as his wife.

I wrote a letter of apology, but the solicitors replied that this was not sufficient. Dorothy Squires was going to sue me in the High Court. I therefore consulted my old friend, Michael Havers.

'Will you handle the case?' I asked him.

'With pleasure.'

When the case came to court, the judge took time off to see a re-run of the TV film at the Hilton. Michael warned me:

'Now when you go into the witness box tomorrow, don't start giving a histrionic performance, Kenny. I know you're an actor, but don't begin spouting a lot of bloody nonsense. Just answer the questions I put to you. Nothing less, but nothing more.'

Michael knows the sort of person I am, and he was absolutely correct to advise me as he did. But the moment I stood up in the box and took the oath, I was carried away by emotion and the drama of the whole scene. I thought, this is the only chance I may ever have of addressing a captive audience in a real court of law. Despite what Michael says, I must make the most of it.

I gave them what I thought was a magnificent oration. I admitted that I might have been wrong. Dorothy had a point. And then I looked down and saw Michael Havers literally cringing under his wig. When I came out of the box he said, 'I told you to say nothing except answer my questions. Kenny, I am never, *never* going to defend you again.'

Anyhow, we won. The jury took thirty minutes to decide that what I had said was not defamatory and Dorothy Squires was faced with a bill of £3,000 or more, for costs. She accepted this situation stoically and like the trouper she is.

In 1970, after a musical film, *Scrooge*, with Albert Finney, in which I played the Spirit of Christmas Present, I went into a revival of *The Winslow Boy* at the New Theatre. This arose from a promise made years earlier to Binkie Beaumont, after my first theatre success in London in *The Deep Blue Sea*, that I would do another play for him. The revival ran for nine months, and happily once again I was directed by Frith Banbury.

My next play was *Getting On* by Alan Bennett. This was set in the early 1970s and was about a disgruntled Labour MP. This also ran for nine months and did very well, but I can't say that I got on as well with the author as I should like to have done. We were polite to each other, and I admired his ability, and of course, still do, but somehow we just did not hit if off. This situation stemmed from an incident that happened in Brighton before we brought the play to London. I went into Mona Washbourne's dressing room just before we were due to open and found her in tears.

'Darling, what's the matter?' I asked her. 'We are opening in an hour. This is no time to be crying.'

She explained the reason for her tears.

'Alan's just been in and reduced me to nothing. He said I am playing the part all wrong. Now I feel completely lost.'

To me this was the most disgraceful thing to do to any artiste when he or she is about to appear on stage. I went at once to see Patrick Garland, the play's director, and told him what had happened.

'Pat,' I said. 'You have got to get Alan Bennett out of this theatre tonight, otherwise I'm not going on.'

'I can't do that, Kenny', he said. 'He's an old chum. We were at Cambridge together.'

I was furious and over-reacted, I suppose, but I was protecting my cast. Patrick Garland realised I meant what I said, and told his old friend. I have never really forgiven Alan Bennett, and I don't think he has ever forgiven me. This was one of those unfortunate things that can happen in the theatre when everyone is strung up, the author no less than the cast.

My next play was *Sign of the Times* by Jeremy Kingston. One day at rehearsal, I was suddenly attacked by the most fearful pains in my back. I doubled up in agony, grey-faced. Somehow I managed to reach my doctor. He diagnosed a stone in my kidney, and advised me to have an immediate operation.

John Gale, who was staging the play, waited several months until I was fully fit, and even kept the cast together so that we could open with the same team. Unfortunately, the play was not a success but I shall always be grateful to John for this very generous act.

After an earlier operation of the same kind, in 1962, I was at a dinner party given by Jack and Doreen Hawkins and found myself sitting next to Sir Carol Reed, the film director. The conversation turned to the subject of health.

'I've been told I have a kidney stone,' Carol announced rather gloomily. He was a hypochondriac, and hated anything to do with knives, doctors, medicine or blood.

'You don't want to worry about that,' I told him breezily. 'I have just had the operation myself. Nothing to it.'

'You mean that?' he said, brightening up visibly. 'Nothing at all?'

'Nothing,' I said. 'Here, I'll prove it.'

I lifted my shirt to show him my scar. I was so used to this scar that I failed to realise the effect it would have on a man as sensitive to matters of health as Carol. The scar for this particular operation is very long and makes the surgery appear much more serious than it actually is. For a second, Carol stared at this livid weal that looked like a grinning tiger – and then he damn near fainted in his chair!

In the summer of 1976 Stuart Lyons, an old friend and producer, told me that Bryan Forbes had asked whether I would star in a film he was going to direct, *The Slipper and the Rose*. This was a musical version of the Cinderella story, and involved a lot of location work in Salzburg. The cast would include Margaret Lockwood, Michael

Hordern, Gemma Craven and Dame Edith Evans.

During this picture, we needed to film some scenes inside a large cathedral. No one would allow this until the Bishop of Southwark, Mervyn Stockwood, gave his permission to film in his cathedral; I think he is a bit stage-struck. It was a very hot summer, and we were filming inside with candles burning, incense smoking and arc lights blazing away. Edith Evans was pretty old and she sat next to me. She was playing the Dowager Queen and I was the Lord Chamberlain. Michael Hordern was the King.

Edith dozed in the heat. Whenever she woke up she would say her one line whether she was on cue or not: 'I think that girl should go.'

She hadn't much to say, but she remembered it well. Whenever I saw her head nod, I rather naughtily nudged her. Edith would immediately perk up and say smartly and with perfect enunciation, 'I think that girl should go.'

The previous year, I appeared on TV in Terence Rattigan's play *In Praise of Love*, with Claire Bloom. Angela then announced that she was going off on tour for eighteen weeks with Anna Neagle in *The First Mrs. Frazer*. Now, for the first time in my life, I felt I had enough money and enough time to achieve a boyhood ambition.

There used to be a regular advertisement, usually in *The Daily Telegraph* under the intriguing title: 'A thousand miles up the Amazon.' From the moment I read this at the age of thirteen or fourteen I had regarded this trip as the ultimate adventure.

'Take a couple of thousand quid out of your bank, darling,' Angela suggested, 'and go up the Amazon. After all, you have talked about it for years.'

So I decided to make the trip, and on my own, as I had always planned it. Because I would arrive in Rio during the carnival, I found it impossible to book any hotel accommodation there. However, I had met the Brazilian ambassador at a party in London some weeks previously, and had told him my ambition, and now I approached him again, and asked whether he could help me find a room. He succeeded in booking me into the Intercontinental Hotel, and I thought, now my trip is made.

I reached Rio at the start of the carnival. This meant that there were no taxis or buses, and no means of reaching any hotel except on foot. The streets were full of revellers, and I stood at the side of the road with my heavy suitcases, wondering where the Intercontinental Hotel might be. Then my guardian angel saw me in this situation, and came to my aid. A lorry trundled slowly through the crowds. I waved to the driver. He stopped.

'Will you take me to the Intercontinental?' I asked him.

'Everyone is at the carnival, señor,' he replied, which did not answer any question.

'You're not,' I pointed out. 'Here's £10.'

I handed him a couple of fivers in English money, and climbed aboard his truck and he drove me to the hotel. At the reception desk when I gave my name, the clerk sent for the manager, who was British.

'Ah, yes, Mr. More, we are expecting you,' he said. 'You are booked in by a friend of our ambassador in London.'

'So I understand. But I just want a small single room, you know. Nothing fancy.'

'Yes, of course, Mr. More. Please come with me.'

I followed the manager into the lift. He pressed the button for the top floor.

'Where are we going?' I asked rather nervously.

'The presidential suite, Mr. More,' he replied.

'The presidential suite?'

Alarm bells sounded in my brain.

'I think there has been some mistake. I only want a single room.'

'There is no mistake, Mr. More. This will only cost you the price of a single room.'

'Are you sure?'

He bowed.

'Certain, Mr. More.'

We reached the top floor. He unlocked the door of a suite of five bedrooms, four bathrooms, two sitting rooms, and a dining room. Priceless paintings hung on the walls, silver bowls were filled with fresh flowers. The view across Rio was worth a king's ransom.

'This suite is reserved for the President of Brazil,' the manager explained. 'We always keep it available for him. But he is not using it at present, so it is at your disposal.'

'But what can I do in return? You can't give me all this opulence for the price of a single room.'

'Well,' he said, 'if you could manage to pose for a few photographs around our pool for our house magazine, I'd be delighted.'

'For this suite, I'll give you a whole week's session.'

I lived here in prodigious splendour for a week, moving out for one night because the President required the suite for one of his family. From this unprecedented luxury I flew up to Manaus, the capital of the new Amazonia. This is a down-at-heel city, but possesses a wonderful opera house, built in the days when Manaus was the centre of the Brazilian rubber industry. This prosperity vanished when a British visitor brought back some rubber plants to Kew Gardens and cuttings were transported to Malaya in the belief

221

that they would grow there because it had much the same climate as the Amazon. This theory was proved correct, and brought prosperity to the east and ruin to rubber growers in Brazil.

There are some strange things to see in Manaus. When the dustbins are emptied, for example, the streets stream with cockroaches. The humidity is almost unbearable. Locals say that in the dry season it rains, and in the wet season, it pours. Something like five inches of rain fell in half an hour when I was there.

During my stay I found a little Indian guide who wore green overalls, a Brazilian Chaco Indian, and gave him some money every day, and he took me through the water jungle and I saw wonderful butterflies and the deadly piranha fish. Their teeth are so sharp, and their appetites so voracious that they can strip a body of all its flesh within minutes. In this, they strongly reminded me of some people I have known in the film business.

I flew back to Rio, where I was entertained royally and gave a farewell party to everyone who had been so kind to me. I invited fifteen people to Régine's, a branch of the famous Paris night club, and thought I could easily pay by American Express, because I simply had not enough travellers cheques left.

Then I saw the bill. If Chivas Regal cost thirty-five pounds a bottle in the hotel, it was twice as much as this in the night club, and everyone had been drinking Chivas Regal as though it was water. This bill was so astronomical I had no idea that any bill for one meal could possibly be so large. However, I pulled out my credit card, and as I did so a hand came over my shoulder and took away the bill. Another hand gave me back the card.

I looked up in amazement. A little man with a dark moustache was standing behind me.

He bowed.

'Please, Mr. More,' he said. 'You do not know me, but I am the film critic of the main daily newspaper here. I would like you to be *our* guest for this evening.'

To my knowledge, I had never seen him before.

'That is very kind of you,' I said, 'but I am the host.'

'Not in Rio, Mr. More,' he replied. He picked up the bill and I breathed again.

14

FOR TWO OR THREE years before I went on holiday I used to have a telephone call from time to time at half past eight in the morning. It went like this.

'Good morning, Ken. This is Lew Grade speaking.'

'Good morning, Lew.'

'Good morning, father.'

'What?'

'Good morning, father.'

'What do you mean, *father*?'

'You are going to be Father Brown for me, Kenny,' he said.

'I don't know anything about that.'

'Oh yes. We have the rights of Father Brown.'

'I can't play Father Brown.'

'Oh, yes, you can . . . father.'

He kept on ringing to say, 'Good morning, father. How's father this morning?'

Finally I said to my agent, 'What do you think about the idea?'

He had discussions with Lew – now Lord – Grade and that is how I became television's Father Brown.

I have seen many changes in my profession since the day when Vivian Van Damn gave me a job moving scenery at the Windmill, and one of the greatest has been the way that actors and actresses now use their names, their voices, and themselves in TV advertisements.

For a long time, we thought that this was not quite the thing to do, but then Olivier, who is without question our greatest actor, lent his name to a series of advertisements for Polaroid cameras in the United States. After this, those who had held back felt the way was clear to follow his lead.

I agreed to advertise Mellow Bird's Coffee. Before the war, this sort of sponsored advertising was on a very small scale. It was also amateurish and rather fun. Today's TV advertising is extremely complicated and professional. They use well known film directors – for instance, Kevin Billington has directed me in the Mellow Bird's advertisement – and they have a complete script and a large unit to produce a film that will only last for thirty seconds.

When I made my last commercial, a car and chauffeur picked me up in London at half past eight in the morning and took me to the studio. It next had to be decided what clothes I should wear for the film. Just before this, Angela had been out in Hong Kong for a month appearing in a play. She brought me back some shirts, and I wore one of these and cavalry twill trousers. Then Kevin Billington suggested I put on a V-necked pullover because it would look more homely. The set of a kitchen was ready and so many people were involved, you would think we were filming *Gone With the Wind*.

I was made up and handed my lines, which were simple enough. The difficult thing was to be correct on timing, because millions of housewives would see the action, which was apparently taking place in the kitchen of a house like theirs, and if there was the slightest thing wrong, they could turn against the product.

For example, there might not be enough bubbles in the coffee, or no steam coming from the cup. So we had a coffee-making-person on the set, a steam-person and a bubble-person.

Our particular coffee lady was called Myrtle. She would come in at the very last moment, just before the camera started to turn, and put a cup of hot coffee in front of me. If the steam was not right, or the camera didn't catch the cup at the right angle, we had to do it again – and again.

This went on for twenty or thirty attempts, and when the steam was right, then the bubbles weren't. So a scheme was devised whereby Myrtle whipped up bubbles in a spoon and dropped them into my cup at the last moment. There were a lot of jokes: 'Come on, Myrtle. Get your bubbles going. Let's see your bubbles,' and so on.

Finally, it was right for the camera man, for the producer, the director, and for me, who had been drinking cup after cup of hot coffee all day long. This represents only one day's work, but every actor who has made a TV commercial agrees with me that it can be the most tiring working day of their lives.

It is, however, a financially rewarding day. The money one can make from such an advertisement means that a 'star' actor can pick and choose roles for the rest of the year.

It is always the little unexpected happening one remembers from a play or a film. For example, in between making *Doctor in the House* and *Reach for the Sky*, I made a little film for Wendy Toye, called *Raising a Riot*. This concerned me as a naval commander, whose wife went abroad and I had to look after our children.

My old friend Ronnie Squire was in it, and we were on location on the Thames Estuary in Kent. Wendy Toye has strong links with the north of England, and Lowry the famous painter was a close friend. He came down to spend a few days and made sketches of us all. He pictured me lying down, as usual, for a nap after lunch, and all the men and women in the unit around doing their particular tasks. So we joined the legion of his matchstalk men and match-stalk cats and dogs.

Then there was the occasion in *The Admirable Crichton* when I nearly drowned. This scene was shot off a jetty in Bermuda. The yacht owned by my master in the film, Lord Loam, was supposed to be sinking in a hurricane and as his loyal and imperturbable butler I had to swim ashore in full tails.

The sea was churned up by outboard motor propellers, and fans created a wind, with the result that the waves pounded the yacht as though a Force 10 gale was raging.

Diane Cilento was the maid, who leaped into the water wearing a period nightdress and nightcap. Being an Australian, Diane's ability to swim can put a fish to shame. I jumped in with her and almost instantly the ridiculous tails of my jacket became water-logged, and the weight dragged me down beneath the surface. Here I was, trying to play the scene as though I was drowning, and I *was* bloody well drowning!

I called pitifully to the director, Lewis Gilbert, 'Help! Help!' But he, as a true professional, refused to let reality affect illusion.

'Marvellous!' he cried. 'He's drowning! Kenny's *drowning*! Keep those cameras turning! What a wonderful shot!'

No one came to my aid as I went up and down in the water, gasping desperately for breath. If it hadn't been for Diane, who kept me afloat, I would not be alive to tell about it. Afterwards, Lewis said, 'I didn't realise you were in real trouble.'

On another occasion, we were making *North West Frontier* in India. The story demanded that rebels should ambush a train in the desert, and we had to set fire to a lot of brushwood near the railway line to keep these rebels at bay. This means that a stunt man impersonating me was due to lie across the rail, already very hot in the sun's heat, and shoot a service revolver at the rebels through flames which were steadily moving closer to him as the bush burned.

The stunt man refused to do this. It was too dangerous, he declared. So I said to the director, Lee Thompson, 'I'll have a go.' And I did.

But that stunt man was no fool. By the time the scene was finished the flames had come so near that they burned off the front of my hair and my eyebrows. From then on, the make-up people

225

had to give me pencilled-in hair and new eyebrows.

In *Reach for the Sky* there is a famous scene when Bader lies in hospital after the flying accident in which he lost both his legs. He is dying. In a kind of coma he dimly hears two young nurses laughing in the corridor outside his room, and then a senior nurse reprimanding them.

'Less noise, please. A young boy's dying in there.'

At that moment – in real life, as in the film – Bader realised that everyone had already given him up and written him off. He was as good as dead. This realisation spurred him to recover.

'I'm *not* going to die – just to please a few nurses in the corridor.'

This was the turning point in his life.

We were filming this scene in Pinewood Studios at about half past ten in the morning. At that hour, what we called the tea boat would always come round with cups of tea and coffee and – a great luxury – about eight pieces of bread and dripping. You had to rush to be one of the lucky ones for this, because there were no seconds. I liked my bread and dripping, and had asked my stand-in, Jack Mandeville, to queue up for it.

'Don't you worry, Ken,' he assured me. 'I'll get it for you.'

Thus reassured, I lay back in my hospital bed while we played the scene, with the camera close-up on me and a girl's voice off-screen saying, '. . . A young boy's dying in there . . .'

I had to show my thoughts on my face through the merest flicker of an eyelid, a faint, stubborn tightening of my lips. This was the moment of truth, the scene on which the whole film pivoted, and I put everything I had into it.

At the end, when Lewis Gilbert said in a very quiet voice, 'Cut,' I opened my eyes, and I saw that people in the unit were crying, they had been so moved. I had done it in one take. There would be no need for any more. So immediately I leaped out of bed.

'Jack!' I shouted. '*Have you got my piece of bread and bloody dripping?*'

Everybody was in hysterics. They couldn't understand this almost instant transition from acting to reality. But I can switch off easily. Of course, I believe totally in the character *when* I am acting. I become that person. But when the moment passes of wearing someone else's skin, and saying someone else's words, I can switch off immediately.

In everyone's life, there is a vast uncharted land of regret to which the passwords are, 'If only.' All of us wonder how our lives would have evolved if we had done this instead of that, if we had only taken one direction instead of another at some faraway crossroad of decision. There is one great decision in my own life that I can never recall without a feeling of pain, and an unanswered question in my mind. I have never spoken about it before, but an autobiography should be like Cromwell's portrait, warts and all, and so I feel I must mention it now.

After I had made *Doctor in the House*, I was under contract to Korda, and one day he told me he had received a long letter from David Lean, who is in my opinion Britain's greatest film director.

Lean was in India where he was preparing to make a film of the bestseller, *The Wind Cannot Read*. This was a novel by Richard Mason, who later wrote *The World of Suzy Wong*. It tells of a young RAF officer in India during the war, who has a love affair in Delhi with a beautiful Japanese girl interpreter working for the Allies. But all the while she is seriously ill, and ironically, while he survives action in Burma, she dies on the eve of peace.

This was a story of youth and first love, and Korda told me that it presented a chance for me as an actor that offered incalculable rewards.

I remember his voice so well with its thick accent, his finger jabbing at me to ram home the importance of David Lean's offer.

'This is the greatest opportunity you will ever have, Kenny. It is a chance to work with the finest director there has ever been. He's already spent two years working on the project. He has found a Japanese actress and all the locations. All he needs now is – you. He tells me he considers you are perfect for the part. He is going to write to you himself to explain his views and how he feels you should play it. This is your chance to become an international star overnight.'

I was living then with Bill in Wargrave, and sure enough, within a few days a letter arrived from David Lean in India explaining his feelings, and a copy of the script. I read this at once and I think it was the best script I have ever been offered. I could not find a flaw in it.

He explained in his letter that when I came out to Delhi, I should bring some small presents for the Japanese actress, maybe bottles of perfume or some such thing, for this was the Japanese custom and it would be appreciated, and we would start on a good footing from the beginning.

Everything pointed to my making this picture. I would never have a chance like this again. Yet – I hesitated. Why?

I explained my doubts to Korda. The public had just seen me as a beer-swilling, back-slapping extrovert in *Genevieve*, then as another beer-swilling extrovert medical student in *Doctor in the House*. How could they possibly now accept me as a sensitive young pilot, a kind of Rupert Brooke of the RAF, who had fallen in love with a Japanese girl? Impossible.

227

'Of course they'll accept you,' Korda insisted. 'You're an actor, aren't you? Just put yourself in David Lean's hands and you're home.'

I was still unsure. One night I actually started out of my sleep, and woke up Bill and told her: 'I *can't* make this picture.'

'But you *must*,' she replied with equal emphasis. 'Everyone says so. This is your great chance, what you've worked for since the Windmill.'

It was at this moment of indecision that I was given the chance of making *Reach for the Sky*. If I had been sensible, I would have done Lean's film first and *Reach for the Sky* second, and so given myself a double chance to succeed in both, but I was not sensible; I still lacked self-confidence. Once more, I explained my reasons to Korda.

'You're mad,' he told me flatly. 'Here is a chance to establish yourself as an international star. Instead, you want to play a man without any legs.'

I wrote a long letter to David Lean in India, and told him why I felt I could not take the part. He did not reply, and I now realise I was virtually implying that I had no faith in his ability to make me believable in a new kind of role. Worse, he scrapped the film. He sold the rights elsewhere, and a shortened and greatly altered version appeared with Dirk Bogarde.

This was the greatest mistake I ever made professionally.

All actors and actresses need talent, luck and good health. I should also like to stipulate a less obvious requirement – hot water. Acting can drain a person emotionally and physically, and when you are very tired you are always cold. When an actor comes back late at night from the theatre or a TV or film studio he is cold and weary, and the first thing he thinks about is having a hot bath. This is often a throw-back to the days when he was poor and did not have the money for a hot bath. In my young days and in theatrical digs, you had to put a sixpence or a shilling into a geyser slot-meter and if you hadn't the money, you couldn't have a bath. Young struggling actors on tour today still have the same problem.

When I arrive back home, I luxuriate in the knowledge that I can enjoy a hot bath whenever I want one. I sometimes have three a day. Whenever I feel lonely or depressed, I run a hot bath and lie back in it, remembering days when I could not afford such indulgence. This is not only good for the soul – it cures my depression!

How many people in Britain ever pause to consider just what a privilege it is to belong to the West rather than to a country behind the Iron Curtain? While I was writing this book, I had an unex-

pected opportunity of visiting West Berlin. My agent, Michael
Whitehall, who looks after me so expertly, was going to see David
Hemmings, whom he also represents, and who was directing a film
there with Kim Novak, Marlene Dietrich, Kurt Jurgens and David
Bowie, and I asked if I could come along for the ride.

In Berlin, David had laid on a visit through Checkpoint Charlie,
the gateway between West and East Berlin, an essential excursion
that every visitor should make.

There is one restaurant in East Berlin that serves teas to visitors
from the West, and taxi drivers are instructed by the East German
authorities to take tourists there, and then drive them back to the
checkpoint. But if you know your way around, as David Hemmings did, you are aware that there are one or two other restau-
rants which will accept Western patrons. We went to one of these,
said to be the best restaurant in East Berlin. I was surprised to see
what a pathetic place it was. Everyone seemed grey and sad-
looking and the decorations were drab.

The exchange rate is entirely in the favour of the West. It was
then about one West German mark for ten East German marks, so
we had lunch and all the wine we could drink, and with this rate of
exchange, the whole meal cost us only £1 a head. The food was
badly cooked and tasteless. The ice-cream was not really ice-cream,
but just a water ice, and the frothy topping was without flavour.
The chocolate was of the hard kind I always associate with cheap
eclairs, without substance or sweetness.

The wine was good though, and the waiters were polite and
willing, but like the diners, they all looked infinitely sad, as though
they were doing penance rather than a job they liked. To them, we
certainly appeared visitors from another world.

At the end of lunch, I felt so depressed with this atmosphere of
defeat and apathy that I suggested we give the waiters ten West
German marks each. They were overwhelmed with our generosity.
They could sell these for more than 100 East German marks, about a
month's salary.

Apart from my trip to Yugoslavia, this was my first glimpse of life
east of the Iron Curtain, and it terrified me. This uniform drabness,
the empty shops, the shabby houses, the feeling of hopelessness
heavy as a fog over everything, depressed me beyond measure. For
the first time I could understand why people would risk their lives
to escape from such death-in-life. If Communist conformity
brought anything like the blessings its vociferous advocates in the
West claim, why must those who should enjoy it have to be kept
literally imprisoned in their country by high walls and barbed wire
and armed guards? And why, I wondered, as I drove silently back

to West Berlin, should some of us be so fortunate, while others are destined to live out their lives in grey and drab regimentation?

To a large measure, I think our lives *are* in some way predestined. Somerset Maugham told of the rich Damascus merchant who sent his servant down to the bazaar one morning to make a purchase. The servant returned quickly in a great state of fright.

'Master,' he explained. 'Death jostled me in the bazaar, and I am afraid. Lend me your horse, I pray you, and I will ride to Samarra and escape him.'

The merchant willingly lent a horse to his servant and then went to the bazaar himself. There, among the stalls, stood Death, and the merchant rebuked Death and asked him why he had frightened his servant. Death replied: 'I did not frighten him. I was simply surprised to see him here in Damascus this morning when tonight I have an appointment with him in Samarra.'

I believe that one may try to run away from one's destiny, to escape what one imagines the future holds, when all the time it is waiting for us where we thought it would never find us. Instead of running away from fate, we may simply be racing towards it.

I see my own life in two stages. The first stage is of early struggle, when I changed from engineering to a job I really wanted to do. Then came the war, the Navy, and six years doing something entirely different. When I returned to acting I was that much older, and while I had changed, so had the whole world, and especially my chosen profession.

The second stage in my life began with the extraordinary telephone call from Bob Lennard on a Saturday morning. I had prayed for a clear sign, and a clear sign I was given. So far as I was concerned, this was destiny. Why else should I have been chosen out of hundreds of better-known actors?

That call changed my whole life, because if I had not received it, on the Monday of the following week I should have returned to the Navy. Instead, on that Monday, I was standing on a high shelf in a 'prison' in Hemel Hempstead.

Up to that telephone call, life had been a harsh struggle and a fight for survival. After that call, my rent was paid for two months and my whole career sailed out of the doldrums. Since then I have mercifully never been short of money, although I still have the fear that one day I might be.

All actors and actresses know this fear far more acutely than people in secure jobs. It tends to make them either over-generous or over-mean; or, to be more polite, over-cautious in their spending.

I remember another episode that reinforced my belief in some superior force in the world – or out of it – which influences us in ways we cannot yet comprehend, and which, if we let it, can keep our lives on course. This occurred when Angela and I were going through a rather down period, and having too many rows. At night we used to go to sleep, turning our backs on each other. 'Good-night darling,' we would say, and that was that.

For a long time, I had been extremely friendly with Frank Lawton, who was married to Evelyn Laye. He in turn was very fond indeed of Angela, and he and 'Boo' Laye were two of our closest friends. His death a couple of years earlier had shattered all of us. Now the thing that would have upset Frank more than anything if he had lived would have been that Angela and I were quarrelling. He could never bear to think that we might fall out.

That night I had a dream about Frank Lawton and Angela heard me say, in the middle of the night, while I was asleep, and speaking in Frank's voice, which was very distinctive: 'Ken and Shrimp, you must make it up. Your troubles are my troubles. What you are doing now is making me very unhappy.'

Then I awoke. I found myself sitting up in bed, and Angela was also sitting up.

'You have just spoken in Frank's voice,' she said in a frightened, puzzled tone. She told me what I had said. I did not remember a thing beyond the vague recollection of my dream in which I had met Frank. But the experience shocked us both; after it, our disagreements ended.

I do not believe that acting is the be-all and end-all of my life. It is a very important part of it, but not everything. Thus, the working atmosphere of a play or a film is far more important to me than the part I am asked to play. I would never appear in a production in which I felt in advance that there was going to be bad temper or bad feelings. I have to be happy in my work, and then, in the only way I am able, I try to make audiences happy, too.

I have been fortunate in my wives, and in my delightful daughters Jane and Sarah, and especially fortunate in my present wife, my little Shrimp. She was born to give happiness and laughter and to me she has given both. Of course, we have disagreements and bleak days as well as sunny ones, as all couples do after years of marriage. But we share a tremendous bond which no one could ever destroy.

Shrimp gave me her youth. She was twenty-one when I met her, and I was forty-seven. With that youth she has also given me a golden bonus I had no right to expect, the priceless gift of love.

She is in a way totally innocent, not of life, but of everyday things that can happen in life; an original innocent in the purest meaning of the words.

Some years ago *Punch* published a number of letters from husbands to their wives and asked me to contribute. I put everything I felt about Shrimp into this letter.

'Darling Shrimp,' I wrote: ' "Shrimp", I call you, and nobody else is allowed that privilege.

'Living with you is an experience, never dull, never predictable, always unusual. You can be Old Mother Riley, or the Impossible Dream. When Saint Patrick planted the McDonaghs in Galway, he must have had me in mind. Who else but you could ask me, "How do you spell?" fourteen times whilst writing one letter, and keep me smiling? Who else but you could look at me with big blue eyes, standing in the High Street at Mahé, in the Seychelles, and in reply to my "What would you like, darling? I'll buy you anything you want," come out with . . . "I think I'd like a paw-paw milk shake" . . . You could have had a gold bracelet, I was in that kind of a mood!

'Only an Irish girl could confront a husband who came home with the milk by picking up something to throw at him, then, realising it was something of hers, put it down and pick up something of his! I love you for that . . . and only a "Shrimp" could go out and buy a fella a fur coat with her entire earnings from a gruelling television show. What unbounded joy is your innocence, Heaven protect me from the woman who knows it all, I want no part of her! Kenny.'

I have been fortunate, too, in my career. Peter Hall asked me recently whether I would play Claudius to Albert Finney's Hamlet at the National. One part of me said that I would like to, but the other part said that there are so many wonderful Shakespearean actors in this country who could obviously do it much better, so let them get on with it. I, for my part, will stick to the roles I think I can play better than them.

I am also lucky to have an extremely talented young agent, Michael Whitehall, to manage my affairs. He is not only good for me, he happens to be that rare character who is respected by those with whom he has to do business, producers and casting directors, and, what is more, he can drive a damn good bargain when the need arises!

I love acting, and that is sufficient recompense for me. I am not the sort of man who needs a Rolls or a yacht. I had a Rolls once and got that out of my system. Angela laughs now when I say that so long as I can have my poached egg on toast and 'three up and two down', I'll be happy, especially if there is a view of the traffic going by.

I enjoy entertaining my friends, and I like to take them out and pick up the bill. I can never forget that evening years ago when I was left with the bill at the Caprice, and the knowledge that I could not pay it. I like to pick up the bill when it is presented, not for any question of showing off, but to prevent somebody feeling embarrassed because he may not be able to afford even his share of it.

I also love the Garrick Club, and this has long been part of my life. If I only had enough money left in the world to pay the club subscription and nothing else, I would pay it. I like meeting the cross-section of people one finds there, all at the peak of their particular professions. The lines of longitude on any map all meet at the top. The country's most eminent judges, barristers, solicitors, other actors, surgeons and editors tend to meet daily at the Garrick. You never feel stagnant there; you are always plugged into life. You do not need to read newspapers to know what is happening or watch the news on TV; there you can meet the men who make the news others read about.

The Garrick is really one of the main reasons why I would never leave England permanently. Another is the fact that I owe so much to this country, and so much to the British public.

The British are the most loyal public in the world, because they identify with those with whom they have grown up. *Genevieve* to my contemporaries is not a film made years ago, but last week, or last year. They see me as I was then, not as I am now; which is why so many say almost in amazement: 'You haven't changed a bit.'

I am also their reassurance that *they* have not changed. In an upside down world, with all the rules being rewritten as the game goes on and spectators invading the pitch, it is good to feel that some things and some people seem to stay just as they were. Of course, I have changed, just as they have changed. By my basic philosophy, which Ronald Squire first taught me, is still unaltered: *Throw the ball about a bit. Give everyone a share of the limelight or the fun or the good fortune.*

That hasn't changed, and so far as I am concerned, it never will.

In Jaipur years ago, when I was filming *North West Frontier*, an old soothsayer, whose hand had been mightily crossed with rupees, concluded the session with a large wink, and these words: 'Do not forget, Sahib, always light your lamp before it becomes dark.'

I'll try to live up to that advice . . . more or less!

Index

241

243